Herodotean Inquiries

Herodotean Inquiries

Seth Benardete

ST. AUGUSTINE'S PRESS
South Bend, Indiana
2009

Manufactured in the United States of America.

1 2 3 4 5   15 14 13 12 11 10 09

Library of Congress Cataloging in Publication Data
Benardete, Seth.
   Herodotean inquiries / Seth Benardete.
      p. cm.
      Originally published: The Hague: Nijhoff, 1969.
      Includes bibliographical references (p.) and index.
      ISBN 1-890318-32-9 (alk. paper)
   1. Herodotus. History. 2. Greece – History – Persian Wars,
      500–499 B.C. – Historiography. 3. History. Ancient –
      Historiography. I. Title
   D58.H57B47 1998
   938'.03 – dc21   98-15614

Paperbound edition published 2009. ISBNs 978-1-58731-362-2;
1-58731-362-6.

∞ The paper used in this publication meets the minimum requirements of
the American National Standard for Information Sciences – Permanence of Paper
for Printed Materials, ANSI Z39.48-1984.

St. Augustine's Press
www.staugustine.net

To
Leo Strauss
(1899–1973)

CONTENTS

INTRODUCTION

Herodotus has so often been called, since ancient times, the father of history that this title has blinded us to the question: Was the father of history an historian? Everyone knows that the Greek word from which 'history' is derived always means inquiry in Herodotus. His so-called *Histories* are inquiries, and by that name I have preferred to call them. His inquiries partly result in the presentation of events that are now called 'historical'; but other parts of his inquiry would now belong to the province of the anthropologist or geographer. Herodotus does not recognize these fields as distinct; they all belong equally to the subject of his inquiry, but it is not self-evident what he understands to be his subject: the notorious difficulties in the proem are enough to indicate this. If his work presents us with so strange a mixture of different fields, we are entitled to ask: Did Herodotus understand even its historical element as we understand it? Without any proof everyone, as far as I am aware, who has studied him has assumed this to be so. In the writings of Felix Jacoby, *honoris causa,* we can see the difficulty that such an assumption leads to: "Whoever makes of the historian (Herodotus) a philosopher, moralist, preacher, folk-psychologist, ethnologist, 'morphologist of human fate,' or anything else, puts in the middle what belongs at best to the periphery; his mistake about the character of his (Herodotus') great achievement is worse, in my opinion, than he who insists that the historian has still not completely understood the methodical foundations, the nature, of his science. That he is and wishes to be an historian, Herodotus in his proem has said with the same clarity as Thucydides has in his; this must be agreed upon."[1] Herodotus then would be an historian who did not fully understand what an historian must be: "His critical sense," Jacoby says, "still stands in children's shoes." Had Herodotus fully understood the "methodical founda-

---

[1] *Charon von Lampsakos,* p. 235, fn 81, *Studi italiani di filogia classica,* N.S. 15, 1938 (1939) = p. 200 *Abhandlungen z. Griech. Geschichtschreibung,* ed. Bloch. The rest of Jacoby's opinions here referred to are found in his article on Herodotus in *R.E.,* Suppl. II, coll. 205ff.

tions of his science," he would have written a different work; but perhaps Herodotus did fully understand them and hence wrote the work we have. Perhaps his foundations are not those of modern historiography but foundations that suited the intention he had in mind. His intention may not only appear in the proem but in his whole work. To consider the proem alone without comparing it to the whole might be like regarding the first lines of the *Iliad* or *Odyssey* as sufficient for understanding the whole poem. One may have to consider the proem in light of what follows rather than the other way round. Herodotus' intention may be far from clear.

Jacoby can only conclude that the proem presents Herodotus' complete intention by assigning parts of the *Inquiries* to different periods. He is convinced, for example, that Book II, on Egypt, has no place in the whole work, but that it was conceived of and written as an independent study; and he goes so far as to claim that none of the first four books has anything to do with the Persian Wars. "No longer will anyone seriously assert," he says, "that the books on Egypt and Scythia, that the Libyan, Babylonian, Mesopotamian, and Libyan λόγοι, have any inner relation with the conflict between Asia and Europe—to make the basic theme of the present work as wide as possible—and that the historian of the Persian Wars would have needed or even desired those journeys."[2] Instead of starting with the most obvious. the presence of a four hundred page disquisition on those countries, Jacoby tries to explain it away; he does not stop to consider that an interpretation of these books might explain Herodotus' intention more adequately than a single sentence. He does not consider this possibility because he does not believe Herodotus has to be interpreted; but in spite of this belief he does interpret Herodotus. To interpret an author implies that his argument is not immediately clear to us; either because his suppositions are unstated, or because his work invites us to think out his argument, which may lie as much in the stories he tells as in what he openly

---

[2]*R.E.*, col. 365, 11. 32–41. Those who have been less extreme than Jacoby in denying a connection between Books I–IV and V–IX, have not, I think, made a strong case; see especially, Pohlenz, M., *Herodot, der erste Geschichtschreiber des Abendlandes* (Leipzig, 1937); also: Fritz K. von, *TalPhA*, 1936, pp. 315–340; Regenbogen, O., *Doe Antike*, VI, 1930, pp. 202–248; Schadewaldt, W., *Die Antike*, X, 1934, pp. 144–168; Reinhardt, K., in his *Von Werken u. Formen* (Godesberg, 1948), pp. 163ff.; Focke, F., *Herodot als Historiker* (Stuttgart, 1927); Hellmann, F., *Herodots Kroisoslogos* (Berlin, 1934); Pagel, K. A., *Die Bedeutung des aitiologischen Momentes für Herodots Geschichtsschreibung* (Leipzig, 1927). For more recent work on Herodotus see now *Herodot, Eine Auswahl aus der Neueren Forschung*, ed. Marg, W. (München, 1962).

says. Jacoby at once decided on the first and rejected the second possibility; it never occurred to him that the second might allow the only approach to the first. He knows, for example, that "no great historical work has ever arisen *sine ira et studio.*" He denies what Tacitus explicitly says was the spirit in which he wrote, and he knows that Herodotus was a "Periclean," though Herodotus never says he is. He knows that Herodotus' opinion about the gods was the same as Sophocles': but we do not know what Sophocles thought about the gods. He does not mean Jocasta's but the chorus' opinion was Sophocles' own, just as he identifies Solon's speech to Croesus with Herodotus' opinion: he knows that Herodotus disagreed with Cambyses. Admittedly, the difficulty of the *Inquiries,* where Herodotus sometimes speaks in his own name, is less than in the plays of Sophocles, where Sophocles never speaks: and yet Herodotus contradicts himself. To accept as his true opinion what we find it convenient for him to believe is arbitrary. To wrench a sentence out of the context in which it appears, without paying attention to what precedes or follows it, completely destroys the argument of the *Inquiries.* It replaces a whole with a series of fragments that can be shuffled about at will. It has led to the study of the lost sources of Herodotus but not to the study of what we have before us. One passage is labelled a 'folk-tale,' another is 'sophistic,' a third an 'Ionian rationalization': but it is rarely considered how these passages fit together. In order to verify or refute what Herodotus says, he has been compared with other authors who report the same episode; but few have considered how Herodotus understood it. To say that Herodotus borrowed his description of the crocodile from Hecataeus does not help us to discover why Herodotus described it. If Herodotus thought of his work as an encyclopedia, which contains everything that he knows, perhaps such an analysis would be impossible. But Herodotus tells us again and again that he omits what he knows, and he sometimes justifies his omissions by referring to the necessity of his λόγος.[3] It is important to take seriously this necessity. which implies that everything that is told has a place in the *Inquiries.* Its apparent lack of necessity shows only that there is a problem; it does not show that a necessity does not govern it. That every sentence belongs by necessity to the work, we should hesitate to affirm. Many facts are simply facts that had to be mentioned though they do not contribute directly to his argument: but that almost every paragraph belongs we have set out to indicate. We can, indeed, only indicate that the argument is a perfect whole, for there are many things that still remain obscure for us and others that only require a hint from us for the reader to see their connection with the whole. In trying to exhibit the argu-

---

[3]Cf. I.51.4; 177; II.3.2; 47.2; 132.3; 171.1; IV.30.1; 43.7; VII.96.1; 139.1; 224.1.

ment we have concentrated on Books I–VII, since it will be clearly seen that VIII and IX are only the culmination of what has preceded them. The victories at Salamis and Plataea are Marathon and Thermopylae writ large, and they complete without altering the argument of the *Inquiries*.

We shall try to show that the argument of the *Inquiries* is crudely this: Books I–IV present the thinking of Herodotus himself, Books VI–IX reflect and supplement that thinking in the great and marvelous deeds of Greeks and barbarians, and Book V is the transition between Herodotus' thinking and Greek-barbarian deeds. Herodotus' thinking, however, is only presented through the thinking of Greeks and barbarians, but the plan and intention of the *Inquiries,* once understood, will explain why Herodotus did not explicitly state it. The *Inquiries* present the evidence for an argument that is in the evidence and not imposed on it. The universal λόγος which Herodotus tries to uncover lies completely embedded in the particulars that he narrates. To understand the particular evidence is to understand the universal argument. The power of Herodotus' argument is shown in its ability to understand the given without destroying the given. The argument is not only an understanding of things but the way to that understanding. It shows both what it is and how Herodotus arrived at it. It contains both a teaching (λόγος) and an inquiry (ἱστορίη): they are inseparable. A story is told in such a way that we not only understand how the characters in the story understood themselves but how Herodotus understood them. A custom is presented in such a context that we see the interpretation both its practitioners and Herodotus gave it. In order to show this doubleness in his argument, our inquiry will have to show that Herodotus was more serious and more playful than has been realized. It might be recalled that Rabelais is said to have planned a translation of the *Inquiries*.

An example perhaps may better explain Herodotus' way, for it is precisely his way to proceed by examples. In the eighth book (118–119) Herodotus tells a story that he himself finds unconvincing about Xerxes' return to Asia after his defeat at Salamis. Xerxes is said to have sailed home from Eion, and when a storm came up which the captain warned would swamp them unless the ship were lightened, Xerxes requested the Persians on board to show their concern for his safety by jumping into the sea: and when they obeyed him and the ship made port, Xerxes "because the captain had saved the king's life rewarded him with a golden crown, but because he had lost the lives of many Persians cut off his head." If we accept Herodotus' reasons for rejecting this as a fable, we might then wonder why he should bother to tell it. As it cannot be true, we can only account for it by considering its "meaning": only what it says, as opposed to its veracity, warrants its inclusion. What it says is simple. Xerxes is shown acting out a perfect caricature of justice. Either of his actions, taken by itself, is just, but together each just action cancels out the other, and absurdity follows. The story is told, then, because it points to a truth about justice: the strict application of a just rule, to pay back what is owed, leads to a contradiction. That this misunderstanding of justice peculiarly belongs to the Persians will become clear later, so that we shall see that even so false a story tells the truth about the Persians (cf. III.36.5–6).

If the reader, however, now admits the relevance of the story, he may still doubt whether its place in the *Inquiries* has any connection with its surroundings, since he might think it had to appear where it did if it were to appear at all. If this were so, to try to work out the plan of the *Inquiries* would be hopeless, even though Herodotus clearly had less freedom in the last books than in the first four. But on glancing back at what precedes this story, we see that a well-ordered series of stories leads up to it. Herodotus tells how a Delphic oracle made the Spartans send a herald to Xerxes to ask a recompense (αἰτέειν δίκας) for Leonidas' death, and that the oracle advised them to accept whatever Xerxes offered (114). The Spartan herald addressed him thus: "King of the Medes, the Lacedaemonians and Heraclidae from Sparta ask a recompense (δίκας) for a death, because you killed their king who was trying to save Greece." Xerxes laughed at his speech and then, after a long silence, pointed to Mardonius saying: "Then Mardonius here will pay a penalty (δίκας δώσει) of the kind that suits them." Xerxes tells a truth unwittingly, for Mardonius later dies at Plataeae; but we should not be so taken with this coincidence as to neglect Xerxes' initial laughter. Does it mean that he is indifferent to Mardonius' fate, as Artemisia's advice suggests he should be (102.2–3)? Or rather does it mean that the Spartans' request for justice is absurd? The oracle's command seems as much a caricature of justice as Xerxes' reward and punishment of the captain: indeed, one might ask whether it illustrates the Spartans' understanding of justice as much as the other illustrates the Persians'. It seems to assume that the justice which almost everyone would admit a city justly exacts from its own citizens equally applies to its foreign enemies. Again we are forced to think about justice.

Now between these two episodes there occur at least two more that concern justice. Xerxes had left his sacred horses and chariot in Macedonia, and though the Paeonians gave them to the Thracians, they claimed, when Xerxes asked for them back, that some Thracians had seized them while they were grazing (115.4). A clear case of injustice, if as the Persians believe lying is always unjust, proves difficult because of the circumstances. What justice if any obtains between victor and vanquished? This same difficulty in fact lay behind the Spartans' request for recompense. Following at once on this account, Herodotus tells of an "unnatural deed" that the king of the Bisaltae did (116). He had forbidden his sons to take part in Xerxes' invasion of Greece, but they "disregarding him as they especially wanted to see the war" joined Xerxes' army; and on their safe return, all six of them had their eyes dug out by their father "for this cause." Once again we have a caricature of justice. The father's prohibition apparently came from his desire to keep his sons from harm, but in spite (or because) of their safe return he regarded their disobedience as more important than the reason for his prohibition. A just rule—obey one's father—overrides all sense of justice.

These six paragraphs, then, though they do not prove our claim to the presence of a plan in the *Inquiries,* at least suggest that it is not absurd to look for one. They make one look back, for example, to the story of Hermotimus, who obtained the greatest recompense for an injustice that Herodotus knew of (105–106), and forward to the way in which the Greeks estimated the worth of Themistocles (123), to say nothing either of Aristides, whom Herodotus held to be the best and most just man in Athens (79.1), or of Timoxenus, whose betrayal of Scione went unpunished lest the Scioneans be forever held treacherous (128). These stories, then, begin to look as if they form part of a reasoned whole, a whole that is only presented in partial stories. They begin to reveal how Herodotus has marshalled particulars, and even a false particular, into a coherent whole that compels us to reflect on a universal question; how an inquiry and a λόγος are made to join; how Herodotus combines an insight into the actors' point of view with his own point of view; and how much that depends on his ability to combine and distinguish the playful and the serious.

* All references are to C. Hude's Oxford text.
** The commentaries of Stein, How-Wells, Sayce (Books I–III), Macan (IV–IX), and the notes of Legrand to his translation. (Budé) have been consulted, but I have usually not repeated what can be found in those works.
*** In noting linguistic peculiarities of a statistical kind in the different books, it is to be understood that, as the book-divisions are not Herodotus' own, we have only used them (especially V–IX) to indicate roughly the limits within which a part of Herodotus' argument is contained.
**** In each chapter all references are to the Book under consideration unless otherwise stated.

I. HERODOTUS

*La pudeur sied bien à tout le monde; mais il faut savoir
la vaincre, et jamais la perdre.*

Montesquieu

The first sentence of Herodotus' *Inquiries* runs: "Here is the showing-forth of the inquiry of Herodotus of Halicarnassus, so that neither what human beings have done might disappear in time, nor the deeds great and admirable, partly shown forth by the Greeks and partly by the barbarians, might be without fame: his inquiry shows forth both other things and through what cause they warred against one another."[1] The so-called Persian wars were wars of Greeks against barbarians; not all the Greeks nor all the barbarians, but primarily the Athenians and Spartans, who were by far the best of the Greeks, and the Persians, who were the best among the barbarians.[2] The war between them might be thought to have been between natural enemies, a war between men with different natures: but they are equally human beings. Although they are human beings, that might seem less important than that some of them are Greeks and some barbarians. Their deeds as those of human beings are neither great nor admirable, they are simply τὰ γενόμενα, which Herodotus does not wish time to eradicate; but as Greek or barbarian deeds they are to be famous, since they are great and admirable. Not human beings but Persians ruled over all Asia, not human beings but Greeks won at Salamis and Plataeae. The difference between Greeks and barbarians overrides their sameness as human beings when we consider the war. It overrides their sameness when we consider the justice or injustice of those who fought. The Greeks fought against the Persians for the sake of their freedom. It appeared to them as it appears to us a just defense. The Persians would seem to have been responsible for that war; but the Persians deny their guilt (1–5). They say the

---

[1] For the syntax see Erbse, H., *Festschrift Bruno Snell* (München, 1956), pp. 209–233.

[2] Cf. Strabo XV.3.23 (735).

Phoenicians were responsible for the original antagonism—they abducted Io—but the Greeks were "greatly responsible" for its permanence. Instead of weighing their own seizures of Europa and Medea against the Phoenicians' seizure of Io and Alexander's of Helen, they destroyed Troy in order to recover Helen; and from that time on the Persians have regarded Greece as their enemy. "for they regard as their own both Asia and the barbarian tribes that dwell there, while they believe Europe and Greece are separate."

The Persians sharply distinguish between Europe and Asia, between what is their own and what is alien. They say the origin of their hatred stems from the Greeks' conquest of Troy, for the rape of Io was a slight injustice, about which no sober man would care, but the destruction of a city—and for so trivial a reason—awakened their desire to punish the Greeks on a large scale. Now Herodotus refuses to say whether or not the Greeks were originally responsible. Instead he seems to make a new beginning: "I am not going to say whether it was in this way or some other, but who I know first began unjust deeds against the Greeks, with just an indication of who he was I shall go on in my *logos,* going alike through small and large cities of human beings." It seems that Herodotus does not think the question of justice very important; practically, to be sure, he counterposes the injustice of Croesus toward Greeks against the injustice of Agamemnon; but he will only indicate Croesus' guilt before he passes on to another theme. This other theme is the small and large cities of human beings, not the cities of Greeks and barbarians. "Cities that were in ancient times great have now become small, and those great in my time were formerly small. Knowing, then, that human happiness never remains in the same place, I shall make mention of both alike." He has in mind the Lydian and Persian empires, of which he shows the Lydian in its destruction (he first half of Book 1) and the Persian in its expansion (the second half). He disclaims that his interest lies in determining who was guilty of the Persian wars. Not the small and large unjust deeds of Greeks and barbarians, but the small and large cities of human beings plot the course of his first *logos.* His indifference to small and large injustices appears in our own uncertainty about whom he thought to be the first wrongdoer among the barbarians. If we believe that the payment of tribute is unjust, then Croesus was the first: but if we believe that even the capture of a city is unjust, as the Persians do (with regard to Troy), then Gyges was the first (6; 14.4).[3] Since all Greeks were free before Croesus' reign, he might be thought more guilty than Gyges; but it remains unclear whether he was not justified in some of his conquests, even if in others he brought forward petty complaints (26.3). Unless the enslavement

---

[3]Consider Thucydides I.15.2; cf. Maddalena, A., *Interpretazioni Erodotee* (Padova, 1942), pp. 1–16.

of a city is never justified, Croesus' responsibility might be only slightly more than Gyges': Herodotus does not give the grounds for either's actions. His silence makes it impossible for us to judge the injustice of either Lydians or Greeks. He deliberately turns us away from a particular question of right and wrong to the universal question of human happiness. He chooses Croesus because his reign brought the independence of Lydia to an end, and not because he enslaved Greek cities. Human happiness, however, cannot be considered apart from all other human things. Herodotus would have to understand somewhat the horizon and the character of human things before he could say something important about human happiness. The first sentence tells us that his *Inquiries* would prevent the things that human beings have done from disappearing; and his narrative about the fall of Lydia and the rise of Persia would seem to fulfill that promise. And yet he talks about Lydians and Persians and not about human beings. Human beings always come to sight as members of some nation or tribe; they never come to sight as human beings. To reveal to us the nature of human beings, Herodotus must first reveal to us what kinds of human beings there are. If he abandons the attempt to discover who first wronged whom, in order to discover the nature of human things, he must first still begin with Greeks and barbarians. He cannot bypass that difference even if it no longer has the same importance for him as it has for the Persians.

What distinguishes barbarians from Greeks is the difference in their customs. Customs are the obstacle to understanding directly the nature of human things. Human beings disagree about the nature of human things. They disagree about what is just and unjust. What each nation considers just is embodied in their customs. The Persians believe ($\nu o\mu i\zeta\varepsilon\iota\nu$) that only unjust men would abduct women, but only foolish men would retaliate, while sensible and sober men would not care. The stories they tell are meant to illustrate these beliefs, and for Herodotus to agree with their version would entail his agreement with their beliefs. He would have to agree with Persian laws about what is just and unjust, what is folly and sobriety. He is now in no position either to agree or disagree. He knows that Persian customs do not agree with Greek customs, just as their version does not agree with the Greek. The Greeks say that Hera drove Io to Egypt, Zeus brought Europa to Crete, and Aphrodite gave Helen to Paris. Not men but gods were responsible for what the Persians believe unjust. The question about justice, which depends on what Greek or Persian laws say is just, proves to conceal the question about the gods. The Persian gods and the Greek gods are not the same. Not only do human things first appear clothed in customs but divine things as well. Neither men nor gods appear as what they are; indeed, men do not appear as what they are because not all men have the same gods. The difference in gods prevents Herodotus from showing forth at once human things. Human things look different in the light of different gods.

Not only human things in general but justice in particular depends for its interpretation on the gods. Homer offers a beautiful illustration of this. Hephaestus puts on the shield of Achilles a city at war and a city at peace. The city of peace has no gods, the city at war shows Athena and Ares leading the troops, and Strife, Din of Battle, and Doom mingling among them (*Iliad* XVIII.515,535). In the city of peace a court is shown in session, where both parties to the dispute have agreed to abide by the decision of the judges (497–508). Since the law of the land is not in question, the gods, who are directly or indirectly the founders of the law and the interpreters of justice, do not have to appear But in the city of war the very existence of its way of life it at stake, and no agreement underlies the dispute between it and its enemy. The gods, therefore, must appear in order to support the laws and customs which they have sanctioned. In a struggle between cities each side must appeal to the gods who support them (cf. I.26.2). Herodotus, however, cannot as Homer does call upon the Muses to let him know who the gods are and what they have decreed. He must come to the gods through the customs and laws of men. He must come to an understanding of justice and human things through what men say about the gods and divine things. Medea's association with Persia (VII.62), Europa's and Helen's with Greece, and Io's with Egypt are the first indications that these three countries form the basis of Herodotus' analysis of human things, for they differ most in what they believe about the gods. What Cicero has L. Furius Philus say in his *Republic* sums up their differences in an Herodotean way: "The justice we are discussing is something political, not natural; for if it were natural, just as hot and cold, bitter and sweet, then just and unjust things would be the same for all. Now, however, if anyone, drawn in that famous Pacuvian chariot of winged snakes, could survey and examine with his own eyes many diverse peoples and cities, let him first look at the Egyptians, who have in writings the memory of the most centuries and happenings, and though the most uncorrupted of men, they believe a certain kind of bull to be a god, whom they call Apis; and many other monsters among them and animals of every kind are numbered among the gods; secondly, let him look at Greece, where there are, as among us, magnificent temples dedicated to images in human shape, which the Persian believed impious; and solely on this account Xerxes is said to have ordered the Athenian sanctuaries to be burnt, because he believed it impious for the gods, whose home is the whole world, to be shut up and imprisoned within walls," (III. 13–14; cf. *Leg.* II.26). Furius contrasts the Egyptians, Greeks, and Persians just as Herodotus himself does: most of what he says comes from Herodotus. The Greeks (we might think) hold a somewhat middle position between the "excessive piety" of the Egyptians and the impiety of the Persians; but Herodotus cannot rest content with their apparent superiority. He must show the how and why of it. The opinions each nation holds about the gods affect the way each understands all things, including human things. Herodotus must understand and judge their customs and laws if he is to go beyond a mere presentation of their incompatibility. Here the greatest difficulty confronts us in reading his *Inquiries*. Herodotus says that everyone would choose his own laws and customs as the most beautiful, even if he could choose from the customs of all others, but he himself does not follow his own opinion: he praises laws that do not agree with Greek laws (two Babylonian, two Persian, one Egyptian and one Scythian), and he blames one of the Babylonian laws that is also found among the Greeks.[4] We might attribute this inconsistency to Herodotus' forgetfulness, but unless we assume that Herodotus was extraordinarily loose in his thinking, we have no right to do so. When he makes a mistake in calculation, it can be simply corrected, but his praise and blame of customs which are not his own, in spite of his belief that Cambyses was obviously mad because he blamed Egyptian laws, cannot be corrected. The contradiction between his own activity and his criticism of Cambyses can only be understood. We try to arrive at such an understanding.

Candaules was in love with his own wife and thus believed her to be the most beautiful of women (8–14).[5] To his most trusted bodyguard Gyges he constantly praised her, and finally he ordered him to behold her naked, so that Gyges could more truthfully agree that she was the most beautiful, "for human ears are less to be trusted than eyes." Gyges was appalled at this command and shouted out: "Oh master, what unhealthy words have you spoken, bidding me to behold my mistress naked? When a woman removes her clothes she removes her shame as well (i.e. the respect we must have towards her). Long ago the beautiful things (morality) were discovered by human beings, from which you must learn; and among them is this one: let each man look at his own. I am persuaded that she is the most beautiful of all women, and I beg you not to demand unlawful things." Candaules believed the eyes more trustworthy than the ears, Gyges was content with report. If the king insisted that his wife was most beautiful, then she was; for beauty was not to be tested but authority trusted. Gyges believed in the beauty of Candaules' wife in the same way he believed in ancient maxims: they were both equally beautiful and equally unseen. Although he had not beheld Candaules' wife nor discovered for himself these maxims, he believed both were what they were said to be. He identified the beautiful with what he had heard, whether it was the voice of Candaules or the voice of the past. Convention and authority were for him the

---

[4]III.38; cf. I.137.1; 196–197; 199; II.64–65.1; 177.2; IV.46.2.

[5]Cf. Pomp. Trogus I.7.15–17; pseudo-Dionysius περὶ λόγων ἐξετάσεως XI, 4 (378, ed. Usener-Radermacher); Harder, R., *Studies Presented to D. M. Robinson* (St. Louis, 1953), vol. II, pp. 446–449).

standard: each laid down with equal force what was to be regarded as true. Gyges, who feared what might happen were he to consent to the king's proposal, knew that Candaules' desire to be confirmed in his view was at odds with his power; for his power could guarantee the only answer he wanted. If his love made him believe his wife most beautiful, he wished Gyges, without being in love, to believe it as well; for to believe without passion would be to believe what was true. Candaules loved what was his own, and because it was his own he thought it most beautiful. He ranked his own wife as Herodotus says men rank their own laws; but his love led him to violate one of those laws, which commands that things not one's own ought not to be seen. He but not Gyges may see his own wife naked. The unlawful thing was for Gyges to see what was not his own—to see what the law says was not his own. The law not only establishes what is one's own, but it itself is one's own: it establishes that one may look only at one's own laws. Gyges violates Lydian but not (in so strict a way) Greek law when he looks at Candaules' wife: "Among the Lydians, and almost among all other barbarians, even for a man to be seen naked leads to great shame."[6] Candaules cannot persuade Gyges by appealing to Greek law; he must only look to Lydian laws, which forbid the Lydians to look at women or men naked. To see them naked is to see them as they are, stripped of the concealment of clothes. And laws are like clothes: they too conceal from us the way things are. All laws say that certain things cannot be seen; before certain things one must have shame. Shame ($\alpha i \delta \omega \varsigma$ occurs nowhere else in Herodotus), which underlies all laws, says each must look to his own laws and no other. The almost universal prohibition among barbarians, that human beings are not to be seen naked, only expresses in a particular way the truly universal prohibition that things alien are not to be seen. But if Gyges unwillingly violates a Lydian law, Herodotus willingly violates the universal prohibition which Gyges himself has formulated. The *Inquiries* of Herodotus continually show him looking at alien things. He looks at the customs of non-Greek people. He agrees with Candaules and not with Gyges that eyes are more trustworthy than ears; but he does not look in order to confirm but to test the beliefs of others. He has lost his shame. He has followed the gods who came to look, and not the goddesses who stayed home out of shame, at Ares and Aphrodite ensnared in the net of Hephaestus (*Od.* VIII.324). He has taken to heart the advice of Athena, who told Telemachus when they had landed in Nestor's kingdom: "No longer do you have need of shame, Telemachus, not even a little, for you sailed over the sea to learn of your father" (III.14ss; cf. VIII.322–327). A traveler, in leaving home, leaves behind all that is familiar and customary; but he still may not be open to the

---

[6]Cf. Thucydides I.6.5–6; Plato *Republic* 457a6–b5.

unfamiliar. His purpose might be, like Telemachus', to find his father, to buy or sell goods, like the Phoenicians', or to take vengeance, like Paris'.[7] Only if he has come like Herodotus to look and for no other reason might he learn how to comprehend both the known and the unknown. Only then might he be able to discover the human beneath the infinite disguises of custom.

Herodotus first showed himself as indifferent to the truth of the Persian account about Io, Medea, Europa, and Helen. He was as indifferent as the Persians say sober men should be to the rape of their own women. He was indifferent to their radical interpretation of Greek stories. He did not become indignant and shout as Gyges did when Candaules urged him to violate Lydian law. He could hear and be silent about what was his own. He now shows that he can also see what is not his own. A story about Gyges turned out to be also about himself. We were able to see this because in a particular story were embedded the universal statements of Gyges and Candaules, whose universality demanded that we compare them with Herodotus' own particular doing. The comparison told us that he would not follow the advice of Gyges. He would not look at his own. He began with Gyges because his Greek readers would see at once that the dilemma of Gyges arose from Lydian laws. They could laugh at Gyges and Candaules, Gyges who had to choose between killing Candaules or himself, and Candaules whose blind love compelled him to violate the law. When Herodotus says, "For it had to turn out badly for Candaules," the reader knows that the necessity is only the necessity of Lydian law. If they had all been Greeks, there would have been no necessity. Herodotus has made his Greek reader look at a Lydian law, which differs from Greek law; and the Greek law, or rather the absence of any such prohibition among the Greeks, would seem as superior as it is. Herodotus has not yet made the reader look at Greek laws in the light of better laws. He has not yet converted him to see even his own as doubtful. He began with the Persian account of the enmity between barbarians and Greeks, which turned on the question of justice, but he soon replaced it with another, the question of human happiness; but that again has been partially replaced with the question of custom. He chose Lydia for two reasons. First, one of its customs pointed to the difference between most barbarians and Greeks, and hence to the difference between Gyges and Herodotus; second, "The Lydians use almost the same customs as the Greeks, except that they prostitute their daughters" (94.1; cf. 35.2; 74.6). The Lydians have the same gods as the Greeks: the oracle at Delphi allows Gyges to retain the throne of Candaules. Thus Herodotus can use the Lydians to show the Greeks to the Greeks. Before he can persuade the Greeks to look on everything as not their own, he must let them look on what

[7]Cf. III.139.1; Iamblichus *de Pyth. vita* XII.58.

resembles and yet differs from their own; for that slight disparity affords the
necessary purchase for a complete conversion.[8] The Lydian *logos* will subtly
lead us away from the Greek to Herodotus' own perspective. It will bring us
round to the seeing of the naturally self-evident.[9]

Gyges could persuade neither Candaules nor his wife to desist in their
intentions; he felt there was no choice but to obey Candaules and then to kill
him. They compelled him to prefer his own life to the maintenance of the law.
Herodotus tells shortly afterwards how Arion overcame a similar dilemma (23–
24; cf. 141).[10] Arion was the best luteplayer of his day, and "the first human
being of those we know who made the dithyramb, gave it its name, and performed it in Corinth." Having spent some time at Periander's court, he went to
Sicily and Italy, and having made a great deal of money then wished to return
to Corinth. Since "he trusted no one more than he did Corinthians," he hired a
Corinthian ship, but the sailors decided to throw him overboard and keep his
money; Arion begged for his life even at the loss of his money; they refused
and gave him the choice of killing himself on board ship ("so that he might
obtain burial on land"), or jumping into the sea; he chose the latter with the
further request that he might first sing, dressed in all the garments of his art.
The sailors, turned pirates, graciously allowed it, "as they were going to hear
the best singer among men," and retreated from the stern into the middle of the
ship. Arion then sang a song, and dressed as he was threw himself into the sea,
and they say a dolphin taking him up on its back brought him safely to
Taenarum. Arion trusted Corinthians the most, for he had become familiar
with their customs and believed that they would practice the same uprightness
at sea as they did at home. He discovered that they lost all sense of justice as
soon as the possibility of punishment disappeared. He discovered that he could
not put his trust in customs (νόμοι) away from home. Finding that he could no
more persuade the sailors than Gyges could Candaules, once they were set on

---

[8]That the Heraclidae obtained the Lydian kingdom "from an oracle"
(6.4), whereas Gyges was confirmed in his usurpation by the "oracle of Delphi" (13.1), shows how far Herodotus' account has moved within the orbit of
Greece; compare ταῦτα μέν νυν Πέρσαι τε καὶ Φοίνικες λέγουσι (5.2) with
ταῦτα μέν νυν Κορίνθιοί τε καὶ Λέσβιοι λέγουσι (24.8); about Io οὐκ
ὁμολογέουσι Πέρσῃσι οὕτω Φοίνικες, but about Arion ὁμολογέουσι δέ σφι
[Κορινθίοισι] Λέσβιοι; cf. 1.3; 2.1; 7.2.

[9]Cf. Aristotle *Physica* 184a16–b14.

[10]The story seems to be a reworking in human terms of the *Hymn to
Dionysus* (VII); consider especially vv. 5–8, 48, 53; the dithyramb was sung
in praise of Dionysus. On the nome see Proclus *Chrestomathia* (ed. Severyns,
vol. II); Wilamowitz, U., *Timotheos* (Leipzig, 1903), pp. 89–105.

violating the laws, Arion turned to another kind of law. He put his trust in "the shrill tune" (νόμος ὁ ὄρθιος)—nowhere in Herodotus does νόμος mean "tune"—, which persuaded a dolphin to save him. A dolphin (δελφίς) not Delphi saved him (13). Arion had greater resources than Gyges. Gyges could only appeal to the beautiful things discovered long ago, Arion could appeal to the sailors' pleasure in his excellent singing, and rely on his own inventiveness to attract a dolphin. Arion was a poet, and it is not too fanciful, I think, to consider Herodotus as another Arion. He too has his music, even though it is less powerful than Arion's. To us there is something childish and superstitious in Herodotus' attributing to Arion the magic of Orpheus. If he had said that his singing made the pirates relent, we could have readily accepted such a change of heart; but for a dolphin to come to his rescue hardly adds to the charm of the story as it taxes our credulity. The story seems to point to Arion's powers and then to cast doubt on them: in looking to his own in a nonGygean way—his own νόμος—, his self-reliance is suggested to be inadequate. Arion, however, needed this fabulous savior because he was in an extreme ἀπορίη, where no ordinary music could have saved him. But if Herodotus is another Arion, could it be that the dolphin is meant to indicate the lesser risk Herodotus ran, who therefore did not have to employ so magical a Muse? For Herodotus too was faced with an ἀπορίη. He has shown in the story of Gyges that he no longer can trust customs; he has set sail on the open sea where customs cannot be a guide, and he wishes to persuade the reader to abandon his trust in them as well. He must entice us to listen to his own *logos* and not to the familiar tunes of our laws. He must sing to us and so charm us that we will not object to our own conversion; or if he cannot convert us, we shall at least be charmed enough to let him pursue his inquiries. Everybody knows that he has charmed all his readers, but his great success has hidden the purpose of that charm. We are not immediately aware of the way his *logos* is taking us. The stories of Gyges and Arion, taken together, indicate his way.[11] Herodotus tells us through them that he will proceed both cautiously and boldly. His caution arises from his unwillingness to offend the customary beliefs of his Greek reader, who may not wish to be anything more than entertained;[12] his bold-

---

[11]That a connection exists between the Gyges and Arion stories is indicated by Plato in the *Republic*. After Socrates has proposed the first of the three waves, the common education of men and women, he compares the ridicule it will encounter with that which greeted naked gymnastic exercises (452c4-d1); and then in going on to defend his own proposal against a possible objection, he says to Glaucon: οὐκοῦν καὶ ἡμῖν νευστέον καὶ πειρατέον σῴζεσθαι ἐκ τοῦ λόγου, ἤτοι δελφῖνά τινα ἐλπίζοντας ἡμᾶς ὑπολαβεῖν ἂν ἢ τινα ἄλλην ἄπορον σωτηρίαν (453d9-11).

[12]For Herodotus' caution see Pearson, L., *TAPhA*, pp. 335-355.

ness arises from the necessity to expose those beliefs to the test of truth; but he cannot be both cautious and bold without resorting to "poetic" devices. These devices are his stories which, by standing halfway between fact and invention, untie as they unite them. It is a monstrous union that because of its monstrosity lets us understand that belief, error, and custom have precisely the same character as Herodotus' stories. They imitate belief, error, and custom. They reveal as well as conceal their "meaning." They are indebted for this doubleness to Arion's νόμος, which showed Herodotus how he could remain within Greek νόμος even though he had broken with it. Arion saved himself in the midst of lawlessness by poetry, Herodotus saves himself and his *logos* in the midst of contradictory laws by the same means. His *logos,* however, requires more than poetry to save it. It requires, as we shall see, nature, φύσις, whose discovery shapes the argument of his *Inquiries.* Before he embarks on its discovery he prepares us for it with the story of Croesus. It is Herodotus' "shrill tune."

Solon once came to Croesus' court (29–33).[13] He had made the laws for the Athenians at their own request and then stayed abroad for ten years, using as an excuse his desire to look, but in fact he went "lest he might be compelled to dissolve any of the laws he established." Croesus does not know this; he says of him what we could truthfully say of Herodotus: "Athenian stranger, much talk has come to us about you, on account of your wisdom and wandering, how in desiring to be wise (φιλοσοφέων) you have travelled broadly for the sake of seeing (θεωρίη)." Solon did not travel in order to look but in order to escape from an ἀπορίη. He wanted the Athenians to accustom themselves to his laws and not force him, in irritation at their novelty, to change them. As a legislator, a maker of new laws—the word occurs here for the first time—he resembles Arion who invented the dithyramb. Arion escaped from lawless sailors by singing, Solon escaped from an Athens that had not yet accepted his laws by going abroad. Arion discovered that he could not trust Corinthian laws but only a musical tune away from home, Solon left his new "tunes" at home and went to look at the laws of other nations. He even went so far as to introduce an Egyptian law into Athens (II.177.2). Even in travelling, then, he carried the concerns of Athens with him. He travelled not merely to see but to make use of what he saw on his return. He may have been wise, but he was not a philosopher in Herodotus' opinion.[14] He was one of the seven so-called wise men, six of whom Herodotus mentions in the first half of Book I;

---

[13]Cf. Aristotle *Ath. Pol.* XI.1.

[14]Cf. Plutarch *Solon* 3.6–8. Solon uses only Greek examples of happiness, though he could have used Psammetichus or Psammis (II.161.2; cf. 177.1; III.10.2).

Periander, Bias, Pittacus, Solon, Chilon, and Thales.[15] We would seem to be presented with wisdom itself at the very beginning of his *Inquiries*. What Solon says to Croesus appears to be the definitive opinion of Herodotus himself on human happiness, just as the story of Croesus appears to confirm that opinion. All the rest of Herodotus, if this were true, would be superfluous to his argument. There would have been no need to go beyond Lydia in order to discover the nature of human things. That the Egyptian Amasis and the Persian Artabanus apparently agree with Solon seems to support this.[16] In spite of the fundamental differences in Greek, Egyptian. and Persian gods, a Greek, and Egyptian, and a Persian all speak of divine jealousy—it strengthens our contention that Greece, Egypt, and Persia are the major countries of Herodotus' *logos*—; and yet we soon realize that Amasis is still Egyptian and Artabanus still Persian in the way they understand divine jealousy. Could Solon then be also still Greek in his understanding? Herodotus gives us several indications that he is. He has Solon use the word ἄτη, "doom," which often occurs in Solon's poetry but never again in Herodotus.[17] The word is almost entirely poetic, endowed with the meanings which Greek poets have given it, and Herodotus makes it clear in Book II that he does not always agree with them. He makes us consider, then, how much credence we ought to give to Solon. He emphasizes the Greek and hence partial view of Solon by attributing to him a mistake in calculation. Solon tells Croesus there are seventy years in a man's life, and in trying to bring home to him its instability he calculates the number of days they make up. His use of the Greek calendar for his reckoning compels him to add separately the days in an intercalary month, which he says occurs every other year "so that the seasons might come out as they should." Their addition makes the total too large by 700 days. That Herodotus deliberately had Solon make this error he indicates in Book II, where he says the Egyptians deal with the solar year more wisely than the Greeks; for they divide it into twelve equal parts of thirty days each and then add five days at the end of the year (II.4.1). The Greeks' inability to adapt astronomical evidence to their own use brought about Solon's error. Should we suspect, then, that Solon's insistence on the disproportion between the divine and the human, which is divine jealousy, had its origin in that inability? At any rate, the Egyptians, with their more accurate calendar, believed they could predict from the

---

[15]20; 27.2; 59.2; 74.2; 75.3; 170; Diels-Kranz, *Vor-Sokratiker*[2], vol. I, pp. 61–66.

[16]III.40.2–43; VII.108; 46.4; cf. pp. 132-3; 181–2 *infra*.

[17]Cf. Solon fr. 1, 13, 68, 75; 3, 35. θεοσεβής occurs only at 86.2 and II.37.1; θεοφιλής at 87.2; the plural μοῖραι at 91.2; and πεπρωμένον at 91.1,3; III.64.5.

moment of birth the fate of every man (II.82.1).[18]

Solon presents a Greek understanding of divine jealousy, but he does not persuade Croesus that one must look to the end before calling a man blessed. His failure to persuade, though he said what was true and did not flatter, differs from the way Bias (or Pittacus) dissuaded Croesus from attacking the Greek islands. He told Croesus that the islanders intended to attack him; and when Croesus expressed the wish that they would be so foolish as to meet his Lydian cavalry, he said the islanders were equally pleased when they heard that he was building ships to attack them. Croesus took the hint and formed alliances with them. Bias or Pittacus made up a story and convinced Croesus, Solon told the truth and failed. Solon lacked the art to adapt the truth to Croesus.[19] We may well wonder whether Herodotus followed the way of Bias or the way of Solon. The way of Bias consists in first accepting the premises of him who is to be persuaded, and then in finding or inventing an example that, on the very same premises, compels him to revise or abandon those premises. Herodotus indicates that this is his own way as follows. Only six of the seven wise men are mentioned by name, and we might wonder why he omitted a seventh, no matter whether he would have been Cleobulus, Myson, or someone else, especially since he says all the wise men (σοφισταί) came to Croesus' court. He does, however, mention someone who could qualify for the seventh. A Lydian, whose name might have been Sandanis (71.2),[20] advised Croesus not to attack Persia; he reasoned in the same way as Bias had, trying to show Croesus how he would lose everything if he failed and gain nothing if he won.[21] We realize that only his being a Lydian precludes his being one of the seven wise men. They are the seven wise men of Greece and not wise men simply, as the reader begins to suspect when he reads Herodotus' account of Sandanis: "customarily regarded (νομιζόμενος) to be wise even before, and after this piece of advice having a very great name among the Lydians." If only the Lydians thought Sandanis to be wise, and his wisdom were as provincial as his fame, then the same might hold true for the seven wise men of Greece. They too might be only wise Greeks. The reader becomes forced to

---

[18]It is well-known that Solon could never have met Croesus since Solon lived about thirty years too early; but may we not regard the false synchronicity as another example of Herodotus' using the Greek point of view in his Lydian history? Cf. Plutarch *Solon* 27.1; for a similar 'error' see Chap. II, fn 54.

[19]Cf. Plutarch, *Solon* 28.1; Aul. Gellius II.29.

[20]Cf. Jacoby, F., *Hermes* 51, 1916, pp. 477ff. = pp. 169ff. of *Abhandlungen z. Griech. Geschichtsschreibung*, ed. Bloch, 1956.

[21]Cf. 207.3–7; IV.83. Note the similarity between 27.3 and 71.4.

think through again their proverbial wisdom, which may have its only support in his familiarity with it; or if he finds it adequate, he must recognize that the Greeks have no corner on such wisdom; it can also be found among the barbarians. In the same way Herodotus later mentions six Greek and one foreign oracle that Croesus consulted, and in the absence of any report about what they said, we have to conclude that perhaps all seven told the truth, including an oracle among the barbarians (46.2–3). Herodotus has led us to this conclusion without saying anything himself. His silence must not be confounded with thoughtlessness. He has let the evidence speak for itself, just as he usually abstains from telling us his own opinion about the truth or falsity of what he relates; rather, his silence urges us to think it out for ourselves, using as a guide what he has told us elsewhere (II.123.1; VII.152.3). We must always keep in mind two things in reading Herodotus: what does each story or episode mean in itself and in its context, and how does its meaning fit in with what Herodotus himself does or says. Neither Herodotus nor his characters always say the same things about the same things. We have no more right to attribute Solon's opinions to Herodotus than to deny Amasis' opinions to him; nor to take less seriously what he says in Book II, for example, than what he says in Book VIII. We must be prepared to find his intention as much in the plan of his *Inquiries* as in his explicit statements.

"After Solon had departed a great nemesis from god seized Croesus, as one might guess, because he believed himself to be the most prosperous of all human beings" (34–45). So Herodotus begins the story of Adrastus and Croesus' son Atys: nowhere else does he use the word νέμεσις, which like ἄτη, is mostly poetic. It is well-known that the story abounds in poetic phrases, even to its breaking into tragic trimeters from time to time; and that it contains a phrase from Sophocles' *Meleager,* whose famous boar-hunt seems to have been the model for the Mysians' hunt here.[22] Indeed, the name Atys suggests ἄτη, and the name Adrastus means "inescapable," so that we are inevitably reminded of the Greek proverb "Adrastean Nemesis" ('Αδράστεια Νέμεσις), which was applied to those whose fortune like Croesus changed from good to bad.[23] All the elements of the story would be so familiar to the

[22]Cf. 36.2 with Sophocles fr. 401 P; see also *Iliad* IX. 538–546; XXIII.85–90; and on 45.2, Hermogenes περὶ μεθόδου δεινότητος 32, in *Rhetores Graeci* (vol. III, p. 438, Walz; vol. II, p. 452, Spengel); Forstemann, A. G., *de vocabulis quae videntur esse apud H. poeticis* (Magdeburg, 1892); Aly, W., *Volksmärchen, Sage, u. Novelle bei H. u. seinen Zeitgenossen* (Göttingen, 1921), pp. 38–40.

[23]Zenobius I.30; Macarius I.28; Apostolius I.31 in *Corp. Paroem. Graec.*, vols. I, II (ed. Leutsch et Schneidewin); cf. *Iliad* II.828–834; see further Blomfield's note on Aesch. *Prom.* 936 (972).

Greek reader that he would accept them as the way things must be, and he would not think at first that the tragedy of Adrastus depends as much on custom as the comedy of Gyges. Adrastus unwillingly killed his brother and with "unclean hands" came to Sardis, where he asked Croesus to purify him "according to the native customs": "The manner of purification is much the same among the Lydians as among the Greeks." The coincidence of customs sets the stage for the tragedy that follows, whereas the difference of customs in the story of Gyges allowed the reader to see the lack of necessity in Gyges' dilemma. Here Atys and Adrastus seem truly caught because their sense of shame agrees with the reader's. Atys reproaches his father for not letting him go on the hunt: "The most beautiful and noblest things, father, had previously been mine, to win renown in wars and hunts; but now you have shut me out from these, observing neither any sign of cowardice nor reluctance in me. Now then what kind of eyes must I show in going to and from the market-place? What opinion will the citizens have of me? What will my bride think? What kind of husband will she believe that she lives with?" Atys is filled with civil shame, fearful lest others despise him. His excellence must be confirmed in the eyes of others, just as the beauty of Candaules' wife needs Gyges to bear witness. We are in the realm of opinion, δόξα, which ultimately depends on custom. Herodotus later remarks on the widespread but not universal belief in the nobility of the warrior class: "Thracians, Scythians, Persians, Lydians, and almost all the barbarians believe artisans are more despicable than the other citizens, while those who are far removed from handicrafts they customarily regard as noble, especially those dedicated to war" (II.167.1; cf. I.41.3). Only because most Greeks, as Herodotus says, agree with this custom does Atys' shame appear natural. And, similarly, when Adrastus kills Atys by accident, the shame that drives him to suicide, "acknowledging himself to be the most heavy with calamity of those he knew," appears equally natural (cf. 82.8; 213; VII.232). His shame might lie deeper than that of Candaules' wife, for hers seems to arise solely from custom, while not even Croesus' forgiveness can remove Adrastus'. There were customary rites to cleanse Adrastus of his first murder, but none seems able to cleanse him of the second. His story, when compared with Gyges', raises one of the questions that most occupies Herodotus: How far is shame something natural? And what is its source? But the conventionality of this story, to say nothing of its poetic form, shows how far Herodotus is from regarding it now as more than a question. It does not seem accidental, moreover, that the first story entirely Greek in tone should be tragic; not only because we might regard it as "typically" Greet, endowed as it is with the sense of doom, but because tragedy suits, as the Athenian stranger of Plato remarks, the majority of men and educated women (*Lgs.* 658d3–5; 817b1–cl). The tragedy of Adrastus better accords with common views than the comedy of Gyges. Laws and customs suggest by their own inexorableness—they tacitly say their way is the only way—that the same holds true for man's destiny. Both tragedy and the law assert that what is must be and what must be is. Herodotus could not have shown us more clearly how much our customs and laws penetrate everything we think and do.[24] Adrastus' story gives the impression it does as much from the way the reader takes it as from the way Herodotus tells it. The story is a double mirror. It reflects at once the Greek and Herodotus' own perspective. Where the reader at first will only see 'fate,' Herodotus sees a question that the reader himself must finally be persuaded to ask. The first half of Book I has too often been taken for Herodotus' final opinion, and its questioning and provisional character has been overlooked. We go on to indicate with a few more examples how it naturally compels the Greek reader to question Greek customs and prepare him for listening to Herodotus' own *logos*.

Herodotus began with what the Persians and Phoenicians say, but he at once dismissed it and began again with what the Lydians, Milesians, Delphians, Lesbians, and Corinthians say; he did not even doubt the story of Arion; indeed, he has so far only corrected the common name 'Corinthian' for the treasury at Delphi (14.2).[25] Only gradually does he lead us to question the veracity of what he reports. Croesus tried to test the truthfulness of seven oracles, six Greek and one Libyan, and of these he judged only the Delphic and Amphiaraean worthy of trust; but Herodotus remarks. "What the other oracles prophesied is not said by anyone": and he later adds, "With regard to the reply of Amphiaraeus' oracle I cannot say what it told the Lydians after they did the customary things at the shrine, for not even this is said, except that he (Croesus) believed that Amphiaraeus also possessed a true oracle (47.2; 49)[26] We must wonder whether the other five oracles lied, including the oldest Greek oracle at Dodona (II.52.2), or whether they told the truth but Croesus could not interpret them correctly, just as he later misunderstood the responses of Delphi. Herodotus does not now make us doubt the veracity of the Pythian oracle but of the Delphians themselves. Their assertion that a bowl Croesus dedicated was the work of Theodorus now needs his independent testimony, for some Delphian, whose name Herodotus "willingly" forgets, forged an

---

[24]Aristotle *Metaphysica* 995a3–6.

[25]Cf. p. 151 *infra*; also 72.1 with V.49.6; VII.72.1.

[26]Herodotus himself uses λέγεται in these two places for the first time; the third occurrence is at 60.3, the next at 61.1 (cf. V.71. 1); see 31.2. There are four main ways in which Herodotus uses λέγεται: a) of what he has not seen; b) of what is divine or miraculous; c) of a double account; d) of what is the best or the worst or a superlative in some way; approximately 60 out of a total 150 instances fall into the first two classes, and twenty into the third.

inscription in order to gratify the Spartans on one of the two sprinklers Croesus dedicated, the inscription now reading that they were the offerings of the Spartans. We are a far cry from Herodotus' previous remark: "I know it happened thus having heard so from the Delphians" (20; 51.3-4).[27]

The oracle told Croesus to make an alliance with the most powerful of the Greeks, and Croesus, finding the two most powerful to be Athens and Sparta, set out to learn which he should choose (53.3-70). Before he tells what Croesus learned on inquiry, Herodotus broaches a theme that becomes increasingly more important—the origin of Greece, i.e., the origin of Greek customs. He tells us that the Athenians were originally barbarians (Pelasgians), while the Spartans belong to the Dorians, who as Dorians may have always spoken Greek. The Greeks as Greeks claim to be superior to the barbarians, but Herodotus shows that, though linguistically separate from them for a long time, they were until recently in point of wisdom as foolish as any barbarians. Their folly consists in what they believe about the gods. "The most simple-minded trick by far, as I find," brought about the return of Pisistratus, even though "Greece had been separated from the barbarians from rather ancient times, cleverer as it is and more removed from simple folly," but nevertheless the partisans of Pisistratus then succeeded "among the Athenians who are said to be first of the Greeks in wisdom." The Athenians believed that a tall and beautiful woman, dressed in full armor and drawn in a chariot, was Athena herself, who had appeared to bring Pisistratus back to Athens. Their belief was based on the conviction that the gods have a human shape: even the Delphic oracle could wonder whether to address Lycurgus, the maker of new laws for the Spartans, as a human being or a god (65.3).[28] Herodotus mocks the Athenians but not the Delphic oracle, and yet the difference seems slight: Phye with less than four cubits' height was human, but a seven cubit skeleton convinced the Spartans that it was Orestes' bones (68.3; cf. VII.117; IX.83.2). Thus Herodotus begins to disturb the reader, making him laugh at the Athenians and question, on the same basis, the Spartans' piety. He cannot but wonder if the difference between impiety and piety is only three cubits. Croesus, at any rate, on learning how matters stood, preferred to make an alliance with Sparta; for the Spartans like himself always consulted Delphi before they undertook anything, whereas Pisistratus only pretended to have

----

[27] Cf. II.52.1; III.117.6.

[28] The name of the Athenian woman Φύη suggests the second half of the word ἀνθρωποφυής, which the Persians believe no god is (131.1); and this is strengthened by the fact that Phye is the only woman in Herodotus called ἡ ἄνθρωπος (60.5); Herodotus elsewhere uses the more common ἀνθρωποειδής (II.86.7; 142.3).

divine guidance. "A divine escort" for him was nothing but the cast of a die. He heard an oracle-monger say, "The cast is thrown," and hence concluded he should attack the Athenians while some were asleep and others were playing dice (62.3–63).[29] He succeeded at every turn by spreading false rumors; while the Spartans, though they too fabricated a false charge, had the support of Delphi. That the Greeks are skilled in lying the next episode shows, where Herodotus hazards for the first time his own opinion about a double account among the Greeks; the Spartans insisting that the Samians robbed them of the bronze crater they sent to Croesus, and the Samians insisting that the Spartans sold it when they heard Sardis had been captured: "Perhaps those who sold it would say on their return to Sparta that the Samians had taken it" (70.3).[30] As he concludes the first half of Book I, Herodotus continually increases the distance between himself and the Greeks-Lydians, as he casts more and more doubt on what they say. He indicates there are other ways of taking an oath than the Greek way—the first indication (since the Gyges episode) that not all men have the same customs—, and for the first time he sharply contradicts a Greek story.[31] The Greeks, then, represent Herodotus' standard neither in wisdom nor justice. Their understanding of divine things will prove to fall far short of the Persian and Egyptian, and their practice of justice cannot match the Persians'. The Persians do not believe in gods of human shape, the Egyptians know the gods must be much older than the Greeks say they are, and the Persians are accustomed to tell the truth, which they say is necessary for justice.

What we have said suffices to indicate how Herodotus has tried to convert the Greek reader to the seeing of things not his own. He has not yet answered the questions he has raised, nor even formulated the questions precisely; for he could not do so until he had persuaded us to listen to the questions. With the fall of Sardis and the Lydian empire, he is prepared to start afresh, expecting us to have realized not only the uncertainty of human happiness but the provinciality of our understanding of human things. He now begins from the Persian side, whose customs completely differ from the Greeks' (except in one particular); and he states a new principle of narration: "As some Persians tell, who do not want to exalt or magnify what concerns Cyrus but want to tell the story that is true (τὸν ἐόντα λόγον), so I shall write, though I know how to speak about Cyrus in three other ways" (95.1).[32] Herodotus in his Lydian

---

[29]βόλος and βολή are used of dice; cf. Xenophon *Memorabilia* I.iii.2. Pisistratus had the nickname Bacis, Schol. Aristoph. *Pax* 1071.

[30]Cf. 65.4; 138.1; 153.1–2.

[31]74.5; 75.3–6; 87.1 (cf. 86.3; also Thucydides II.77.5–6); 91.1; 94.2; cf. 89.2–3; 92.4 with Plutarch *de Herodoti malignitate* XVIII.1–3.

[32]For σεμνοῦν cf. 122.3; III.16.7; also I.99.2.

account did not speak of the Greeks' or Lydians' veracity; he recorded with
increasing doubt what they say, but he never mentioned the possibility he
might have written the story of Croesus otherwise, that there might have been
a version which did not bring in the gods. There was no one among the
Lydians or the Greeks who wished to tell an unadorned truth: in the Persian
account there are dreams but no oracles, and the magi incorrectly interpret a
dream (120; cf. 208). Everything now appears in a different light, the light of
the truthtelling Persians. Herodotus transposes two Greek stories into a Persian
setting—those of Thyestes and Oedipus—in telling the story of Cyrus' child-
hood. By letting us hear directly what Astyages, Harpagus, Cyrus, the
shepherd and his wife have to say, with almost no comments by himself, we
willingly accept that transposition. We understand the necessities under which
they acted as though they were our own, and we soon forget the Greek versions of Oedipus and Thyestes. We become slightly Persian. The story takes us
in as the first account of the Persians did not. There we were told of Io,
Europa, Medea, and Helen without any details, and the Persian interpretation
sounded strange to our ears; for we had not yet been loosened from our trust in
the familiar, and even Herodotus was unwilling to commit himself as to its
truth; but now he trusts unreservedly the Persians. They must be the same Persians as those he then called learned (οἱ λόγιοι) who did not magnify the heroic
age.

Before telling how the Persians took over the Median empire, Herodotus
goes back as many generations as he had at the start, to the time of Candaules
and Gyges, after he had mentioned Croesus as the first barbarian to enslave the
Greeks. Now he begins with Deioces who partly resembles Candaules and
partly Gyges (95.2–101). At the break-up of the Assyrian empire, a certain
wise man, Deioces, conceived a love for tyranny, and "knowing that the unjust
is inimical to the just," he practiced justice in the midst of anarchy, and so
successfully that his neighbors brought him all their disputes to settle, which
he judged "in accordance with the right," until they consulted no one else and
everyone came to him, "because they heard that suits always turned out in
accordance with the truth." Deioces then refused to be bothered further with
judging, but when lawlessness and rapine broke out again, the Medes decided
to elect him king, so that they could attend to their own affairs as Deioces
would maintain justice among them. The Persians had traced the enmity
between themselves and the Greeks back to the Trojan war, and Herodotus did
not then decide for or against their version; for he know it depended on
customs alien to the Greeks, not only those dealing with the gods but also with
justice. He now, however, returns to their understanding of justice in the story
of Deioces. Deioces, "because he longed for rule, was straight and just."
Basing himself on what the Greeks would regard as the greatest injustice,

tyranny, Deioces was just.[33] Though he knew the just and unjust were at war with one another, that did not prevent him from being just in all particular cases, so that he could completely conceal his injustice in general. Even after he became tyrant he continued to be just but harsh in its maintenance. His harshness stemmed from his making himself an exception to the enmity between justice and injustice. He first established the law that no one should have access to the king nor should anyone see him; and besides he established it as shameful to laugh or spit in his presence: "He thus made himself awesome lest his comrades, in seeing him, brought up as they were with him and in no way of worse family nor deficient in excellence, be pained and plot against him, and that they might think him, in not seeing him, to be different." As the unjust source of all justice, Deioces could not be seen; he was the measure of without being himself measurable by right and wrong; his spies reported everything they saw and heard to him, but no one could see him. He surrounded himself with as much mystery as Lydian laws had surrounded the nakedness of men and women. He established as shameful the seeing of what was alien, namely himself, who had always to be regarded as beyond laughter. The essence of a way of life is shown in that at which one is forbidden to laugh, for that is what everyone is expected to look up to; and what one looks up to both literally and figuratively are primarily the gods (cf. III.37-38). Deioces, as the founder of a new way of life, imitated the gods (cf. 65.3). Even the new city he established, with its seven concentric walls rising to his palace at the top of a partly natural and partly artificial hill, was modelled on the seven planets (98.4-6). As the gods constitute the heart of every set of laws and customs (cf. II.52.1), Deioces' imitation of the gods points to a deeper understanding of shame than the story of Gyges. Gyges had maintained that the beautiful things were one's own, and the law forbade one to look at the beautiful things of others; but he had not gone on to say that the forbidden things, at which one could not look, might be forbidden because they were ugly and not beautiful. Deioces supplies that addition and deepens the intention of Herodotus. Deioces instilled shame in his subjects so that they would not know of the defectiveness of the justice he dispensed. He hid from them the ugly basis of the beautiful. Herodotus, then, will not only look at what is not his own, in disobeying Gyges' precept, but he will look at its sources, the possible defects in what each set of customs takes to be beautiful. He will disobey Deioces as well as Gyges.

Gyges and Deioces resemble each other in one other respect. Although Gyges wanted to be just, he was compelled to become a tyrant, which was the

---

[33]Cf. Plutarch *op. cit.* XVIII.4; for a similar contradiction cf. VIII.68α1; see Chap. VII, fn 16.

conscious ambition of Deioces. Under the compulsion of custom, Gyges proved to be as unjust as Deioces. Gyges and Deioces illustrate the story of Gyges that Plato's Glaucon tells in the *Republic* (359a6–d7). If a just man had the ring of Gyges which would make him invisible, he would act, according to Glaucon, in the same way as the unjust man similarly equipped (cf. III. 72.4– 5). Herodotus' Gyges was compelled to become unjust not because he had the ring of invisibility but because he saw that which should have remained invisible, and Deioces was able to be unjust with the greatest appearance of justice because he had learned how to make himself invisible. The violation of the *arcana* led to the same result as the creation of the *arcana*. Gyges and Deioces together, then, show as much as Glaucon's story does the precariousness of justice. They show that Herodotus' concern with law and custom coincides with his concern for justice.

Herodotus exemplifies the question Deioces' tyranny raises in his discussion of two Babylonian laws, one the wisest and most beautiful, the other the ugliest or most shameful (196–199). The most beautiful law consists in this: each village offers for sale its most beautiful maidens to the highest bidder; and the money collected from them becomes the inducement for the poorer citizens, who have no need of beauty, to marry the ugliest, the girl going to whoever would marry her for the least amount, though he had to furnish guarantors of his intention to live with her. The ugliest law, on the other hand, demands that every native woman lie with a stranger once in her life, sitting at the temple of Aphrodite; and if a stranger drops any sum of money in her lap, no matter how small, saying, "I call upon the goddess Mylitta," she must lie with him. If the woman has any beauty at all, she soon fulfills her obligation, but if deformed she may have to stay there for as long as four years (cf. IV.117). The most beautiful law levels as it preserves the natural differences in beauty, the ugliest law, which is a sacred law, heightens as it destroys the same natural differences. The first law ranks the girls in order of their beauty by means of money, and then tries to compensate for the rankings by distributing the money in an inverse order of beauty. The second law not only does not equalize differences but ignores them: the most beautiful can be had for as little money as the ugliest. The first law depends on a fair measure of prosperity, so that the fathers of beautiful daughters would be willing to lose whatever money they could make if they sold them privately; the second law can exist even in the worst times. Herodotus says the first law fell into disuse, and the poorer classes now prostitute their daughters; he implies that the second law is still in effect in his own day. He finds here, just as he did in the case of Deioces, the ugly and the beautiful subsisting together. It is his own distinction and not one the Babylonians themselves would accept. They established both laws and in Herodotus' opinion would have chosen both as the most beautiful from all laws. He has not explained how the Babylonians could confound the ugly with the beautiful to such an extent as not to see the difference between these two laws. He has only presented the problem which the later books (especially II) try to solve.

The second half of Book I, the rise and consolidation of the Persian empire, describes a great variety of customs—e.g., Babylonian, Persian, Massagetaean—all of which serve to complete the conversion of the reader that the first half began. As we shall see, these laws present all the major differences among laws which Herodotus tries to account for in Books II–IV; but now they indicate how he intends to proceed in his *Inquiries*. It looked at first as if he intended to maintain a temporal order in his narration, having indicated who first wronged the Greeks to go on to those who came later; and to some extent he has done so—Croesus, Cyrus, Cambyses, Darius, and Xerxes; but the sentence, which says he will indicate who was first, ends with the statement that he will proceed alike through the small and large cities of men. Geography seems to replace temporality. We must consider what that partial replacement implies. The Persians spoke of events that had happened in the Greek heroic age; but Herodotus, by his indifference to the truth or falsity of what they say, suggests that he will not concern himself with heroes, and except for brief notices now and then he does not enter deeply into that part of the Greek past. His *Inquiries* cover intensively less than 150 years, within which time he finds all the evidence he needs for the discovery of human things. In dismissing the heroic age he turned to Lydia, whose customs so nearly resembled the Greeks'. One of the first sight-worthy things he mentioned was the welded iron support for a silver bowl at Delphi: "The work of Glaucus of Chios, who alone of all human beings discovered the welding of iron" (25.2).[34] After the heroic age, in the Hesiodic scheme, came the iron age, the age to which Herodotus seems to have turned in abandoning that of the heroes. There arc a number of indications that he has done so. Croesus dreamed that an iron spear would kill his son, but Atys convinced him that on a hunt he would run no danger, since boars have tusks of horn (34.2–3; 38.4).[35] Moreover, we learn how a Spartan was able to discover the bones of Orestes (67.3–68). While on tour of duty in Tegea Lichas watched in amazement as a blacksmith hammered iron; the blacksmith, seeing his wonder,

---

[34]Consider this in relation to the story of Arion which precedes it.

[35]Note in addition that among the tribes Croesus subdued were the Chalybes (28), "craftsmen in iron," as Prometheus calls them (Aesch. *Prom.* 714–716), and reputedly the first to work in iron, a tribe that was usually placed on the other side of the Halys. Consider what was said above about αἰδώς and νέμεσις with Hesiod *OD* 197–201. "Iron" occurs ten times out of a total 31 in the first part of Book I (1–94).

stopped his work and said: "You would have very much wondered, Spartan stranger, if you had seen what I saw, since now you are amazed at the working of iron." The blacksmith wanted to dig a well in his courtyard and came on a coffin in which there was a seven cubit skeleton. Lichas at once realized what the enigmatic words of the Delphic oracle had meant, which said that the Spartans would find the bones of Orestes where "two winds blow by strong necessity, strike and counter-strike, and woe is laid on woe." Seeing the bellows, anvil and hammer, he understood the oracle's description of a forge, comparing the hammering of iron to woe laid on woe, "since iron was discovered for man's grief." Beneath the floor of a blacksmith's shop lie the bones of a hero: the iron age has literally buried the heroic.

The word for blacksmith is χαλκεύς, "bronze-worker," which indicates, as does the wonder of Lichas, that iron was discovered more recently than bronze. According to Hesiod, the warlike bronze age disappeared without a trace, "nameless" he calls them (*OD* 143-155). Herodotus, in going as far back as he could by hearsay, discovered that the Carians, then called Leleges, were subject to Minos and manned his ships, being "the most renowned race by far at that time" (171-174; cf. V.118-121; VII.93). They made three discoveries in military equipment which the Greeks took over: plumes on helmets, insignia and handles on shields. The Carians had lost by the time of the second conquest of Ionia all of their renown: "Having shown forth no brilliant deed they were enslaved by Harpagus." As the only people Herodotus knows of who sacrifice to a martial Zeus (Ζεὺς στράτιος), they would correspond to Hesiod's bronze age (cf. II.152.3-4), but with this difference: the Carians have not disappeared. They still survive, though greatly reduced in fame and power. Herodotus, then, has partially replaced the temporal order of Hesiod with a geographical distribution; or, more precisely, the variety of customs has replaced the differences in genealogy. The Persians, for example, partly correspond to the men of the silver age, who, filled with arrogance, according to Hesiod, "were unwilling to sacrifice on the sacred altars of the blessed gods, which is right for men (to do) according to custom" (127-142);[36] so the Persians have no altars on which to sacrifice, and Croesus calls them arrogant by nature (φύσιν—its first occurrence) (89.2: 132.1). And finally the Massagetae resemble the men of the golden age, uncorrupted as they are and using only gold and bronze, for their land lacks silver and iron (215; cf. III.23.4; Strabo XI.8.7(513)). The Massagetae did not live in the time of Cronus, nor were the Persians made and then destroyed by Zeus; they live simultaneously with the Lydians, Greeks, and Carians in different parts of the earth. The surface of the

---

[36]Cf. line 130 with 136.2 here, Plato *Leges* 694d1-7, and Proclus' scholium to Hesiod *ad loc.* (Gaisford, T., *Poetae Minores*, III, 104).

earth presents together all the Hesiodic ages, which are not distinguished so much by what metals they use as by their customs. The Lydians first appear as the representatives of the iron age, and their customs show some of the consequences of that condition. They were the first men Herodotus knows of who coined gold and silver money, as they were also the first shop-keepers (94.1; cf. 79.3; 155–156). At the time of Cyrus' conquest they were the strongest and bravest nation in Asia, but on the advice of Croesus Cyrus ordered them to wear chitons and high shoes, teach their sons to play the lyre and harp, and live the life of shop-keepers. Cyrus transformed the Lydians into the effeminate people Herodotus knew, just as he had corrupted the ancient Persian austerity (71.2–4; 125–126; 207.6–7).[37] Hence there must be a temporal element in the *Inquiries*. Herodotus is not unaware of the changes time brings, in human happiness as well as in customs and inventions, but he sees in customs something more permanent than he could find in empires and wars. Customs form the horizon within which these historical events occur, and without which they could not be understood. They point to the human understanding of all things, no matter how partial and fragmentary that understanding might be. They point to the understanding of those things which determine the limits and nature of human things; and as evidence for this discovery of the naturally self-evident, they are more reliable than the past, since, as Candaules remarked, "eyes are more trustworthy than ears." What Herodotus says at the end of Book I indicates the spirit in which we, following him, try to understand them. The Massagetae "reverence alone of the gods the sun, to which they sacrifice horses; the meaning (νόος) of which sacrifice is: to the swiftest of the gods they assign the swiftest of all mortal things" (216.4). To discover, then, the νόος of customs is to be on the way to discovering the νόος of Herodotus' *Inquiries*.

Herodotus presents a νόμος whose νόος he has discovered, and it is this νόος that reveals Herodotus' own intention; but he also presents a series of λόγοι from which, I claim, he lets us extract their νόος. It is the articulation of these meanings that constitutes Herodotus' true *logos*. Even if the reader will grant, however, that some kind of *logos* is present in these λόγοι, he may well ask the following question: Once the *logos* has been extracted, what status should then be accorded to the λόγοι that underlie it? Are the λόγοι to be taken simply as a convenient way to uncovering the *logos*? Or are they indispensable in Herodotus' opinion even after the *logos* has emerged? The *logos* that I shall try to show lies behind the *Inquiries* might seem to make the λόγοι ironical, i.e., masks that can be dropped in the last analysis. They might seem to be only illustrative of a *logos* that any other series of λόγοι could equally reveal.

---

[37]Cf. IX.82; 122; Xenophon *Cyropaedeia* I.v.7–14; see also III.72.

This is what I think Thucydides would most object to in Herodotus. He would deny any inherent connection between what Herodotus thinks is the nature of things and the artful means Herodotus employs to present it. He denies that the Persian Wars had a sufficient magnitude in themselves to show up man as man (I.23.1). They were for this purpose as inadequate as the Trojan War which needed a poet to force it to say something universal. Herodotus, by rejecting Homer as much as Thucydides did,[38] should have relied on what actually occurred as much as Thucydides claims to have done. But Herodotus—the story of Gyges suffices to prove it—did not. He wove together the fabulous and the literal in a manner neither Homeric nor Thucydidean. From Thucydides' point of view, Herodotus sacrifices the advantages of fable without grounding his account on the literal truth. He could not do so, again according to Thucydides, because the literal truth did not offer any self-evident way to universalize it. Its recalcitrance to being a basis for reflection made Herodotus mix in elements that would allow him to reflect; for only in that way could the particular become the root for the universal.

These Thucydidean charges against the *Inquiries* cannot, I think, be entirely met by Herodotus. He does not explain how his λόγοι can generate their exemplifying character; how, in other words, his Egyptian, Persian, Scythian-Libyan λόγοι do not ultimately appear as metaphors for his *logos*. And yet Herodotus is not without all defense. He can point to Themistocles' reply as a partial justification of his own way (VIII.125). When a jealous man of Aphidna charged that the honors Themistocles had obtained from Sparta were given to him because of Athens and not because of himself, Themistocles said: "So it is, you see: Had I been of Belbina I would not have been so honored by the Spartans, nor would you have been, though you are an Athenian." Athens was a necessary but not a sufficient condition for Themistocles' honors; without her he would have been nothing, but she did not automatically guarantee his becoming somebody. There is no simple account of his greatness. In a similar way, Herodotus could. say that there was no necessity nor can there be for the link between the λόγοι which are the condition for the *logos* and the *logos* itself. The grace of things, their χάρις, which admits an insight into those things is finally inexplicable; and if this is unsatisfactory, it would be a long question whether Thucydides himself or anyone else has ever done away with this disproportion between things and their *logos*. Herodotus was more concerned, in any event, with pointing to it than explaining it. And for that we should be grateful.

---

[38]Cf. pp. 46–51, 127–130 *infra*.

II. EGYPT

Before Psammetichus made his experiment, the Egyptians were of the opinion that they were the first of all human beings; but after he had isolated two children, so that they only saw goats and a goatherd (whom he forbade to speak in their presence), he concluded from the first word they spoke—"bekos" (Phrygian for bread)—that the Phrygians were older than the Egyptians, but the Egyptians were older than all others. It is with this story that Herodotus begins the second book; and he begins with it because it illustrates in small compass everything he wishes to say about Egypt. It stands as a frontispiece before his whole Egyptian *logos*; and we shall have to keep it in mind as we go on in our analysis.

Two things in the story strike us at once. First, Psammetichus is guilty of a logical error: the experiment does not warrant his belief that the Egyptians were the second oldest people; for there might well be people older than the Egyptians though younger than the Phrygians, for all that the experiment can tell. It is impossible to distinguish by its means among the claimants for second place. The Egyptians appear to be so reluctant to abandon their supposed priority that they console themselves with second place with as little evidence as they once had had to arrogate to themselves the first. To be first in their account means to be oldest: it does not mean to be a source or origin for others. They do not conclude that they are derivative from the Phrygians, but they regard themselves as independent. They are not concerned with explaining how the Egyptian language arose. They certainly did not think that the second word the children spoke was Egyptian; and it remains as obscure as before how they account for the diversity of tongues.

The Egyptians are shown as believing—this strikes us second—that speaking is natural to men; that even in isolation and without learning from others men speak. They go, however, further than this. Not only is speaking natural but speaking a particular language is natural as well.[1] They fail to distinguish

---

[1]Cf. 57.2; Fronto I.10.5 (ed. van den Hout): οὕτως μὲν δὴ καὶ τὸ βαρβαρίζειν τῷ βληχᾶσθαι προσήκασι.

between speech and this speech, between λόγος and γλῶσσα. This failure is
based on another mistake. They do not consider the possibility that the children might have imitated the goats, which to us seems so obvious an explanation. They do not see the connection between learning and imitation,[2] between
the derivative and the original.

Herodotus also saw how the children's imitation of the goats could
account for the word "bekos"; for he labels the Greek version of this story
foolish precisely because, if only women whose tongues Psammetichus had cut
out took care of the children, there could be no accounting for the word at all
(2.5). The Greeks, in making the story more fabulous, remove the one element
that permits us to explain it. Even if the Egyptians interpret it incorrectly, they
still preserve something that can correct their account; whereas the Greeks
make the story unintelligible. If it loses its point in the transmission, perhaps
by returning to Egypt, Herodotus seems to suggest, we can recover the source
not only for this story but also for all the Greek customs that he thinks were
originally Egyptian. Not that the Egyptian account will prove to be correct,
but that the Egyptians are somehow nearer to the sources of things than the
Greeks. The true beginnings are somehow imitated more exactly among those
who are older.

The distinction Herodotus makes between the Egyptian and Greek
accounts resembles that which Thucydides draws between Greek poets and
storytellers (I.10.3, 21.1). The Greek poets exaggerate, it is true, but their
exaggerations can be removed and the facts on which they based their tales
uncovered, for their tales retain some traces of these facts. The storytellers, on
the other hand, make their stories more with an eye to the attractive than to the
truth, and they are so successful that nothing of the original version can be
recovered. If Thucydides corrects Homer, he still uses him, whereas he mentions no logographer by name. Herodotus, then, looks here to Egyptians as
Thucydides looks to Homer, and rejects a Greek story because its mythical
character has completely effaced the meaning embedded in the Egyptian
account.

Herodotus says that he heard this story of Psammetichus from the priests
of Hephaestus at Memphis, but though he went to Thebes and Heliopolis for
confirmation, he does not tell us whether the Thebans or the Heliopolitans,
who "are said to be the most learned among the Egyptians," (3.1, cf. I.1.1),
agreed with them or not. Whatever this silence might indicate (there were great
differences between Memphite and Theban theology),[3] it is not accidental that

---

[2]Cf. Apollonius Rhodius, Schol. Vet. IV.257c (ed. Wendel); Aristotle *de
arte poetica* 1448b-9; *Metaphysica* 980b21-25.

[3]Cf. Kees, H., *Der Götterglaube im alten Ägypten*, 2nd ed. (Berlin,
1956); Sethe, K., *Amun und die acht Urgötter von Hermopolis*, APAW 1929,

the priests of Hephaestus should tell the story. Hephaestus for the Greeks is the first craftsman, the maker *par excellence*; and among the Egyptians it is his temple that their first human king built at Memphis.[4] As the god of building and making, Hephaestus is the source of all human making (Prometheus steals his fire), and hence the author as well of imitation. Imitation, however, was not distinguished in the first story from the original; the Egyptians did not think of the bleating of the goats as the model for the children's sound; and their confusion here was repeated in their thinking that some one language was the first language. As the first language it would be a discovery rather an invention, a natural rather than a made language. Its vocabulary would be the natural vocabulary of things; everything would have its correct name. Not only would human things have their correct names but divine things. The gods would not have conventional but natural names.

Once one sees that the story of Psammetichus' experiment points to the assumed identity of the first language with the natural language and hence with the language of the gods,[5] Herodotus' next remark perfectly fits in with this train of thought. He says that he is not eager to report "the divine things in their accounts, except their names only, believing that all human beings know equally about them" (3.2), where the ambiguity in the phrase "about them"— does it refer to "divine things" or to "their names"?—indicates how Psammetichus' experiment leads to this remark.[6] Herodotus does not agree that the names of the Egyptian gods are the correct names. He distinguishes between "the divine in their accounts" (τὰ θεῖα τῶν ἀπηγημάτων) and "all the human things" (ἀνθρωπήια πρήγματα) the Egyptians said, "agreeing among themselves" (4.1; cf. IV.46.2). Unlike human things, where it is not difficult to separate what is heard from what is seen, or what is done from what is said,[7] divine things are mostly heard; and they are heard in a certain language whose speakers must lay claim to its being the speech of the gods, who are thought to be the beginnings of all things, if they claim as well that they are the first men; otherwise, there must have been a translation of the names of the gods from a

---

4. Hephaestus as Ptah was thought of at Memphis as "Bild der schaffenden Urkraft" (Kees, p. 287); as well as the "heart and tongue" of all the gods (pp. 291ff.).

[4]99.2-4; Hephaestus is mentioned fourteen, the Hephaesteion four times in II; cf. 32.6-33.1 with III.37.2-3.

[5]Cf. *Iliad* 1.403ss.; II.813ss.; XIV.291; XX.74.

[6]Cf. Plato *Cratylus* 400d6-401a5, which is like a commentary on Herodotus; Origen *Contra Celsum* V.45-46; Linforth, I. M., *Greek Gods and Foreign Gods in Herodotus* (Publications in Class. Philology, vol. 9, n. 1, Univ. Calif.); also compare IV.85.1 with *Odyssey* XII.60ss.

[7]Cf. 52.1 (with I.216.4); 99.1; 122.2; on πρήγματα see Chap. IV, fn

more original speech (cf. I.171.5–6). In leaving it open whether or not "divine things" are ever separable from "divine accounts."[8] Herodotus denies the identity of the oldest (recorded) things with the first things or the beginnings absolutely. The ἀρχαῖα are not the ἀρχαί.[9] The relation between them might be understood as the same as that between languages and speech. Even as speech itself might be natural to men, though every manifestation of it be conventional; so all the accounts of divine things, though disagreeing among themselves, might point to one true account. It might be that a single meaning lies hidden beneath the diversity of laws and customs, a meaning that all the laws and customs point to but do not express.[10]

The Egyptians claim that they were the first men to have discovered or invented seven things: the year, the twelve months, the names of the twelve gods, altars, statues, temples to the gods, and the "carving of living things in stone" (4.1–2). These discoveries are not of human things, but the human discovery for human use of non-human things. They cannot help but remind us of the seven Persian gods: sky, sun, moon, earth, fire, water, and winds.[11] Even as sky, sun and moon belong together, being the sources for the telling of time, the first three Egyptian inventions—year, months, names—belong together, being the Egyptian understanding of what is accessible to all men everywhere. Earth, fire and water appear to be the terrestrial counterparts of the three celestial gods of the Persians; just as the Egyptian assignment of altars, statues and temples to the gods is their understanding of how divine things come to light on earth for men.[12] Perhaps, too, the Persian worship of winds—the god that moves between heaven and earth—finds its parallel in the Egyptian "carving of living things in stone"—what moves and breathes being transformed into what it motionless and dead.

However this may be, Herodotus goes on to say that most of what the Egyptians claim, they prove in fact; a remark that suggests that the rest of the second book will in some way substantiate their originality. The book, as is well known, falls into four parts. Paragraphs 4.3–34 are devoted to the land and the river; 35–98 to their customs; 99–146 to their history as told by themselves; and 147–182 to the history of Egypt as agreed upon by both themselves

---

49.

[8]Cf. 46.4 (i.e., γυναικὶ Μένδης ἐμίσγετο ἀναφανδόν); 65.2; 146.1; IX. 100; Hesiod OD 763ss.

[9]Cf. Aristotle Metaphysica 1074a38–b14.

[10]Cf. Euripides Bacchae 481–484; Plato Minos 316a2ss.

[11]I.131.1–2; cf. IV.59.1 Consider what Hephaestus, with the help of fire and bellows, first puts on the shield of Achilles, Iliad XVIII.483–484; also 417–420.

[12]Cf. 109; 142.4; [Lucian] de astrologia 7.

and other men. The first two parts have almost the same number of lines as the last two: 1,434 lines in paragraphs 1-98, 1,464 in paragraphs 99-182. Our task will be, then, to articulate this plan as we proceed to discover Herodotus' intention.

The first part falls again into two subdivisions: paragraphs 4.3-18 concern the nature of the land, paragraphs 19-34 the nature of the Nile.[13] They are both made up, on the one hand, of what Herodotus sees and thinks, and, on the other, of what the Egyptians and Greeks say. Herodotus shows himself to be uninfluenced by what they say, and he is careful to indicate that his judgments were independent whenever an Egyptian story agrees with them.[14] In fact, he uses the word "I" and its declension more frequently here than in any other book.[15] His agreement with the Egyptians shows up the provincialism of the Greeks, who fail to see Egypt as any larger than the Delta, and of that only the part to which they sail (5.1: 6.1; 15.1). But their mistake is not only provincial but theoretical as well. They fail to see that their assertion would lead to turning the Egyptians into a fairly recent people; which would leave unexplained why the Egyptians insist so much on their being thought the first human beings.[16] They fail to take into account the opinion the Egyptians have about themselves (cf. 45.2-3), whereas Herodotus' opinion, that the Egyptians have been always "ever since the race of men has been," both makes use of their belief and corrects it. It is not sufficient to account for what is seen; it is necessary to account for what is said. The nature of a land cannot be understood unless its opinions and customs are also understood. Even if sight has priority over hearing, it should never become so divorced from what men say that one could not explain their error. Thus the Greek belief makes Egypt part Libyan and part Asian, with the Delta as an inexplicable fourth addition to their triple division of Libya, Europe, and Asia (16-17.2). By looking only to natural boundaries, without attending to the people who occupy the land, they make it impossible to understand the customs of the people; while Herodotus' respect for their beliefs lets him see that their peculiarity has its origin, if not its full explanation, in the peculiarity of their land.

This attack on Greek beliefs does not imply that Herodotus sides completely with the Egyptians; for although they know that the Delta up to the lake of Moeris is the "gift of the river," they do not see that the same holds true for another three days' sail; to say nothing of Herodotus' view that much

---

[13]Cf. 5.2; 9.1; 19.1, 3; 35.2; 104.1.

[14]Cf. 5.1; 10.1; 15.2; 18.1; 33.2.

[15]ἐγώ occurs 28 times; ἔγωγε twice; (ἐ)με ten; μευ four; ἐμοί seventeen; μοι forty-two; ἔμοιγε four; the plural occurs only nine times.

[16]15.2; cf. Aristotle *Meteor.* 351b25-353a28.

of Egypt up to Elephantine has been produced by the action of the Nile (5.1; 10.1; 11.3–4). They are also guilty of provincial blindness in saying that unless "god rains," Greece would have no water; which, though true, has its counterpart among themselves, for if the land below Memphis continues to rise in the same proportion as it has done in the past, lower Egypt will also become a desert (13.2–14.1). Their failure to observe this is all the more surprising because Herodotus can show up their error only on the basis of what they themselves have told him; just as it is from what the Greeks say that he can point to their mistaken arithmetic (13.1; 16). Moreover, the Egyptians do not even attempt to explain the nature and power of the Nile, which the Greeks, even if erroneous in their theories, at least see as a problem. Its solution, as Herodotus presents it, turns on the course of the sun (19.3; 24–5). It turns, in other words, on a celestial phenomenon, on that which the Egyptians deny has any effect on them. The Egyptians do not see their land and themselves within the larger context of the cosmos (cf. 77.2–3; 109.2–3; 144.2; I.138.1). They have no cosmology. Not Zeus the god of heaven but Demeter and Dionysus, the dry and wet principles of the earth, are the only gods that all the Egyptians worship (44.2; cf. 123.1; IV.54.1).[17] It is perhaps for this reason that they believe that a man's life is determined at the moment of his birth, and that even the wise Amasis believes one can control one's destiny (82.1; III.40.2–4; cf. I.131.2; 207.2).

If neither the Greeks nor the Egyptians suffice to explain Egypt, Herodotus must turn to his own observations. But simple inspection can only show what is there before him; it cannot by itself supply any account of the antecedent, nor tell anything about the future course the land or the river might take. Herodotus must use conjecture; but conjecture that has its ground in what he has seen. This kind of conjecture proves to be comparison and proportioning. The first thing he does is to give the measurements of the Egyptian coastline, not only in Egyptian "schoeni" but in parasangs, stades, and fathoms, along with an account of how they are related to one another. He shows how the extent of one's land determines the standard used; or, in other words, he compares the small with the large and indicates that proportion allows him to interpret so singular a country as Egypt in the light of many other, apparently dissimilar, places. Even the immense distance from the sea to Heliopolis, which seems at first incomparable to anything known to the Greeks, proves to be just a little more than the distance from Athens to Olympia (6–7; cf. IV.31; 86.2–3). This set of equivalent measures presents Herodotus' first attempt to

---

[17]Cf.Euripides *Bacchae* 274–280; Isocrates *Busiris* 13; Porphyry says that the Egyptians called the Nile the "sweat of the earth" (apud Proclus *in Pl. Tim.*, ed. Diehl, I,119).

translate the particular into the universal—to move from γλῶσσα to λόγος—, which Psammetichus' experiment had raised as a question. but not only are measures translatable but the nature of Egypt itself. The silting up of the Nile can be compared with what happens around Troy, even though it is to compare small with great; just as its "great deeds" can be matched by those of the Achelous and many other rivers (10; 29.3).[18] Far from its action being unique, Herodotus can imagine the Arabian gulf becoming another Egypt if only the Nile were diverted into it (11; cf. 26.2). These similarities between Egypt and other regions and rivers show that there is a fundamental agreement in the nature of earth and water. Indeed, they have a nature precisely because they agree in their effects everywhere: ὁμολογία indicates that we are concerned with φύσις.

The connection between φύσις and ὁμολογία is beautifully if comically shown in the story of Amasis and his Greek wife (181). After Amasis had married a woman from Cyrene, he found that he could not have intercourse with her; and this failure finally led him to accuse her of witchcraft, and when her denials did not appease Amasis, she prayed in her heart to Aphrodite and vowed to send her a statue to Cyrene if she granted her wish. The prayer and vow apparently worked, and Amasis had no more trouble in sleeping with her. If each country were *sui generis*, then a man and a woman of different people could not generate. A god would be necessary to overcome their natural incompatibility. The Egyptians with their abhorrence of all alien customs (91.1) are the perfect representatives of this view. Indeed, this story is but the human counterpart to their denial that there are heroes, beings that are the offspring of gods and men (50.3).

As long as Herodotus discusses the nature of the land, his observation suffices; it has a certain "look," black and friable, equally unlike the reddish, sandy soil of Libya and the clay-like, stony subsoil of Syria and Arabia. Its very look shows that it comes from the slime and mud of the Nile. All of Egypt above Memphis was once a bay, evident in the shells and salts found on the mountains and pyramids (5.2; 7.1; 12.1–2). It is the product, the ἔργον, of the continuous action of the Nile, prolonged over a period of ten or twenty thousand years (11.4; 142.4)[19] To some extent the Egyptians also see this, certainly better than the Greeks; but they are blind to the Nile itself. To them it is not a problem. They are aware of permanence but blind to change; the results, the static earth, are familiar to them; the sources, the kinetic river,

---

[18]Cf.I.5.3; IV.99.5; VI.109.1; also Thucydides II.102.3–4; Polybius IV.39–42.

[19]Cf. Aristotle *Meteor.* 352b20–22, where he calls all of Egypt τοῦ ποταμοῦ ἔργον.

remain unknown and unexplored. To understand the power, δύναμις, of the
Nile, Herodotus must rely on other rivers. He must understand the unknown in
the light of the evident (cf. 33.2; cf. 24.1). He must try to convert die
invisible into the visible, the apparently contrary power of the Nile into the
known power of all other rivers; from which conversion it will turn out that
the Nile has no peculiar property in itself that makes it rise in the summer and
continue shallow during the winter. The anomaly proves to be based on the
sun's irregular course, or rather on the disproportion between its course and
the earth's surface; so that if an alteration of the seasons and sky made what is
now north into south and what is now south into north, the Danube would
undergo all that the Nile now does (24–26). The upside-down character of the
Nile, its apparent look of difference, obtains an explanation that, without
destroying this appearance. fits it in with all other rivers. The way up and the
way down are one and the same.[20]

Herodotus gives two explanations of the Nile, a short account that makes
"the god" its cause, and a long account that assigns the cause to the sun (cf.
161.3 with IV.159). The short account can be short because it is presented in
terms of the familiar; while the long account attempts to free the reader from
the familiar and present its reasoning unencumbered by any reference to
opinion. Herodotus says in the short account that to whatever land "the god"
comes nearest, he is likely to dry up the native (ἐγχώρια) streams; but in the
long account he says that the sun goes up into the middle of the sky. In looking at the sun as a god, it is the land that is important; while as the sun itself,
it is the sky. There is a change of perspective. Such a change, however, cannot
be wholly accomplished. Herodotus must still rely on the customary and
likely. "It is customary" (ἔωθε), he says, for the sun to do what it does during
the summer; "in all likelihood" (οἰκότως) the winds that blew from upper
Egypt are the wettest of all winds; and again "in all likelihood" the Nile alone
of rivers should flow less in winter than in summer; and it is "not likely" (οὐκ
οἰκός) that prevailing breezes blow from warm regions, but "it is customary"
(φιλέει) for them to blow from the cold; and he concludes his account by
saying, "I am accustomed to regard (νενόμικα) the sun as the cause."[21] Since
Herodotus entertains the possibility of a complete revolution in the heavens,
even what most appears natural and permanent—the daily course of the sun—
assumes the character of only the familiar. To free himself and the reader from
the Egyptian cast of thought—the usual and customary—he must imagine
everything turned round. Once the looks of things are penetrated up to their
sources, we can see that a different order would not effect any change in the

[20]35.2–36; cf. 38.2; I.177; III.3.3; VII.40.2; 41.1.
[21]Cf. 3.2; III.38.2; IV.27; VII.129.4; 153.4; 153.4; VIII.79.1.

way they work. Only the locale, not the principle, would change. The sun would now turn Scythia into Egypt and Egypt into Scythia, and yet something "Scythian" and something "Egyptian" would still, though translated, remain.

Herodotus resorts to the familiar for yet another reason: the Greeks so much disregard it. All their three accounts completely ignore what is known about the Nile and other rivers. They fall into the same mistake they had made in paying no attention to Egyptian opinions about their own land; just as later, in telling a fabulous story about Heracles, they show themselves ignorant of the nature and customs of the Egyptians (45.2-3; cf. III. 2.2). Even if the etesian winds could do what their exponents claim for them, the Nile would be left as anomalous as it was before, since these winds clearly do not act the same way on other rivers; nor can the melting of snow be reconciled with either the warm winds that blow from the south or the migration of cranes southward for the winter; and the appeal to Oceanus explains the obscure by the more obscure (20-23). The impossibility of refuting this last opinion shows the necessity of the familiar as a starting point; for Herodotus suggests that the "invisible" or "occult" belongs to poetry, wherein the poet has so transformed his own starting point and denied us even that access to the understanding of his myth, that we are as much at a loss now as we would have been, had we only the Greek version of Psammetichus' experiment.[22]

Although Herodotus has given some account of Egypt—the look of the land and the power of the Nile—, there still remains some mystery about it. He knows nothing of the sources of the Nile. He has only a playful story from the treasurer of the sacred money at Sais to go on (28; IV.53.5). Its source, according to him, is two mountains between Syene and Elephantine, where Psammetichus' could not plumb its depths, though he played out many thousand fathoms of line. Psammetichus' failure recalls his other experiment, in which he tried to discover the original language (cf. 15.2; 28.4). In both cases we can sense an attempt to go back to the beginnings; to discover the single source for what appears in fact as an infinite variety of phenomena: either the whole set of different languages or Egypt itself, with its great number of customs and monuments. Somehow all of the latter must be traced back to the river and the land, but to look for one origin of them all is as mistaken as to look for one language, from which all others would have sprung. The multiplicity of things cannot be reduced to one. And yet the obscurity about the

---

[22]Cf. ἐς ἀφανὲς τὸν μῦθον ἀνενείκας with ἐς ποίησιν ἐσενείκασθαι (23); cf.III.115.2; IV.8.2; Thucydides I.21.1. For the second account, see *Iliad* III.1-5; and IV.50.2-4, which suggests that Herodotus' argument might be polemical, directed against the Egyptian disregard of the sun, 142.4.

Nile's sources indicates that some mystery about the sources of Egyptian customs may always remain. How mysterious these origins are, the story of the Asmach shows (30). Psammetichus had stationed them as guards at Elephantine, on the border of Ethiopia; and they, unrelieved from guard duty for three years, revolted and fled south; and when Psammetichus begged them not to leave behind their ancestral gods, children and wives, "one of them is said to have pointed to his private parts and said, 'Wherever this will be, there we shall have children and wives.'" Their spokesman is silent about the ancestral gods. Are the ancestral gods, then, also to be understood as having their origin in the same place, and the spokesman's silence only a sign of his decency (Cf. 48.2–3; 51)? Are the ancestral gods the ancestors?[23] Or is their origin as obscure as that of the Nile itself, and the spokesman's silence an admission of his ignorance? Perhaps what Herodotus means is that just as he knows the ultimate cause of the Nile's flowing (the sun) but not its geographical source, so he recognizes the ancestors as the ultimate ground of Egyptian gods and customs, though he cannot trace their present custom in a direct line back to them (cf. 143–144). The great distance in the one case and the long stretch of time in the other join together in keeping Egypt mysterious.

Herodotus, then, checked from presenting a single source for all of Egypt's customs, turns to describing the customs themselves; a turn which suggests that from the results of whatever powers have been at work, the powers themselves can be inferred. But he not only describes their customs in part two but their parochial history, when they had little or no contact with other countries, in part three. Customs and history appear to bear the same kind of relation to one another as the land and the river were seen to have in the first part. Just as they were connected as effect to cause (or better as the permanent to the changing), so customs seem to be the static horizon within which historic events take place. To understand parts two and three in this way, although not wrong as far as it goes, will prove to be inexact, when we find that permanence and change do not allow so neat a division into customs and history. Herodotus finds more than the static and unchanging in custom: he finds nature itself. In looking towards custom in order to arrive at an understanding of nature, he gives a new twist to Heraclitus' saying. "Nature has the custom to hide itself"; so that it might be read thus: even in the customary, where nature lies concealed, does nature show itself.

Paragraphs 35–98 fall into five sections. Paragraphs 35–50 concern the customs and the gods; 51–65.1 the festivals and the way the gods became Greek; 65.2–76 the sacred animals; 77–91 the way of life in upper Egypt; and

---

[23]Psammetichus says θεοὶ πατρώιοι not πάτριοι; cf. I.172.2; consider further 61.1; 86.2; 169.4–170.1.

92–98 the way of life of the marsh-dwellers. Part three also seems to admit of the same number of subsections, a coincidence which suggests that these two themes, custom and history, must be understood together. Paragraphs 99–120 deal with the first kings up to Proteus; 121–123 with Rhampsinitus; 124–135 with Cheops, Chepren, and Mycerinus; 136–141 with Asychis, Anysis, and Sethos; and 142–146 with Egyptian chronology and theology.[24]

The first section of part two begins with a list of seventeen customs that distinguish the Egyptians from the Greeks and other people (35.2–36). How are they to be understood? How is the difference of the Egyptian river and sky reflected in them? How have these natural things been transferred into the habits and laws of the Egyptians? What appears at once is that almost all involve pairs of terms that have reversed their roles or changed their meaning; ϋὸὲ pairs are pointed up by sixteen μέν-δέ clauses.

1. Women buy and sell in the market place: men weave at home.
2. Other men push the woof up: Egyptians down.
3. Men carry burdens on their head: women on their shoulders.
4. Women piss standing up: men sitting down.
5. They relieve themselves in their homes: they eat out in the road.
6. No woman is a priestess: men are priests of both male and female gods.
7. Sons are not compelled to take care of their parents: daughters are compelled.
8. Priests elsewhere let their hair grow: Egyptian priests are shorn.
9. Other men in grief shave their head: Egyptians let their hair and beard grow.

---

[24]Herodotus gives some verbal indications that he had this scheme in mind, though the complete proof of it depends on our interpretation of what he says. 51.1 makes an obviously new start: ταῦτα μέν νυν ἄλλα πρὸς τούτοισι, τὰ ἐγὼ φράσω, Ἕλληνες ἀπ᾽ Αἰγυπτίων νενομίκασι; 65.1, the end of the second section, has: οὗτοι μέν νυν...Αἰγύπτιοι δὲ θρησκεύουσι περισσῶς, τά τε ἄλλα περὶ τὰ ἱρὰ καὶ δὴ καὶ τάδε; the third section ends with the words (76.3; cf. 34.2; IV. 15.4; 36.1; VI.55): τοσαῦτα μὲν θηρίων πέρι ἱρῶν εἰρήσθω; and the fifth begins ταῦτα μὲν πάντα οἱ κατύπερθε τῶν ἑλέων...οἱ δὲ δὴ... Likewise in the third part, section one ends (120.5; cf. IV. 31.2): καὶ ταῦτα μὲν τῇ ἐμοὶ δοκέει εἴρηται; section three begins (124.1): μέχρι μέν νυν Ῥαμψινίτου, and ends (135.6) Ῥοδόπιος μέν νυν πέπαυμαι; and the fifth section begins (142.1): ἐς μὲν τοσόνδε τοῦ λόγου Αἰγύπτιοί τε καὶ οἱ ἱρέες ἔλεγον. These divisions are more in accordance with what Herodotus says than those imposed upon him by Petrie, F., *JHS*, xxviii, 1908, pp. 275ff. See further Chap. IV, fn 13.

10. Other men live apart from animals: Egyptians live with them.

11. Other men eat wheat and barley: Egyptians eat only spelt.

12. They knead dough with their feet: mud and dung with their hands.

13. Others leave their genitals as they are: Egyptians are circumcised.

14. Each man wears two garments: each woman one.

15. Others fasten the rings and ropes of sails on the outside: Egyptians on the inside.

16. Greeks write and count from left to right: Egyptians from right to left.

17. Egyptians have two kinds of letters: sacred and demotic.

Six of these customs concern men and women (1,3,4,6,7,14), three others a change in direction (2,15,16), and most of the rest the care of the body.[25] To make sense of them all, it hardly suffices to appeal to the topsy-turviness of the Nile's way, which the Egyptians themselves are unaware of. Herodotus must show how they interpret their own customs before he can offer a more adequate explanation.

In defense of their fifth practice the Egyptians say: "Whatever is shameful though necessary must be done in secret, but whatever is not shameful openly." The shameful or ugly things (τὰ αἰσχρά) are not opposed to the beautiful or fine things (τὰ καλά), but to the not shameful. Τὰ αἰσχρά must be understood, then, as the shameful and not the ugly, opposed to those things that are free from reproach, and not in contrast with τὰ καλά; for, as Herodotus says, the Egyptians are circumcised for the sake of cleanliness, preferring to be clean rather than becoming (εὐπρεπέστεροι (37.2; cf. 47.2; 89). The secret and the open are closely linked with the clean and the unclean. Only what is clean should be seen publicly, all that is not should be hidden. Although many of their customs thus seem to become intelligible, they do not really do so unless one considers these pairs in the light of a more fundamental one: the sacred and the profane. The sacred is the clean. The Egyptian priests demonstrate their holiness by shaving their whole body every second day, by washing twice at night and twice during the day, and by "countless other ceremonies" (37.1-3). What is clean, however, though it might seem at first

---

[25]That men have become effeminate in Egypt, by taking up certain practices usually done by women, Herodotus stresses by never using the words "virtue" (ἀρετή) and "best" (ἄριστος) throughout the second book because of their connection with the male; while he employs in this book alone the word for "human being" more times than "man," and "woman" the same number of times as "man"; cf. 102.5 with 106.1; 164.2; VII.153.5; VIII.68α1, γ; IX.32; see further Chap. VII, fn 16. For the usual connection between women and piety, see Strabo VII.3.4 (297); Aristophanes *Eccl.* 214-228.

an open and evident fact, and less disputable than the beautiful, proves to belong to the secret and hidden.[26] Mud and dung are listed with the clean, while dough and hair with the unclean. Other men cut their hair in grief in order to make themselves ugly, to show that they do not care for appearances; but the Egyptians, in letting their hair grow on such occasions, show that they regard the body as it naturally is to be ugly.[27] Their asceticism makes them rank food among the unclean, so that they purge themselves for three days every month, "believing that all diseases arise from the food that nourishes them" (77.2). ὧf even to be nourished is almost a shameful necessity, the caring for parents must be imposed upon the daughters of the family, so as to leave the sons free for what is more sacred, hidden and clean. The women are seen in public buying and selling, but the men stay at home; just as they hide more of their body by wearing two garments instead of only one as the women do. The Egyptians, by substituting the clean for the beautiful, have made seeing itself suspect: "The priests do not even tolerate looking at beans, believing that the legume is unclean" (37.5).[28]

Since cleanliness paradoxically leads to the denial of the living body, and through this denial to the hidden and sacred, Herodotus goes on to describe the ceremonies connected with bulls sacred to Epaphus (38–40). A single black hair is enough to mark them as unclean, and if the hairs in the tail "have grown naturally," they are accepted. To be clean is to be κατὰ φύσιν, not to diverge from what the law requires. The sacred as the clean explains why they skin the sacrificial bull, remove its guts (i.e. all that nourished it while alive), and fill its insides with "clean bread" and unguents; while the sacred as something not open to sight explains their cutting off its head and cursing it, for the head carries all the organs of sense.[29] Thus ceremonial purification might be described as the attempt to wipe out everything bodily and sensible, the human imitation, in fact, of the invisible gods. Divine revelation proves to be divine concealment.

The Egyptians tell the story that Heracles wanted to see the face of Zeus Ammon, and being persistent, Zeus put on the skin of a ram and in this dis-

---

[26] Cf. 60.2; 64; 85; I.197-199 (cf. Strabo XVI.1.20 (745); Heraclitus frs. 5, 15.

[27] Cf. I.82.7-8; Plutarch *Lysander* I.2.

[28] The word "clean" occurs only in this section (35–50) in all of Book II, nine times in all. Cf. I.146.1 (κάλλιόν τι γεγόνασι (Ἴωνες) with 147.1 ἔστωσαν δὴ καὶ οἱ καθαρῶς γεγονότες Ἴωνες. It does not seem accidental that Herodotus never uses ἀγνός, and ἀγνεύω only once of Egyptian priests (I.140.3); and that Aeschylus in his 'Egyptian' play *Supplices* has ἀγνός-εύω eleven times, whereas there are twelve in all the rest.

[29] Cf. 39.4; 121.2; III.29.2; Athenaeus II.72 (65f-66c).

guise showed himself (42.3-4; cf. III.26.3). Zeus does not show himself as he is but in a mask, and although the Egyptians portray and worship him with a rain's head they do not believe that that is his true shape; any more than they believe the goat-faced and goat-footed Pan, which their painters and sculptors present, shows the true Pan, "believing him not to be like that but like the rest of the gods" (46.2).[30] Herodotus never says what the Egyptians thought their gods to be truly like; a silence that implies either their ignorance or his own reluctance to deal with divine things. If the visible shapes of the gods give no insight into their one true shape, and all their appearances are utterly distinct from their being, there cannot be any Egyptian heroes, beings who have a human figure though they have become immortal.[31] "About the other Heracles," Herodotus says. "whom the Greeks know, I was unable to hear anything anywhere in Egypt" (43.1; cf. I.182).

When we say that the Greek gods are anthropomorphic, we are usually unaware that the term is ambiguous but assume that the Greek gods are like men because the Greeks are men. It could be, however, that the Greeks are men because their gods are anthropomorphic. Their gods might have been the cause of the Greeks' becoming human beings. What especially excites Herodotus' disgust is the practice of almost all men except the Greeks and Egyptians of having intercourse in sanctuaries. Their reason is that if the gods did not approve of it, they would not allow animals to copulate in their sanctuaries (64; cf. 1.203.2; III.101.1; IV.180.5; IX.ll6.3).[32] Most men do not distinguish between themselves and animals. Their failure to make this distinction is shown in their not having anthropomorphic gods, who establish what they can and cannot do (52.1). Hesiod and Homer, in giving the Greek gods their human shape (53.2), did more than just duplicate human beings. They radically separated human beings from all other living things and stamped them with a specific excellence (cf. Pindar *Nemean* VI.1-7). The gods thus imposed a standard which the Greeks could look up to, so that they could judge whether to respect or despise themselves. The gods established a sense of shame. The Egyptians took another way in separating animals from men (65.2; cf. 46.3-4). They gave their gods, in so far as they had one, an animal shape. They made men look down rather than up, to reverence the subhuman rather than the human, only to despise and never to respect themselves (36.2; 37.1).

---

[30]Cf. 142.3; Hecataeus of Abdera *FGH* II, Fr. 7: κατασκευάζειν δὲ καὶ ἀγάλματα καὶ τεμένη τῷ μὴ εἰδέναι τὴν τοῦ θεοῦ μορφήν; Chaeremon *FGH* IIIc, fr. 2.

[31]44.5; 50.3; 142.3; 143.4; cf. *Odyssey* XI.601ss.

[32]Consider I.182.1; II.63.4; see Griffiths, J. G., *The Conflict of Horus and Seth* (Liverpool, 1960), p. 86.

It is the humanity, then, of the Greek gods that makes the Greeks superior to the Egyptians, just as it might be this same humanity that makes them superior to the Persians, even though the gods of the Persians represent a more natural theology (1.131.1–2). The very super-humanity of the Persian gods might have been that which proved fatal to the Persians.

We saw that Egypt itself is composed of two elements, earth and water, whose relation to one another could be described as that between appearance and power (εἶδος and δύναμις);[33] and we now find that the Egyptian gods contain the same double character. In order to discover the nature of the land, Herodotus had only to look; but to understand the nature of the Nile, he was forced to conjecture. There proved to be something invisible (ἀφανές) about the river, not only in the complete obscurity surrounding its sources, but in the way it openly acts. That the priests could offer no account of its action, though Herodotus was as eager to find this out from them as he was reluctant to tell what they said of any divine matters (3.2; 19.2), finds its parallel in their silence (or his own) when it comes to explaining how the variety of visible shapes which the gods put on (their statues) are connected with and derived from their nature and power. The gods, who are the Egyptian understanding of the first things, but whose power, as opposed to their manifestation, is not shown, can be compared in turn with the almost complete lack of any signs (monuments that can be seen) of the first 330 kings (101.1; cf. 148.2). This absence of any "show of deeds or works," except for one generation succeeding the next, hides the early human history of Egypt as much as the absence of any reports about the gods, who are said to have been the first kings of Egypt (144.2; 156.4), hides the divine. In spite of the human and the divine being utterly separate in Egypt, they do share a certain mysteriousness in common.

At the same time that Herodotus tells of his inquiries in Egypt, he indicates how Egypt differs from and resembles Greece. He gives his reasons for believing that Egypt was the source of all but seven of the Greek gods, from whence the Greeks learned their names and how to portray them (41.2; 43.2; 46.2; 49–50). In the transmission, however, not everything was preserved. Melampus, who imported Dionysus—his name, his sacrifice, and the proces-

---

[33]In the tenth book of the *Odyssey* (302–306), Hermes showed Odysseus the "nature" of the moly: "it was black in its root, but its flower was like milk"; that is its εἶδος; and its power is to preserve the εἶδος of Odysseus, so that he does not assume "the head, the hair, voice, and body of swine," for his companions' νόος is unimpaired (239ss.); cf. Holt, J., *Les noms d'action en* ΣΙΣ (ΤΙΣ) (Copenhagen, 1940), pp. 78ff.; Benveniste, E., *Noms d'agent et noms d'action en i.-e* (Paris, 1949), pp. 78ff.; Holwerda, D., *Commentatio de vocis quae est* φύσις *vi atque usu* (Groningen, 1955), p. 63.

sion of the phallus—changed a few things; Io, whose picture is the same as the
statue of Isis, does not have the central place in Greek belief that Isis has in
Egyptian; for she is reduced to the status of a heroine, the human ancestor of
the Greek Heracles, whereas Isis herself, stripped of her animal character, is
the Greek Demeter; and Heracles in turn does not bear any resemblance to the
Egyptian god except in name; nor does Pan, endowed with the same
appearance both in Egypt and Greece, conceal another shape behind what he
shows. The Greeks take at face value what in Egypt only passes for show. That
the gods do not reveal themselves completely in their human or animal shapes,
the Greeks only preserve in the mysteries (51). They seem to a greater extent
to have brought the sacred into the open and hence given it a new interpretation.

Pheros, the son of Sesostris, went blind after he had angrily thrown a
spear into the rising waters of the Nile; and in the sixteenth year of his blindness an oracle informed him that the urine of any woman faithful to her husband would cure him (111). The purification of his impiety is accomplished by
something indecent; what the Greeks would regard as something to be hidden
restores his sight. The sacred is allied with the ugly but clean, and the open
does not have here the character of the self-evident. When Pheros recovered
his sight, he dedicated "sight-worthy works" at the temple of the sun.

Why the Egyptians portray Pan in the way they do, "it is rather
unpleasant" for Herodotus to say; just as why they abominate the pig in all festivals except the joint festival of Selene and Dionysus he regards as more becoming not to tell.[34] The pleasant and the becoming belong to Greece and not
to Egypt, where so unbecoming a story about the Trojan war is told; for
though Homer knew the Egyptian version, Herodotus believes he suppressed it
because it did not have the same attractiveness as the alternative he used
(116.1)[35] This suppressed version throws light on the Egyptian understanding
of the sacred, as well as on how the Greeks refashioned what they had heard
from them.

When Paris was forced by contrary winds to land in Egypt, his servants
sought sanctuary in a temple of Heracles, and wishing to hurt Paris, they nar-
rated his "injustice" toward Helen and Menelaus to the priests and Thonis,
who sent a message to King Proteus that said a stranger had come, "having
done an impious deed in Greece"; and Proteus demanded that he who had
committed those "impious things" should be brought to him. When Paris tried
to fabricate some parts of his story, his servants refuted him and revealed "the
whole story of his injustice"; and Proteus, in indignation, called him

---

[34]46.2; 47.2; cf. 46.4–48.1; 63.4–64.1 with which cf. I.182.
[35]Cf. 37.2; 137.5 with 137.1.

"wickedest of men," who had done "the most impious deed" (113–15). What at once strikes us in this account is that the Egyptians never use the word "injustice" or "unjust," nor do the Greeks ever say "impious" or "not holy." Even when the priests, in telling Herodotus the rest of the story, do use the words "justly," "justice," and "injustice" they only repeat what Menelaus has told them (118).[36] The replacement of the just by the holy accompanies the replacement of the beautiful by the clean. Herodotus himself, however, indicates that the just and the holy might not be as separable as the Greeks would suppose; for he calls Menelaus "unjust" because he did an "impious thing," though he may do so under the influence of the Egyptians (119.2).[37]

Once the decent and becoming have been removed from the Homeric story, Menelaus, who says in the *Odyssey* that he was prevented from sailing because he had forgotten to sacrifice a hecatomb, now commits in Egypt an impious crime, sacrificing two native children in order to appease the gods. His sin of forgetting is aggravated now in his endeavor to be pious. Menelaus turns ugly in the Egyptian air; even as the Trojan war itself, in becoming more prosaic, becomes senseless; for now the Trojans are destroyed, though they have done nothing wrong and told the truth (both under oath and without swearing), and the whole effort to win back Helen proves vain. The gods' punishment altogether exceeds the Trojans' guilt. Herodotus, in siding with the Egyptian story, takes away every human reason that could justify it. Piety, disassociated from equity, follows its own rules. "The plan of Zeus" can no longer be learned. The gods reward Mycerinus' piety and justice with great sorrows and an early death; but Cheops and Chephren, though impious, live in prosperity to an old age (129–133; cf. 120.5 with IV.205).

Homer's version of the Trojan War makes the gods just and men foolish (cf. I.60.3), for whereas Priam and Hector had to have been fools to have allowed their city to be destroyed for the sake of a woman (120.3–4), even the Persians have to admit that the Trojans were guilty of injustice and hence the gods were just to punish them (I.4.2). The Egyptian version, on the other hand, makes the gods unjust and men excessively distrustful of one another, for the Greeks do not even believe the oaths of the Trojans. Men become more suspicious the more their gods are unjust (cf. 174), for men are not to be relied

---

[36]Cf. III.15.2–4; 19.2–3. The Egyptian judgment about the Olympic games must be considered in the light of this (160); cf. 137.3–4 (a law of an Ethiopian king); 177.2 (a law by the philhellenic Amasis); 110.3; 129.1–2; 151.1 with 133.2. The word "truth" (ἀλήθείη only occurs in the first section of the third part in all of Book II: 106.5; 115.3; 119.1; 120.5; cf. 174.2 where "true gods" means "just gods."

[37]Cf. VI.86.1—α2; VIII.105.1; Thucydides V.104.

on if the gods do not support the justice of men, but treat the truthful oath as perjury. Αἰγυπτιάζειν means to be πανοῦργος, sly and crafty (Cratin. fr.378). The Egyptian version of the Trojan War thus shows the consequences of the Egyptians' rejection of alien customs and their calling everyone who speaks another tongue a barbarian (79.1: 91.1; 158.5). The gods stand in the way of ὁμολογία (cf. III.13.2). And yet Herodotus says, in support of the Egyptian version, that the divine (τὸ δαιμόνιον) brought about the complete destruction of Troy in order that "they (the gods) might make it evident to human beings that punishment from the gods is great for acts of great injustice" (120.5). The destruction of Troy, in other words, was exemplary punishment. The prohibition against adultery is manifested in an example that, from a human point of view, does not illustrate it. By becoming an example, the destruction of Troy can no longer be regarded in itself as either merited or unmerited punishment. It becomes the symbol of justice without itself being just. It loses its surface meaning as it acquires significance. Between its appearance, from which one can only conclude that the gods are unjust, and its "essence," which makes one see the gods as just once again, there lies the unbridgeable gap between what the Egyptian gods are shown to look like and what they in fact are. The Greek understanding of the gods entails that justice be rewarded with happiness and injustice punished with misery, but the Egyptians, whose gods are fundamentally mysterious, avoid the obvious difficulty of maintaining such a view by making human misery and happiness wholly independent of justice and injustice. The rules of piety are to be followed for the sake of piety itself and not for their consequences (cf. Pl. *Rep.* 357d3–358a3). Regardless of whether one can ever strictly separate the two (cf. 124.1; 161.2; 177.1), the command to practice piety for its own sake necessarily leads to a denigration of simply human life, or, because the Egyptians do not distinguish between human and animal life (36.2; 123.2), to the denigration of life as such. The only thing (πρῆγμα) therefore that Herodotus in his Egyptian account calls divine (θεῖον), i.e. concerned with the gods, is the suicide of cats (66.3).

Herodotus' siding with the Egyptian version of the Trojan War forces us to look more closely at Homer, whose decency is shown in his connecting the destruction of Troy with the injustice of the Trojans. And yet Homer makes Helen, the initial reason why the Greek cause is just, offer another explanation for the war that renders it as exemplary and as little concerned with justice as the Egyptian version. She says to Hector that Zeus set upon herself and Paris an evil fate, so that hereafter they might be the subject of song (ἀοίδιμοι) to the human beings who will be (*Il.* VI.357–8; cf. *Od.* VIII. 579–580). Not justice but glory ultimately justifies the Trojan War. Whereas the Egyptians see that war as exemplifying an inhumane theodicy, Helen interprets it as the celebration of human glory (cf. Eur. *Hel.* 36–41). The Egyptians, then, in despising themselves in so far as they are living human beings, despise glory: a shepherd, according to them, built the Great Pyramid (128).

The priests of Theban Zeus told Herodotus that the Phoenicians carried off two of their priestesses, one of whom was sold in Libya and the other in Greece; but the priestesses of Dodona told him that two black pigeons flew away from Egyptian Thebes, and one sitting on an oak at Dodona told them to build an oracle of Zeus, and the other told the Libyans the same (54–57). In order to reconcile these two stories, Herodotus supposes that the Greeks likened the woman's barbaric speech to the jabbering of a bird, just as in saying that the pigeon was black, "they indicate that the woman was Egyptian." Without the Thebans' story, the Dodonan version would appear miraculous; but with its help, he can show that they belong together and are related as original to copy. The original contained no fabulous elements at all; the copy is the result of imitation—the seeing of a likeness—which translated the original into something poetic. Why Greek beliefs are unintelligible by themselves, the influence of the poets explains. They have taken historic events and reworked them so as to remove almost every trace of fact that they once possessed. Herodotus tells this story immediately after he has declared that Homer and Hesiod were responsible for making the theogony of the Greeks in assigning to the gods their appelations, dignities, arts and shapes (53.2–3). Profane Egyptian history becomes sacred Greek history or theology.

Greek gods are not merely duplicates of Egyptian gods; they are poetic renderings of them. Proteus in the Egyptian story was the son of Sesostris and quite as human as he. In the *Odyssey,* however, he is a god, who can change himself into "all the things that creep upon the earth" as well as into water, fire, and trees (IV.417ss.; 456–458).[38] Proteus, the "First" in Greece, is the 333rd mortal king of Egypt. While the Egyptians believe that the human soul enters the body of all the animals in turn (on land, sea, and in the air), Homer has made a god assume bodily these shapes (123.2).[39] Not only has the poet turned history into fable, but all that pertained to the invisible in Egyptian theology, he has made visible. By poeticizing the Egyptian gods, the shameful has been made into the beautiful, and the secret into the open.

In the second section of the third part, which follows the discussion of the Homeric and Egyptian versions of the Trojan war, Herodotus shows in some detail how this transformation took place. There we are told the story of Rhampsinitus, who received from Proteus the kingdom of Egypt. He left two statues as memorials at the temple of Hephaestus; the one turned toward the north they call summer and worship, the other facing south they call winter, to which "they do the opposite." Rhampsinitus' wealth was so great that no later

---

[38]Cf. Homer's Thos *ibid* 227–232 with the Egyptian Thonis (113.3); also Diodorus I.62.

[39]Note the pun on Proteus and πρῶτος at 118.4.

king came even close to equalling it; and he had constructed a large chamber in which he deposited all his money in jars. Omitting for the moment how two anonymous thieves stole it, it is also said that "he went down into the place which the Greeks call Hades," and in honor of his descent and return the Egyptians continue, even to the time of Herodotus, to perform a festival, in which the priests cover the eyes of one priest, and on their giving him a robe they have woven in a single day, it is said that two wolves escort him to a temple of Demeter and back again (121–122). These extraordinary episodes would suggest, we submit, to anyone familiar with Homer (and Herodotus certainly was) the following. In the thirteenth book of the *Odyssey*, in which the Phaeacians bring Odysseus back to Ithaca, Homer describes the cave sacred to the Nymphs. The cave is full of stone jars wherein bees store their honey; and there are huge stone looms on which the Nymphs weave purple-dyed robes. "It has two doors, one facing the north is the descent for men, the other facing south is more divine, nor do men enter there, but it is the way for the immortals" (XIII.105–112; cf. 135–138; 362–371). Surely the similarities between the Egyptian story and this Homeric fabrication are very great: that the statute facing north is worshipped, while the mortals' descent also faces north, which points to the reversal everything undergoes in Egypt, would accord with Rhampsinitus' descent into Hades; just as the more divine entrance to the south finds its inverted parallel with a statue called winter which the Egyptians abuse; that the Nymphs should weave robes just as the priests do to celebrate Rhampsinitus' journey; that there should be jars in both places; that Athena should later hide in the cave the treasures of Odysseus, which surpass even the booty he would have taken from Troy, and seal it with a single stone, just as by the removal of a large block the thieves break into Rhampsinitus' treasury; all would confirm Herodotus' saying that Homer was one of the makers of Greek theology.[40]

If we look more closely, we find other similarities between those two stories. Odysseus like Rhampsinitus also descended into Hades; and like the thief who spirited away his brother's body by intoxicating its guards, he made the Cyclops drunk in his cave; and his conversation with Athena here also shows up his resemblance to the thief. The thief was admired by Rhampsinitus for his cleverness and daring (πολυφροσύνη and τόλμα) and for being the most "knowing" of men; for he had committed with impunity two acts, one the "most impious," the other the "cleverest" or "wisest" of crimes. Turning to

---

[40]Only at 122.1,3; 123.1 does Herodotus use the Greek name Demeter by itself for the Egyptian goddess and not Isis, which he uses everywhere else in Book II except when he explains that she is the same as Demeter (59.2; 156.5).

Odysseus, so often called wise and clever (πολύφρων and πολύμητις) and shown to be daring, who has just lied to Athena, we hear her telling him: "He would have to be cunning and tricky to surpass you in every kind of guile,... (since) you have not forgotten deceptions and cunning words even in your own land." Odysseus, then, seems to combine the wealth and adventures of Rhampsinitus with the cleverness of the thief, though Homer has removed from his hero the indecency of the one (which Herodotus is loth to believe), and the impiety of the other.[41] Thus Egyptian history in becoming Greek poetry loses its grossness and becomes beautiful. Not only more beautiful, however, but less a matter of belief. The statue of Isis which the Egyptians "revere" has the same look as the Io the Greeks "paint": the painters take over the role of the ancestral law (cf. Plato Euthyphro 6b7-c4). The Egyptian discovery of which month and day belong to which god, and what the fate will be of each man born on a certain day, "those of the Greeks who are engaged in poetry employ"; and Aeschylus alone of previous poets has made Artemis the daughter of Demeter, as though the genealogy of the gods did not depend on what is true but only on the convenience of a poet.[42] di quoque carminibus, si fas est dicere, fiunt.

Herodotus often refers to "sacred" stories or names which he prefers not to tell, a silence that seems self-imposed and more in keeping with his own sense of propriety than with any respect for Egyptian customs.[43] It would

---

[41] 121ε1; cf. 126.1. πολυφροσύνη (121ζ1) is unique in Herodotus, as is πολυτροπίη (121ε3); Odysseus is called πολύτροπος in the first line of the Odyssey. That the story of Rhampsinitus may be not only profane history in Egypt is suggested by the following coincidences, though how much Herodotus knew of this, it is impossible to say. Rhampsinitus resembles in two respects the god Hermes: his great treasure and his descent into Hades (i.e., Hermes the treasure-finder and the conductor of the dead); and Plutarch tells us that Hermes played dice with Isis or the Moon, which Rhampsinitus does here (122.1; de Is. et Osir. 12; Hopfner's commentary, vol. I, p. 27).

[42] 41.2; 82.1; 156.6; cf. 123.1 To understand the strange statement that Aeschylus raped (ἥρπασε, 156.6) his assertion from the Egyptians' logos, one has only to consider the similar rape the learned Persians practiced in I.1-4; cf. p. 17 supra.

[43] 46.2; 47.2; 48.3; 61.1; 62.2; 86.2; 132.2; 170.1; 171.1,2; cf. 3.2; 45.3; 51.4; 64.2; 65.2; also Augustine de civitate dei XVIII.5; see also for another kind of silence, 123.3; I.51.4; 95.1; IV.43.7; VIII.128.3; and Linforth, I. M., Herodotus' Avowal of Silence (vol. 7, n. 9, Univ. Calif. Publications in Classical Philology); Sourdille, C., Revue des études grecs, 38, 1925, pp. 289-305.

appear that what was common knowledge in Egypt becomes arcane in Greece. And yet he does sense that silence dominates Egypt more than elsewhere. There are only three sets of speeches presented in direct discourse in the whole of Book II, in spite of so much of it being composed of reports.[44] The first occurrence is in the story of Helen (Thonis and Proteus speak); the second is the exchange between Amasis and his advisers; and in the third Amasis speaks to his wife.[45] What connects all three speeches is Greece. The presence of impious Greeks in Egypt loosens the tongue of Thonis and Proteus; Amasis, a "philhellene" and rather playful in spirit, tries to explain his unkinglike and un-Egyptian behavior to his friends, who have been shocked by it into speech; and Amasis talks to his Greek wife, when he thinks she has bewitched him.[46] Only in the departure from what is established is there speech; only when something must be attacked or defended does λόγος arise: Psammetichus, who first instituted the teaching of Greek (1.52.2), was the first to test the antiquity of the Egyptians and their language. In this way Herodotus' understanding of the "dumb" animals which the Egyptians worship can be found.

Seventeen animals are described or mentioned in paragraphs 65.2–76, all of which the Egyptians honor or hold to be sacred: the word "sacred" also occurs seventeen times in this section. "Were I to tell why they are consecrated, I should be descending with my account (λόγος) into divine things, which I most avoid relating; and what I do say that touches on them, I say overcome by necessity." At the beginning he had said that his references to divine accounts would be compelled by his λόγος; his λόγος would overcome his desire to remain silent (3.2).[47] Its necessity certainly differs from the necessity of the Egyptian law, which commands that whoever kills an ibis or hawk, whether willing or unwilling, must be killed; and yet that law's indifference to one's intention does parallel the indifference of Herodotus' λόγος to his own reluctance. Herodotus seems to connect them when he talks

---

[44]The number of speeches in the other books is as follows (a colloquy is counted as one): I: 45; III: 33; IV: 20; V: 25: (with one five page speech); VI: 18 (with one two page speech); VII: 34 (with colloquies of several pages); VIII: 29; IX: 31; but λόγος and λέγεται occur most often in II. Cf. Creuzer, F., *Die historische Kunst der Griechen*, 2nd ed., ed. Kayser (Leipzig, 1845), p. 129, fn 1 on IV.132: "wo die misslungene Erklärung in indirectem, die gelungene dagegen in directem Gespräche vorgetragen wird."

[45]114.2–3; 115.4–6; 173.2–4; 181.3; consider III.14. Note the conversational ἤτοι and τοι (120.1,3) in Herodotus' opinion about the Egyptian account of Helen; cf. Denniston[2], *The Greek Particles*, pp. 538, 553.

[46]173.1 (cf. 28.2); 174.1; 178.1.

[47]Cf. III.75.1–2; VII.96.1; 139.1.

about the behavior of cats in Egypt. The population of cats would greatly increase, if the females did not refuse to receive the males after they had once borne a litter; to which the males contrive a stratagem if they wish to mate. The female cat has two contradictory impulses; she naturally rejects the male after becoming a mother, but just as naturally she is a lover of children; so that the absence of her offspring compels her to mate again. But this desire for generation is canceled by yet another impulse, when "divine things overcome" them. When a conflagration occurs, the cats try to jump into the fire, though the Egyptians station guards around it to prevent them; and if they succeed in eluding the guards and are consumed, "great grief comes over the Egyptians."[48] This feline auto-da-fé is the only "divine thing" specifically labelled as such in the second book. It is divine because they are compelled to jump; but they are also compelled to generate; and the only difference lies in the one being done willingly and the other unwillingly. They are both compulsions; "willy-nilly" they must do what they do. Their willingness to perpetuate themselves and their unwillingness to die makes no difference to their nature; persuasion and necessity co-exist in it. But the Egyptians, in grieving, do not see this double compulsion; only Herodotus sees it; who is compelled to break his silence about divine things because the divine cannot be separated here from the not divine. His desire to tell only about human things breaks down in the presence of sub-human things, where $τὰ θεῖα$ and $τὰ μὴ θεῖα$ are naturally found together. In animals a contradictory doubleness exists that permits Herodotus to reflect on a similar doubleness in Egyptian customs. The crocodile could be taken as the emblem of that doubleness.

The "nature" of the crocodile is made up of contraries. It lives both on land and in the water; it is blind in the water but "most sharp-sighted" in the open air; alone of all animals it moves its upper jaw and not its lower (a reversal that recalls the Egyptians' pushing the woof down though all others push it up); it grows from an egg no larger than a goose's to seventeen cubits or more; it alone of all the "mortal things" Herodotus knows becomes the largest from the smallest beginning; it is a silent animal, because it alone has no tongue; and though all other birds and beasts avoid it, it does no harm to the "trochilus" that cleans its mouth of leeches. Its peaceableness and ferocity are taken up in the two ways the Egyptians treat it. In some places they regard it as sacred and domesticate it; elsewhere they treat it as inimical and eat it. The distinction between wild and domesticated animals does not rest on that between the natural and the conventional but on that between the profane and the sacred.[49] So too, the hippopotamus, from whose hide they make the hafts

---

[48]Note the repetition of ($καταλαμβάνειν$ 65.2; 66.2; 66.1, 3, 4; cf. III.109–109.

[49]Cf. 69.2 with III.28.1; see also 74.

of spears, those at Pampremis, where the temple of Ares is situated, revere; while others do not believe it to be sacred (71).[50] The monstrous character of both these amphibious animals, the double look they have—the hippopotamus with the hooves of a bull and the mane, tail, and voice of a horse but the size of the largest bull, and the crocodile with the eyes and tusks of a boar but otherwise like lizards, shows how difficult Herodotus sees his task to be of uniting the disproportion between the ultimate causes of Egypt (its land and river) and their results, the customs and beliefs of the Egyptians. The disproportion exists in the animals themselves. The crocodile's scaly, unbreakable skin, which is the product of its power of growth, resembles Egypt itself, with its permanent, unchanging appearance that the moving power of the Nile has effected (cf. III.12; 16.2). Indeed, Herodotus himself underlies the resemblance. The Ionians, in calling them crocodiles because of their likeness to their native lizards, do what Herodotus did in comparing the action of the Nile to that of other rivers in Ionia, "to compare the small with the large" (10.1). Egypt and the crocodile have both become large from the very smallest beginnings.

Animals are living things ($\zeta\tilde{\omega}\alpha$) into which for a period of three thousand years the Egyptians believe the soul or life of a man ($\psi\upsilon\chi\acute{\eta}$) enters; at the end of which time it reenters the body of a man (123.2).[51] The animals, then, would be held sacred as the depositories of life and the soul. The Egyptians see man as composed of body and soul, the one preserved by mummification as an empty shell, the other invisible but always present and becoming in the animals around them. These two kinds of immortality comprise the immortality of continual change and the immortality of static permanence. The monuments of Egypt also reflect this double permanence.

Cheops is said to have closed the sanctuaries and forbidden all sacrifices, compelling everyone to build a pyramid as a tomb for himself (124–125). Can his impiety be connected with his monument? A monument is a memorial, a reminder to future generations that one has once lived. It perpetuates one's name. Even in one's absence it preserves one's presence. Cheops in closing the sanctuaries expressed his disbelief in the immortality of the soul; the building of a monument for himself would be its substitute. It accomplishes the same purpose without the help of the gods.[52] He would no longer need the sacred

---

[50]Cf. 59.3; III.12.4. There are two kinds of ibis, one honored for its defending Egypt from the plague of Arabian winged snakes, the other more usually to be seen in Egypt (75–76). Herodotus does not say which one is the sacred ibis; it is the more familiar one (Hopfner, T., *Der Tierkult*, pp. 117ff.).

[51]"Body" occurs fifteen times, "soul" twice in II; cf. 120.2.

[52]Cf. *Iliad* VII.443–453 (cf. 81–91 with VI.1); XII.3–35.

animals to achieve immortality; so the Egyptians try to thwart his ambition by being very unwilling to mention his name, and they attribute his work to a shepherd (128).[53]

Monumental building is not the only means of perpetuation. Poetry also has the same power. Hence in the section devoted to Cheops, Chephren, and Mycerinus, Herodotus mentions Aesop "the story-teller" (λογοποιός), who wrote fables about animals, and Sappho "the poetess" (μουσοποιός) (134-135). In doing so he refers to Rhodopis, a courtesan, who was so famous that all the Greeks knew her name: Sappho often abused her. She too desired to leave behind a monument, "having made an object (ποίημα) that had been invented by no one else." Again the reason for her desire is clear. Unable to have any legitimate children of her own (one may note that Cheops' father is not given), who would somehow keep her memory alive, she must resort to a unique kind of reminder that could replace the ordinary means of survival. Her monument is just as lasting as any children might have been, and it makes her more notorious than Archidike, whose name was only recorded in song (ἀοίδιμος). So Cheops' daughter, whom he set up in a brothel, left her own pyramid in a effort to be remembered (130.2-131.1).[54] Immortal fame replaces immortality itself: there is only one song sung in all Egypt (79; cf. 129.3).

Even Mycerinus, pious though he was, goes out of his way to commemorate his own daughter who died young. He made for her a hollow, wooden cow and covered it with a purple cloth except for the neck and head which were heavily gilded; and he placed a "gold imitation of the sun" between its horns (129.3; 132; cf. 73). On the day they beat the god "who is not named by me in such a matter" (i.e. Osiris), she is carried out to see the sun; while during the rest of the year they honor her with incense by day, and

---

[53]Cf. 104.1; IV.76.5; Pliny *NH* XXXVI.79.

[54]Cf. I.93.2-4. It has often been noted that Herodotus puts Cheops, Chephren, and Mycerinus in the wrong dynasty, since they belong to the fourth and not to the twentieth as here. This 'mistake' becomes intelligible if one considers that the Egyptians said that up to Rhampsinitus' reign, Egypt was prosperous and well-governed (124.1): their desire to obliterate innovation compels their rearrangement (cf. III.16.5-7), for their premise is that the oldest is the best. Herodotus himself indicates that an error has been made by saying that the Greeks make Rhodopis contemporary with Mycerinus, while she actually lived at the time of Amasis (134.1-3; cf. 140.2). Such is the power of fame that it can make one older, and the power of infamy that it can make one younger, than one really is. Also observe the shift from ἐκδέξασθαι (111.1; 112.1; 121.1; cf. 127.1; I.6.4) to βασιλεῦσαι (124.1; 129.1; 136.1; 137.1; 141.1).

by night a light is kept burning beside her (130.1).[55] She has become endowed, as the commentators remark, with the attributes of Isis. Under the stress of grief, Mycerinus has transformed his daughter into a goddess.

Herodotus' reluctance to declare openly that the gods of Egypt, especially Osiris, are buried, wept for, and have tombs, turns on his reluctance to point to the mortality of immortal gods. The Egyptians fail to see any difficulty in this. They maintain both the death and the immortal life of the gods (cf. III.29). The doubleness of everything in Egypt is reflected in their unawareness of contradiction. They do not see a contradiction as a contradiction.[56] Their belief in the immortality of the soul must accordingly be counterposed with their practice of mummification.[57] The preservation of their bodies would appear, at first, to fit ill with their belief in the soul's immortality. Body and soul appear as two distinct entities without any inherent connection between them. We have seen that the soul is supposed to live on in an animal; but this insistence on preserving the body suggests that the soul does not contain everything that constitutes a man, since its assumption of the shape of all the animals, without its becoming any of them permanently, shows that it has no particular shape. It is simply the power of life itself. The human shape is thought to be the body; not the body with all its internal organs but only the skin and the bones. In mummification, everything corruptible is drawn out of the body or dissolved, and the inside is filled with unguents, in much the same way as they prepare a bull for sacrifice (86–87; cf. 40.3) The most expensively treated corpse they called by a name which Herodotus believes it is not holy to mention; but it is as clear here as elsewhere (where he says the same) that he means Osiris (86.2; 132.1; 170.1).[58] The mummy is a god (cf. IX.120.2). The whole corpse is not a god, but the empty shell, cleansed and emptied of its vital organs, the mere surface of the body, is. When the god stands revealed in a permanent guise and not in an animal mask, he appears dead. Surface and substance are divorced; one becomes superficial, the other unknown. The "look" of the gods seems as lifeless as their statues are, unless one recalls the

---

[55] Cf. 62.1; 86.2; 133.4.

[56] Cf. Xenophanes' remark as variously reported, Vor-Sokratiker[5], I, A13; e.g., Plutarch de superstitione 13 (171E): Ξενοφάνης ὁ φυσικὸς τοὺς Αἰγυπτίους κοπτομένους ἐν ταῖς ἑορταῖς καὶ θρηνοῦντας ὁρῶν ὑπέμνησε οἰκείως "οὗτοι," φησίν, "εἰ μὲν θεοί εἰσιν, μὴ θρηνεῖτε αὐτούς, εἰ δὲ ἄνθρωποι, μὴ θύετε αὐτοῖς."

[57] 76.3 ends with τοσαῦτα μὲν θηρίων πέρι ἱρῶν εἰρήσθω and 77.1 opens with αὐτῶν δὲ δὴ Αἰγυπτίων κτλ; see also IV.15.4–16.1, and Iliad I.3ss.; also Odyssey XI.602.

[58] Cf. 123.1; Heraclitus fr. 15; [Demosthenes] 60.30.

power of life that their animal disguises represent. Anyone killed by a crocodile or drowned in the Nile is treated as "something more than the corpse of a man" (90; cf. III.27-28). Once again look and power (εἶδος and δύναμις have proved to be the two fundamental aspects of Egypt.

The Egyptians show their concern with this kind of preserving not only in their treatment of the dead but in their daily life. "Of all men they exercise their memory the most and are by far the most learned of those I have any acquaintance with" (77.1).[59] To be the most learned (λογιώτατοι) does not mean to be the most reasonable but only to preserve in writings the history of the past. The past becomes so much the model for the present that even miraculous events, if they are similar to some recorded occasions, they think will have the same issue (82.2). The past as the permanent makes them regard all change as corruption. They think that eating is the cause of disease, and attribute to their monthly purges their great health, which Herodotus refers to the unchanging character of the seasons (77.2-3; cf. IV.187. 2-3). They transfer a celestial phenomenon to the earth; so the Greeks learned geometry from them but took their astronomical instruments from the Babylonians (109.3; cf. 35.2). Bread from spelt and wine from barley, dried or salted fish, pickled, broiled, or stewed birds constitute their diet (77.4-5). Everything fluid and corruptible even in their diet is to some extent removed. At drinking parties they are reminded that they soon will be as stiff as the wooden figure they are shown, "painted and worked most accurately in imitation" of a man (78). Mortality, seen as the impermanent and fleeting, makes the Egyptians devote all their effort to transforming it into something stable and hard. The mummy is only the most obvious such effort. Their avoidance of all foreign customs and their strict adherence to "ancestral laws" point in the same direction (79.1; 91.1). Their "excessive piety" makes them not only yield the right of way to their elders but made the law of Asychis effective as well; it allowed credit to be extended if one's father's mummy was offered as security; the penalty for not honoring the debt being the denial of entombment for oneself and one's descendants (37.1; 80.1).

Memory stops the ever-changing flow of events. It fixes and solidifies becoming. It stands to the events themselves as earth stands to water. Asychis wished to surpass the previous kings, Cheops, Chephren, and Mycerinus; so he had built a pyramid out of bricks, on which he inscribed these words: "Do not scorn me in comparison with the stone pyramids; for I exceed them by as much as Zeus does the other gods: they dipped a pole into a lake, and

---

[59]Cf. 3.1; 145.3; I.1.1; IV. 46.1; Orth E., *Logios* (Leipzig, 1926) pp. 12ff.

whatever mud clung to it they collected, from which they drew bricks, and thus they made me" (136.4). The labor involved in such a manner of building dictates Asychis' boast. Its piecemeal character makes it a more glorious achievement than Cheops'. It resembles, in fact, the way lower Egypt was built up, the slow accretion of mud carried down by the Nile. Asychis imitates, to compare small things with large, the very history of Egypt: the transformation of the moving into the stationary.

This episode, which stands at the beginning of the fourth section in the third part, (136–141), typifies all the stories that follow. The blind king Anysis who succeeds Asychis, when driven into the marshes, has every subject who brings him food, carry to his retreat, in secret, dust or ashes, with which he builds up an island ten stades in circumference that for more than seven hundred years went undetected. A monument is no longer intended to be seen, raised for the greater glory of its builder, but only the haphazard accumulation of earth that mutely testifies to the loyalty of his subjects. So, on the other hand, the pious Sabakos, the Egyptian king who displaced Anysis, compelled those who did wrong to heap up mounds of earth at whatever city each came from; which accidentally has the effect to make the temple of Artemis "a great pleasure to behold"; for though the city becomes higher, "the sanctuary was not moved since it was first made," which thus allows it to be seen from all sides. The beautiful proves to be an accidental product of blind makers; he earth that is only meant to pay a fine has an unforeseen result.

How trivial things can have great consequences comes out again in the last story. Sethos, the priest of Hephaestus, held the warriors of Egypt in no account; and when the king of the Arabians and Assyrians invaded Egypt, none of them was willing to aid him. Trusting to a dream, which promised him victory, he was rewarded by discovering that field mice during the night had eaten away the straps of the enemies' shields. "And now this king in stone," Herodotus says, "stands at the temple of Hephaestus, with a mouse in his hand, and these words are inscribed: 'Look on me and be pious.'" *ex mure nascitur mons.* Sethos resembles the other three kings, Asychis, Sabakos, and Anysis, in this: the weakness of their resources and the greatness of their deeds. The fortuitous works of Sabakos and Anysis and the slight material of Asychis and Sethos show up the enduring and unchanging aspect of Egypt—the land, in short—, which the monuments of Cheops, Chephren, and Mycerinus— deliberately planned to usurp the place of the soul's immortality with the permanent becoming of fame—would tend to efface.

Egypt contains two Egypts. The Egyptians themselves, trying to forget innovation, see most clearly upper Egypt, a land that has always been the same for over eleven thousand years (142.3–4). The Greeks only see lower Egypt, a land that has come into existence "virtually only yesterday or the day before" (5.1; 15.2; 53.1: 58). Both are partially correct, and to modify one version by

the other, and yet to hold them together, has been Herodotus' task. He therefore describes the marsh-dwellers and their ways (92–98) after he has dealt
with the cultivated part of Egypt, in which section he had pointed to all that
was ancient and lasting; and that the transient and recent will now predominate
he indicates in its last paragraph (91). There he corrects his former assertion
that the Egyptians avoid all foreign customs: for he adds the words "in a manner of speaking." He goes on to say that in the city of Chemmis ("near New
City in the district of Thebes") he found a temple of Perseus the son of Danae,
for whom the Chemmites hold athletic contests in the Greek fashion. So recent
an intrusion in the very heart of old Egypt—long ago Egypt was called Thebes
(15.3: cf. 9.2)—reveals the inadequacy in the Egyptian account of themselves.
If the Greeks are always children, the Egyptians have not yet lost—nor can
they ever lose—the capacity to change. The principles of things are always present and always at work (28.1: cf. I.140.3).

Among the marsh-dwellers the river naturally dominates. The Egyptian
lotus, papyrus and castor-oil plants (all of which grow in or near the water),
the generation of a certain fish, the manufacture of boats, and how lower
Egypt becomes a sea when the Nile rises, these things the Greeks are more
aware of than the Egyptians: Homer calls the Nile Egypt.[60] Hence comparison
with Greek things occurs here very often. Each Egyptian marries one woman
"just as the Greeks"; the lotus "resembles the poppy-head," its root "about the
size of an apple": lilies here "resemble roses," their fruit "most like in looks
to the comb of wasps." and they have in them "about as much edible stuff as
the stone of an olive"; the castor-oil plants, sown on the banks of the rivers,
"grow without planting among the Greeks," its oil "no less suitable to lamp
fluid than olive oil"; their boats are made from acacia, "whose shape is most
like the Cyrenaic lotus"; and the cities, which alone appear above the flood-
waters of the Nile, then "most resemble somehow the islands in the Aegean."
The sameness of Egypt, what it has that can be likened to other places and
things, is associated in Herodotus' mind with growth and generation; just as in
the early paragraphs of the book he compared the Delta with the Macandrian
plain, and guessed at what its unknown course might be from the Danube's.
And since he thinks of generation in terms of the ever-new and recent, he says
at the end of this section that Anthylla is a "notable city reserved for shoes," a
task entrusted to it ever since the Persians conquered Egypt; and that the city
of Archandrus received its name from the son-in-law of Danaus; or if there
was another Archandrus, the name at any rate is not Egyptian.

The Greeks' involvement in the present, their relative youthfulness as a
distinct people, blinds them to the other, perhaps more evident aspect of

---

[60]*Odyssey* IV.477. Note the use of the second person singular at 5.2;
29.3–6; 30.1; 97.2; cf. I.139; 199.4; III.12.1; IV.28.1.

Egypt: the age and permanence of its human institutions. Even the "λόγος-maker" Hecataeus brought his ancestry back to a god in sixteen generations; whereas the Egyptian priests could show 341 statues of kings with not a god or hero among them; for the Egyptian god Heracles, who belongs to the second generation of gods, was born seventeen thousand years before the reign of Amasis (143–144; 43.4).[61] The Egyptians distinguish more sharply than the Greeks do between the time when the gods ruled Egypt and the rule of men; but they admit that the gods once lived with men: the gods did not rule over other gods (144.2). Although the genealogies of the gods and of men are kept separate, the problem of the gods' origin remains as obscure as it is among the Greeks. They merely push back the problem in time; but antiquity cannot substitute, as the Egyptians think it can, for first principles. Just as they had confused the power of speech with speaking a particular language, so they now confound again the ancestral with the beginnings. They rely on the darkness of a remote past to achieve a supposed clarity about the present and its completely human history. By pulling apart the divine from the human, they can never explain how they can constitute a whole. The gods are merely the strange and the alien.[62] The disproportion between the human and the divine is made into a disjunction; and if the Greeks too hastily join them, at least they are aware that they belong together.

Since the Egyptians have many practices the reverse of the Greeks', the age of the gods among them it also given in the reverse order. Whereas the Egyptians put Pan among the oldest eight gods, Heracles among the next

----

[61]The numerical error at 142.1–3 is only apparent. Although 341 generations of kings amount to 11,366 2/3 years and not 11,340 years as Herodotus says, the difference can be found in the story of Mycerinus (133), who was told that he would live six years and die in the seventh. If 33 1/3 years constitute the average royal span (at three kings to a century), and if the oracle about Mycerinus was fulfilled (Herodotus does not say), then Mycerinus would have fallen short of the average by 33 1/3 − 6 + = 27, i.e., the difference between the 'correct' and Herodotus' figure. For the standard of three kings to a century, note that the Mermnadic dynasty lasted 169 years, distributed over five reigns of varying lengths (I.15; 16.1; 25.1; 86.1).

[62]Cf. *Odyssey* VII.199–206; XVII.483–487. How alien the gods are Herodotus shows in the list of the seven Egyptian classes (164.1): the pilots are concerned with shipping goods from one place to another (cf. 175.3); the interpreters with foreign languages; the merchants with exchange; the swineherds are forbidden to marry into another class (47.1); the cowherds take care of sacred animals; the warriors fight foreign enemies; and the priests are assigned to the gods.

twelve, and Dionysus in the third generation, the Greeks make Dionysus the oldest, Heracles the next, and Pan the youngest (145-146). The Greek gods also lose the accuracy that the Egyptians claim to have about their origins. Dionysus was born "approximately a thousand years before my time," Heracles "about nine hundred years," and Pan after the Trojan war, "approximately eight hundred years before my time." Whatever one may believe about Heracles—he may have been a famous man who assumed the name of a previous god—the Greek stories about Pan and Heracles—their divine birth—make it clear to Herodotus that their origin must be sought in Egypt; and that the Greeks started their genealogy from the time they had first heard about them. If the Greek gods are alien gods; if they can be understood as derivative and as only reworked by their poets, the Egyptian gods as their sources cannot so easily be explained. They must be regarded, finally, as original and indigenous as the earth and water of Egypt.

Pan in Egypt has the same name as "goat"; and it is sensible to attribute something "goatish" to the god (46.4); but the Greek Pan cannot be traced back to something natural, for his name does not point to something outside language but to another proper name, the first syllable of Penelope, from whom he is said to have been born; and similarly Dionysus takes his name from Zeus and Nysa, where he was nurtured, and it is impossible to look beyond his hybrid name. Pan has his origin in Penelope, but the origin is not only sexual but linguistic. The Greeks mistake etymology for genealogy. Whereas the Egyptians, in the story of Psammetichus' experiment, mistake what is derivative for the original, the Greeks ignore the original, in this case the Egyptian Pan, and mistake his derivative, their own Pan, for Penelope's son, where derivation obtains a different meaning. Once one knows of the Egyptian Pan, the Greeks' procedure somehow preserves the truth, for their Pan is in fact only a name, not from Penelope but from Egypt, though they are mistaken in combining generation with it. We shall see in Book IV that the double origin of Pan, linguistic and sexual, unites what is peculiarly Egyptian (the sexual) with what is peculiarly Scythian (the linguistic). This unification will then indicate the derivative character of what we call Greek, derivative not only historically but essentially from 'purer' ways of thinking.

Two works that Herodotus admires, the labyrinth and the lake of Moeris, serve to explain why the Egyptians are less compelled than the Greeks to bring gods and men together (148-150). The labyrinth like the pyramids is "greater than any reckoning" (λόγου μέζω), and the lake of Moeris is "a still greater marvel," in comparison to which even the greatest "show of works" among the Greeks would appear insignificant.[63] The upper part of the labyrinth,

---

[63]Cf. 35.1; VII.147.1; IX.37.2.

duplicated below (or so Herodotus heard) as the tomb of the twelve kings and the sacred crocodiles, "we ourselves see to be greater than human works." "To be greater than λόγος" means to be greater than human. It suggests that the human has almost usurped the role of the divine. What has been made by men takes on the look of the natural: the sixty stade perimeter of Lake Moeris "equals Egypt itself in its coastline" (149.1; 6.1).[64] Everything looks man-made: of the seven mouths of the Delta two are artificial (17.3–6; cf. 149.4). The natural has receded into the past because men have imitated its works so well. And just as Egypt has become what the earth and river have made it, so the stone labyrinth (with six of its halls facing south and six facing north) and the lake, which fills up in six months and empties in six, show, in human fashion, the same doubleness of the permanent and the transient. They are found again in what Herodotus regards as the most marvelous things in all Egypt. The temple of Leto made from a solid block of stone, each wall of which is forty feet square, Herodotus thinks the "most wondrous of visible things"; and the island of Chemmis that is said to float and move secondly amazes him (155.3–156.2; cf. 175.3). The seen and the heard are related to one another as the evident (the stationary) to the obscure (the moving), a proportion Herodotus had hinted at previously when he discussed the visible silting in the Delta and the obscure causes of the Nile's action (5.1; 24.1; cf.. 83–84); but it is important to add that in the Egyptian man-made temple and the sacred story of the island, the visible and invisible are farther apart than in the natural things, earth and water.

We have examined so far the second and third parts of Book II as though they belonged together. By interlacing in our own account the five sections of one with those of the other, we have tried to make it evident how each section of Part II depends on its corresponding section in Part III. Paragraphs 35–50 considered Egyptian customs and gods, which led us to examine in turn paragraphs 99–120 that dealt with the first kings of Egypt. History paralleled without duplicating customs, for the notion that linked them was that of the first things. Gods and kings stood as the divine and human beginnings of Egypt: they were what made Egypt Egyptian. Paragraphs 51–65.1 dealt with the festivals and the way the gods became Greek, which was echoed in the story of Rhampsinitus, the second section of the third part (121–123). Paragraphs 65.2–76 dealt with sacred animals, and the pyramid-builders (124–135) were connected with them, as the pyramids offered the substitute of immortal fame for the immortality that the animals had guaranteed (note that 123 concerns the Egyptian belief in the soul's immortality). Paragraphs 77–91 dealt with the "earthy" part of the Egyptian way of life, which recurred in the brick

---

[64]Cf. 9.2 with 15.3; also Diodorus I.63.7.

pyramid of Asychis and the hidden island of Anysis (136-141); while the marsh-dwellers' way of life (92-98) could be seen again in Herodotus' account of Egyptian chronology and theogony (142-146). This interlacing seems justified by the light it throws on Herodotus' understanding of Egypt, which found the self-evident difference between earth and water manifested everywhere in Egypt. We might ask, however, how Herodotus thought of mummification, for example, as being grounded in earth, or the animal masks of the gods as being related to water. Mummification seems connected with earth because it has the same characteristics as earth-solidity. immovability, and shape—, and not because it may consist of earth; just as the animal masks of the gods are apparently connected with water through the properties of generation, fluidity. and shapelessness. Now to ask further of Herodotus how he conceives water and earth actually imbued Egyptian customs and history with their own properties, would be to ask him a question to which he has no answer; for he could only say that somehow water and earth were able to generate likenesses to themselves throughout Egyptian customs and history; and that these two principles shone through the thought and action of the Egyptians without the Egyptians ever becoming aware of them. But it is this question of the metaphorical power of earth and water that compels Herodotus to search elsewhere for some answer to the riddle of Egypt. It is what dictates, as we shall see, the character of Book IV on Scythia and Libya.

Autopsy and hearsay have been the twin sources of Herodotus' account up to the end of the third part; but the fourth and last part seems to be based on a different kind of evidence (147.1; cf. 154.4). There he says: "All that other men and the Egyptians say agreeing with one another, I shall now relate; and there will also be in addition my own observation." The agreement between Egyptians and others (mostly Greeks) can apparently replace his own judgment and inquiry (γνώμη and ἱστορίη), which played so large a role in the first three parts, and which he never again mentions by name.[65] It cannot be that agreement as such automatically guarantees the truth of what is said; for neither the agreement of the priests of Heliopolis and of Memphis about human things, nor that between the Corinthians and Lesbians about Arion, warrants their truth (4.1; I.23).[66] Herodotus' trust in it, then, must lie rather in the character

---

[65]Herodotus' γνώμη: 18.1 bis; 24.1; 26.1; 27; 43.3; 56.1; 99.1; 120.5; 146.1; his ἱστορίη: 99.1; ἱστορέειν: 19.3 bis; 29.1; 34.1; 44.5; 113.1; but cf. 148.5. At 148.5 occurs the only one of nine πυνθάνεσθαι that Herodotus makes: 8.1; 18.1; 19.2; 29.1 bis; 44.1; 50.1; 75.1; and at 150.4; 156.4 occur the only two of his fourteen ἀκούειν: 2.5; 3.1,2; 13.1; 32.1; 43.1 bis; 52.1; 55.1; 99.1; 104.1; 112.2; and only once his own δοκέειν, 170.2. Of 31 occurrences of νομίζειν only one is in part four (167.1).

[66]Cf. IV.12.3; 105.2; 150.1.

of those who agree than in agreement itself. If the Egyptians resemble their
river and sky, which act so differently from the way they act in all other
regions of the known world, because they do the opposite of what other men
do; then, if these other men agree with them about the facts of Egyptian history, the partiality inherent in either group's reports is removed; and their
agreement, like the agreement of nature with itself in spite of its local differences, testifies to its own truth and does away with the need for independent
reflection. Herodotus' conviction in the first part that the Egyptians were correct about their land was based on the agreement of what they said with what
he himself saw; but here, in the fourth part, "they easily persuaded" him when
they explained where the earth from the excavation of Lake Moeris had been
carried, because he knew "by report that another similar thing had happened at
Nineveh" (12.1; 150.2).[67] Neither report by itself would have persuaded him;
but since he believed the Assyrians and Egyptians had had no contact with
each other, the independence of the two λόγοι turns them into a ὁμολογία that
carries as much weight as his own observation would have done (cf. 160). This
kind of agreement produces, as one of its consequences, Herodotus' introduc-
ing the reign of each king in direct speech; whereas before he always wrote
"they said" or "the priests said," or even when those words are absent, they
must be understood; he now writes, "Mekos was the son of Psammetichus and
became king of Egypt," and the like (158.1; 159.3; 161.1; 172.1). Agreement
has broken the authority of the priests, and he never again quotes them; in
fact, only thrice more does he refer to an unsupported Egyptian tale (147.2;
148.5; 150.1; 156.2,5).

   "The Egyptians call everyone a barbarian who does not speak the same
language (ὁμόγλωσσοι) as themselves" (158.5; cf. 18.2); but when Psammetichus, allied with Greek and Carian pirates, conquered Egypt, he had them
teach Greek to some Egyptian boys, from whom came "the present interpreters
in Egypt" (154.2-4). The first settlement of men of foreign speech
(ἀλλόγλωσσοι) destroys the rigidity as well as the isolation of Egypt. It
permits Amasis, a commoner, to become king, marry a Greek wife, show himself a "philhellene," and promulgate the only Egyptian law that Herodotus
praises (177.2; 178.1; cf. 182). Amasis is something new in Egypt; not
because he is "un-Egyptian" and looks at things in an utterly different light,

---

[67]Cf. IV. 195.2; for ἕτερον τοιοῦτον, see also 11.3; 104.2; 150.4. This
similarity between Assyria and Egypt is not isolated; cf. I.185.1 with II.100.2;
I.182.2; 193.1-2; 198; 200 with II.77.4; 92.5; I.193.4 with II.68.2 and
VII.63; and I.194.1 with II.155.3. Book II is, one might say, Herodotus'
promised Assyrian logos (I.184; cf. 93.2); for a possible explanation of
I.106.2 compare I.107.1 with Diodorus II.28.

but because he brings together what the Egyptians so far had managed to keep apart. When Amasis first occupied the throne, the Egyptians despised him on account of his low birth; so in order to win them over, he had a gold foot basin made into a statue of a god, which the Egyptians came to revere greatly; whereupon he revealed its origin and told them that he resembled the basin, in which they had vomited, pissed, and washed their feet; but now that it had been made into something sacred and he himself into their king, they must honor him as willingly as they now paid homage to the statue (172). Not the sources of things but their present appearance must be one's concern. If the origins are obscure, ugly, or unclean, they must in no way affect one's attitude toward what they have become. The final shape has an autonomy that owes nothing to its past. In maintaining this, Amasis goes no further than the Egyptians themselves, who tell indifferently the obscene and the glorious about their kings; and whose sacred stories Herodotus refuses to divulge, though they are supposedly the reasons for the practices he describes, because they offended his taste and not theirs.[68] What Amasis does in addition, however, is to bring them out in the open, so as to suggest to us, if not to the Egyptians, that the doubleness of origin and result, of the base and the beautiful, belongs together. His insight points to what Herodotus thinks is the riddle of Egypt. It is Amasis who dedicates huge man-sphinxes (175.1).[69]

Amasis used to deal, in the early morning of each day, with the serious business of his office; but afterwards he spent the time in drinking and being playful with his friends; and when his friends reproached him for it, and urged him to act always in a royal fashion, Amasis answered that bows when needed are stretched and when not in use are unstrung; "for if they were always taut, they would break and prove to be useless when needed; so too is the condition of man: were a man to be always in earnest and never to devote himself to play, he would unawares go mad or have a stroke" (173-174).[70] The human condition is not uniform; it is made up of two disparate elements, the playful and the serious. The serious is one's job, whether it be ruling a kingdom or stealing, and whatever makes up a way or form of life; but the playful is trivial and has no specific character or purpose. If the function of a bow is to shoot and kill, its idleness would appear to be no essential part of itself; but if the bow unstrung is necessary for its usefulness, then its two states cannot be dis-

---

[68]Cf. 171.1-2 and fn 44 *supra*.

[69]Cf. IV.79; Hegel, *Phil. d. Weltgeschichte*, pp. 510ss. (ed. Lasson).

[70]Cf. I.133.3-4; III.34-35; VIII.83.1; consider also III.40.2. Herodotus does not allow even Amasis to use the word φύσις but only the phrase ἀνθρώπου κατάστασις (173.4), unlike Themistocles' ἐν ἀνθρώπου φύσι καὶ καταστάσι (VIII.83.1).

joined. Amasis' statue and foot basin belong as much together as the playful and the serious. The high and noble do not exist apart from the base and mean (cf. III.112). They are different, they are not separable. The understanding that can grasp their togetherness, without either confounding them or being blind to one of them, may be called διάνοια (cf. 162.3–5). It is a fundamental part of Herodotus' λόγος; it is his understanding of Egypt.

Herodotus in Egypt was confronted with two things: its nature and its customs. Its nature derived from and was the river and the land; a river that acted unlike any other river, yet whose results were comparable; and an earth that did not resemble its neighbors', yet was not unique. He tried to explain how this sameness and difference came about. His explanation led him, in turn, to understand the customs of Egypt, which looked so unlike the customs of others, in terms of what he had discovered. He tried to derive them from the nature of Egypt, and at the same time to show that they were parallel to it; he did not make the mistake of binding the derivative with the source so closely that they would prove to be the same. He saw that the Egyptians themselves in their customs and history had partially understood this; that they conceived of man as body and soul; and that they discerned the difference between the divine and the human; but he realized, too, that they were bound to the doubleness they had discovered, and were unable to put together what they had so accurately distinguished. The whole eluded them (cf. 84). Herodotus supplied the corrective. His knowledge of φύσις allowed him to see νόμος as its necessary companion: the opinion about things grounded in the nature of things. Nature, by revealing itself partially in Egypt, also reveals in custom part of its *logos*. On that basis Herodotus could account for what the Egyptians believed even while he went beyond what they believed. Through the whole tangle of their monuments, laws, and history, he could follow this double thread and never lost his way.

It might be objected that Herodotus has forced Egypt to fit his theory; and all the extravagances, omissions, and simplification, which his commentators have collected, would seem to confirm this. We should point out, however, that this distortion, if knowingly done, served a useful purpose. It offered us an access to Egypt that the mere piling up of details could never have accomplished. Herodotus selected his facts with a view to presenting a certain aspect of things. It is not the only one. If he understood that, the distortion will prove to be only temporary, and will disappear as he looks in another way; although there again, what he has so far uncovered will be neglected, and another distortion with its own insight will dominate. Only when all the ways of understanding, based on the ways things are, are completed, that is, only when we come to the end of Book IV, do the distortions inherent in each particular way, if taken separately, disappear. It is our claim, as yet unproved, that Herodotus has done this.

Herodotus tries to discover the universal in particulars; a particular was Egypt, its nature and customs. Herodotus found a single kind of error running through all Egyptian customs. This error was to distinguish without bringing together again what had been distinguished; and this error was based on the failure to distinguish between φύσις and νόμος. The Egyptian error was that kind of error which leads to the truth: the truth in its universality was found by reflecting on a particular error. To account for an error necessarily leads to an account more comprehensive than that error; and to account for all errors would lead to the most comprehensive account. The next way of erring is the Persian way, which, by correcting the Egyptians though at the same time committing its own kind of error, brings Herodotus one step closer to that most comprehensive account.

III. PERSIA

Cambyses invaded Egypt because Amasis had deceived him; he had sent the daughter of the former king when Cambyses demanded one of his own; he had hoped that her beauty and height, set off with fine garments and gold, would fool Cambyses; he had not counted on her speaking the truth when Cambyses addressed her as the daughter of Amasis (1). Amasis' trust in her silence seems to have been founded on the silence Herodotus had discovered in Egypt itself. Speaking appeared so alien to Egypt that even Amasis did not consider the error in his deception. But Herodotus adds that this is what the Persians say; the Persians understand the Egyptians in this way; they think the Egyptians are so addicted to show and position that they would overlook the possibility of the truth being spoken. The Persians do not respond only to the surface of things; they are accustomed to tell the truth, and seeing means less to them: apparently an eye-ailment of Cyrus was the ultimate cause of Cambyses' invasion (1.1).

Herodotus does not say whether he agrees with the Persians or not; but he does rebuke the Egyptians for the version they tell (2; cf. II.45.2). It is incorrect because it goes against the laws and customs of Persia, which the Egyptians know better than anyone; and yet their ambition to attach themselves to the house of Cyrus proved stronger than their knowledge. We learn that the Egyptians do not always tell the truth; in the light of Persia they do not show up as well as they did when isolated from other countries. This rebuke is only the first of several they receive in the first paragraphs of Book III. They offer a different version also of Cambyses' sacrilegious treatment of Amasis' corpse, which would make it appear that another mummy was outraged and not his own; but Herodotus thinks that Amasis never ordered this substitution at all, and "the Egyptians fabricate this magnification in vain" (16.5-7).[1] Again the Egyptians are shown to be liars.

If the Egyptians tend to enhance themselves at the expense of truth, they would be likely to think that everyone else acts in the same way; they would

---

[1] Cf. I.95.1; 99.2; 122.3.

have no trust in what others say. When the defeated Egyptians retreat to
Memphis, Cambyses sends a herald to invite them to surrender; but they rush
out, sink the boat and tear the man apart "limb from limb" (13.1-2). They do
not wait to hear the herald's terms, nor to find out whether it is a trick; their
own lying has brought them to distrust everyone else; so that when Psammenitus, the son of Amasis, is captured and receives no violence at Persian
hands, he attempts to revolt, even though the Persians were accustomed to
honor the sons of kings by giving them back their thrones (15; cf. VII. 238.2).
Psammenitus' distrust of the Persians more than outweighed any knowledge he
had of their customs; just as before, Egyptian vanity could override their
knowledge that in making Cambyses their own they lied.

The lying and distrust of the Egyptians stand opposed to the truth-telling
of the Persians; a habit that makes them trust not only the truth but anything
spoken. Cambyses asks for no further confirmation of what the daughter of
Apries tells him; her word suffices to compel him to invade Egypt. "This
speech and this cause," Herodotus says, brought Cambyses greatly wroth
against Egypt; but clearly the phrase is a kind of hendiadys and the words of
Nitetis alone are the cause as far as Cambyses is concerned. Cambyses pays no
attention to the more remote occasion, the resentment of an Egyptian doctor;
the immediate speaking is enough to provoke him. Speech as a cause, rather
than any material pretext, underlies most of the stories in the third book. To
mention only those where a word ($\check{\epsilon}\pi o\varsigma$) actually instigates something, there
are the following: Cambyses sets out on a fatal expedition against the
Ethiopians because of the words their king spoke; the Greeks and Egyptians
both say Cambyses' sister was killed because she criticized her brother;
Croesus almost loses his life because of what be said to Cambyses; Polycrates
loses his friendship with Amasis because he was pleased with what a fisherman
said; Lycophron, the son of Periander, acts the way he does because his grandfather asked him a question; Ocestes desires to destroy Polycrates because of
the reproach Mitrobates leveled against him; Demokedes ultimately owes his
freedom to a word that pleased Darius; and Babylon falls because of a word
spoken in jest.[2] Speech, then, has assumed an importance that it never had in
Egypt; it has somehow prevailed over deed in Greece and Persia.

It might seem at first that Cambyses invades Egypt on petty grounds; on
what looks very much like the reason why the Persians had mocked at the

---

[2]21.3; 32.3; 36.1; 42.2; 50.3 (cf. 51.1); 120.1-4; 130.4 (cf. 134.6);
151.2 (cf. 157.3); cf. 137.2-4. Out of 56 instances of $\check{\epsilon}\pi o\varsigma$ (discounting those
where it means a verse or occurs in verses), sixteen are in III, twelve in VII,
where it never is causative; see e.g. VII.3.2; 120.1; 226.1; for the character of
$\check{\epsilon}\pi o\varsigma$ see Fournier, H., *Les verbes "dire" en grec ancien* (Paris, 1946), pp.
211-215.

Greeks about the Trojan war (I.4.2-3); but we soon realize that neither the beauty of Nitetis nor her being a woman decided Cambyses; it was the way Amasis lied that enraged him. It was not a spoken but a silent lie: Nitetis' appearance was an earnest of her truly being the daughter of Amasis; but Cambyses insisted that the name must correspond to what appears. Telling the truth and the truth must coalesce among the Persians. Although they are taught to speak the truth, they also learn that everything they may not do they may not say; which leads them to assert that no one has ever killed his own mother or father; "for it is improper that a child kill its true parent" (I.136.2-138).[3] The Persians are obliged to ignore Orestes and Oedipus. Their belief that everything true can be said depends on the law that only permissible things are done. Only if the proper and reasonable alone can happen, can the truth as law always coincide with the truth as deed. Even Cambyses, when he wished to marry his sister, asked the expounders of the ancestral sanctions whether there was any law that commanded it—he did not ask if any law prohibited it; and only after their "safe and just" answer did he marry (31). True speech, then, in Persia means lawful or just speech; it does not simply mean the truth. If lying is thought the most shameful thing, owing a debt is the next; for the Persians say that a man in debt is almost compelled to lie (I.138.1).[4] Amasis' deception, so that he did not have to give what Cambyses asked for, may have forced the Egyptians to make up a story to hide his injustice. But that "they pervert the λόγος," in pretending that Cambyses is half-Egyptian, only follows if their disregard of the law they know so well entails a disregard of the truth: only here in Herodotus does λόγος mean the same as truth (2.2).[5]

So great a concern with speech (and hence with hearing) leads to a certain depreciation of sight and visible things. The Persians do not observe, although Herodotus does, that "their names are like the magnificence of their bodies" (I.139; cf. VI.98.3). They do not see their bodies as reflected in their names; unlike any Greek who could not fail to notice the derivation of "Polycrates" or "Periander." The shape of things does not impress them; miraculous mixtures in animals do not trouble them as much as an eclipse of the sun (VII.37.2-3); cf. III.153).[6] Their cosmic gods are not embodied in statues. The sky could only be shown as a cup; sun, moon, and earth as disks,[7] while fire, water and

---

[3]Oedipus in *OT* 1409 says, after telling of his crimes, οὐ γὰρ αὐδᾶν ἔσθ' ἃ μηδὲ δρᾶν καλόν (cf. 1386-1390); cf. Diogenes Laertius I.59:(Σόλων) ἐρωτηθεὶς διὰ τί κατὰ πατροκτόνου νόμον οὐκ ἔθηκε, διὰ τὸ ἀπελπίσαι ἔφη.

[4]Cf. I.96.3-97.1, where κατὰ τὸ ὀρθόν means the same as κατὰ τὸ ἐόν.

[5]Cf. II.115.3; VI.2.2 (with 3.1).

[6]Accordingly, the Persian land has no "marvels" at all, nothing that really distinguishes it; cf. I.93.1; 110.2; IX.122.

[7]Cf. Maximus Tyrius II.86 (ed. Hobein).

winds are either formless or invisible. Their gods are sensible gods, they are not definite: none of them always has the same look. The moon wanes, the sun sinks, the sky is one through day and night. Their gods, therefore, must have a *logos* that is superior to the phenomena. Their blindness (or superiority) to the obvious brings along with it a depreciation of the body; the magi kill every living thing except dogs and men, and let dogs and birds tear apart their own corpses. If the body, then, loses its importance, we would expect that the soul would gain in proportion; and, in fact, the two Persian laws Herodotus praises both concern the soul (I.136.2–137.1). A father does not see his own son for the first five years of his life, lest his death might impose additional sorrow upon him. The natural desire to see one's own son is checked by the stronger consideration of what the familiarity of sight might do to the soul; indeed its tranquility is bought at the expense of any bodily feeling. The other law states that no one, not even the king, may kill a servant for a single cause; but he must first calculate whether the injustices exceed the benefits, for only if they do "may he use his wrath." Passion is meant to be subordinate to reason, and no immediate injury must prevail against the memory of favors received (cf. VII.194.1–2).[8]

The soul usually does not show itself in any way except in speech; but speech may be true or false speech; it may lay bare or conceal the soul. To test the soul a man's speech must be tested. Our own knowledge may sometimes be able to confirm or refute his speech; but most of the time we either trust or distrust what a man says in accordance with what we hold to be believable (cf. I.193.4). The believable is everything in which we put our trust, everything we can be persuaded of; it is what we call the self-evident. Whether it is truly self-evident or only self-evident to us, and should it prove to be the latter, what can be found to take its place, are the questions that dominate Herodotus' Persian *logos*. Against the background of the Persian trust in λόγος, he tries to articulate the true and the false.[9] It is the Persians' 'rationality'—the self-

---

[8]ψυχή and φρήν occur in III twice as often, and νόος as often, as in any other book; ψυχή: 14.1; 40.4; 41.1; 43.2; 108.2; 119.4; 130.4 (VII with the next highest number has four); φρήν: 33; 134.3; 155.3 (no other book has more than one); νόος: 21.3; 41.1; 51.1,2; 64.2; 81.2; 122.1; 135.3; 143.1 bis (only I has many); and ἔμψυχον: 16.3; 100; 106.2 (I, II, IV each has one).

[9]Note that the phrase λόγος αἱρέει, which usually means "reason requires," is once used of a Persian custom and once of Xerxes' whim (I.132.3; VII.41.1; cf. IV.127.3). ἀληθείη, ἀληθής, ἀληθέως, ἀληθίζεσθαι occur most often in III: 1.4; 17.2; 21.2; 22.1; 23.1; 34.3; 35.1; 35.1,2; 62.2,3; 63.1; 64.1; 72.4ter; 72.5bis; 75.2; 156.1; 157.1 (I has twelve instances, VII eleven); ψεῦδος, ψευδής, ψεύδεσθαι again occur most often in III: 27.3bis; 63.3; 72.4ter; 72.5bis; 118.2 (I has seven); see also IV.43.6;

evident character most of their customs have—that lets Herodotus use them as a guide for the understanding of λόγος. In the same way that he guided his inquiry in Egypt by the light of Egyptian discoveries, so here he follows the Persians as far as they can take him. He tries to look in the Persian way before he abandons it for his own; or, rather, his own *logos* accompanies their *logos* as its silent critic, to which we must listen as closely as we do to theirs.

If the first story explains Cambyses' invasion of Egypt in Persian terms, and the second in Egyptian, the third anecdote shares something with each: we might guess it is the Greek version. It agrees with the Egyptians' in making Nitetis Cyrus' concubine, but also with the first in keeping Cambyses Persian (3: cf. II.1). Herodotus finds it an "unconvincing story"; it does not jibe with Cyrus' show of grief at the death of his wife Cassandane; but what it does say nevertheless fits in with the theme of Book III. Cambyses promised his mother that when he grew up he would turn Egypt upside-down. If he had done so, Egypt would have taken on the appearance of all other countries. To turn it upside-down would make it, according to Herodotus, right side up (II.35.2). Its marvels would cease to be marvelous; they would cease to be unconvincing; and Egypt would cease to be a problem. But Herodotus himself has already accomplished that revolution; his *logos* did turn Egypt right side up, though in fact it remains as it was before. Cambyses' promise to do actually what Herodotus has done in thought, points to Cambyses' function: his distrust of the marvelous and unreasonable will force him to destroy everything anomalous and introduce in practice the uniformity of thought. His intolerance will serve as a foil to Herodotus' impartiality.

Herodotus introduces the invasion of Egypt with a series of episodes that sets the course for the rest of the book (4–9). One of Amasis' mercenaries was a certain Phanes who ran away to Cambyses; and when Amasis had him pursued, because he knew all about Egyptian affairs "most accurately," Phanes escaped from "the most trusted" eunuch of Amasis by making his guards drunk. Wine was able to overcome trust; it could set at naught the difference between the reliable and unreliable. Sobriety would appear to be a necessary condition for trust, and water-drinkers the most trustworthy of men. The Persians, before they invaded Lydia, did not drink wine; and afterward they had a custom to deliberate the most important matters when drunk, and then reconsider their decisions when sober; and if they first deliberated when sober,

---

44.1. For the importance of telling the truth among the Persians, see paragraphs LIV–LXVII of Darius' inscription at Behistūn (*The Inscription of Darius the Great at Behistūn* (British Museum, 1907); also König, F. W., *Relief u. Inscrift d. K. Dareius I am Felsen von Bagistan* (Leiden, 1938), esp. pp. 61, 81–83); cf. the remarkable similarity between par. LVIII and I.193.4.

they reconsidered when drunk (I.71.3; 133.3–4).[10] They tried to arrive at decisions that were so well founded that under any conditions they could he trusted. An opinion that can survive drunkenness might be thought unshakable. Although wine is brought to Egypt from Greece and Phoenicia, hardly one empty jar is to be found there: "Where in the world, then, one might ask, are they used up? This too I shall relate" (6.2).[11] Herodotus wishes to remove the disbelief the Greeks might well have if they only saw full wine-jars and no empty ones in Egypt. Their trust in sight would be shaken: they would think they were "seeing things." They must be told how the Persians convert wine-jars into water-jars and have them sent to the dry regions of Syria. Herodotus, then, with a delicate playfulness, brings together the distrust of the Greeks with the drunken-sober state of the Persians. They must trust his Persian *logos* even if they can scarcely believe their eyes.

The Persians must pass through Arabia in order to enter Egypt; and on the advice of Phanes, Cambyses requests and obtains from its king safe conduct. It is obtained by exchanging pledges ($\pi i\sigma\tau\iota\varsigma$), which the Arabians "reverence" as much as any other people. An oath is their pledge ($\acute{o}\rho\kappa\iota\alpha$ $\pi\iota\sigma\tau\acute{a}$); they call upon Dionysus and Uranian Aphrodite to bear them witness; but the ceremony consists not only in speaking to the gods, but in smearing on seven stones some blood taken from the middle finger of both contracting parties.[12] To mingle their blood would seem superfluous if they later invoke the gods, were it not that their gods not only have ears but bodies as well: the way they dress their hair they claim to be the same as Dionysus'. They pledge in token both their body and soul through blood and speech, because they believe their gods are similarly composed (cf. I.74.5; IV.70); white the gods' immortality guarantees their own faithfulness more strongly than any human contract could. To trust the Arabians, however, would not depend on whether one believed in their gods or not; their belief alone is enough to make them keep their oath. Trust, unlike truth, needs no other ground than belief; for a Greek would surely think it strange to swear most strictly by the goddess of love and the god of wine. At any rate, Herodotus cannot truly tell how the Arabians conveyed water to Cambyses' army: there is only a "more convincing" and a "less convincing" story to choose from.

Trust in speech, from the law of the Persians to the oath of the Arabians, has been most prominent in these first nine paragraphs; but a different kind of trust comes to light in the meeting between Persia and Egypt (10–16). The central story there concerns Cambyses' trying-out of Psammenitus' soul. Cam-

---

[10]Cf. Plutarch *Quaestiones Conviviales* VII.10.2 (716B–C).

[11]For κοῦ δῆτα, see Denniston, *The Greek Particles*[2], p. 272.

[12]Cf. *Iliad* V.330–342.

byses forced the king's daughter, dressed as a slave, to carry water, accompanied by other daughters of the foremost Egyptians; and although they wept and lamented as they went past their fathers, who echoed their grief, Psammenitus said nothing but merely looked at the ground; whereupon the king's son and other boys, with their necks in halters and their mouths bridled, were sent to their death, walking past the Egyptians; but again Psammenitus did not speak, in spite of the wailing and indignation of those seated around him; and last, by accident, a friend of the king, now reduced to beggary, came by; which sight made Psammenitus weep and beat his head. Cambyses, astonished at this behavior, asked the reason for it; and Psammenitus explained that evils of a private, familial nature are too great for tears, but the ill fortune of a friend deserves them. Psammenitus says that there are certain things that cannot be expressed in words or signs; that only dumbness and silence are at all adequate. These sorrows are private sorrows; they belong to one's flesh and blood; no one can properly feel them except the members of that family. They are like the pains of the body that cannot be shared with anyone else. Cambyses, in testing the soul of Psammenitus, discovers something that does not show itself in speech; something that all the familiar and private things affect. He discovers, in other words, the body, the most private thing we have. How different this is from the way in which the Persians understand the private can be seen in another story that occurs after Darius has been made king. One of the conspirators, Intaphrenes, mutilated the doorkeeper and page of Darius; and Darius, learning that the other five conspirators did not approve of this action, arrested Intaphrenes, his children, and his immediate relations. His wife so persistently wailed and complained that Darius, in pity, gave her the choice of saving the life of just one of those arrested; she chose her brother. Darius, amazed at this choice, asked her why she picked someone more alien than her sons and less beloved than her husband; to which she answered that she might have another husband and other children, but with her parents dead she only had a single brother (118-119).[13] Here we find just the opposite kind of reasoning from that which Psammenitus gave. He stressed the privacy of his sorrow, she the reasonableness of her choice; he could only be silent, she could explain why the greater claims of her husband and children, if viewed in the light of their being hers, were much less, if the uniqueness of her brother were considered. Psammenitus felt that his son and daughter were the flesh of his flesh, bone of his bone; but the wife of Intaphrenes ranked these bodily considerations lower than the name of a brother, who only in a genealogically legal way belonged to her. She does not say that she loves him. It was the

---

[13]Cf. Sophocles *Antigone* 904-915, where Antigone twice calls her reason a νόμος.

category, the name, of brother that she ranked higher, by his irreplaceability, than the names of husband and children. She wanted the roster of family relations to be complete. Her judgment far outweighed her sense of property; she reduced to absurdity the Persian trust in reason.

The trust in the body implies a trust in the senses and especially in touch. Touch discriminates most of the qualities that come in pairs; hot and cold, dry and wet, hard and soft; all of which cluster about Herodotus' confrontation of Egypt with Persia. First, what was the greatest miracle occurred during Psammenitus' brief reign—it drizzled for the first and last time in Thebes; as though the sky, responding to Cambyses' threat, intended to turn Egypt right side up. Next the Greeks and Carians, in Egyptian employ, in order to show their disapproval of Phanes' desertion, cut up all his children in a bowl, into which they poured water and wine, and then drank the blood so mixed before advancing into battle. Third, Herodotus himself saw a great marvel on the field of that battle; the skulls of the Persians were thin and easily broken, because they always wear hats; whereas the skulls of the Egyptians could hardly be cracked, so hardened were they by the Egyptian custom of always shaving their heads and exposing them to the sun. Fourth, the Egyptians tore apart the Persian herald and the Mytilenaeans. Next, Psammenitus showed his sorrow by a "dry" silence; sixth, he later revolted in distrust of Persian clemency and died drinking ox-blood; and last, Cambyses had the mummified corpse of Amasis burnt in violation of both Persian and Egyptian custom, but not, we may add, in violation of Greek custom (38.3-4). That the Egyptians rely on the body does not imply their greater reliability; quite the contrary, they break faith and lie more readily than the "wet" Persians. It is not the living body but the dry mummy that they trust: Asychis established it as surety for a loan (II.136.2).[14] Whereas the Persians think it unjust to feed the god fire with a corpse as it is an ensouled god—Cyrus did no wrong in trying to burn Croesus alive (I.86.2-6; cf. VII.114.2)[15]—the Egyptians believe that fire is a living beast (ἔμψυχον θηρίον), which feeds on what it gets and dies when it has consumed its food. The Persians see fire as almost bodiless (cf.29.2), the Egyptians see it only as embodied. The Persians believe it eternal, the Egyptians mortal, and hence eternal bodies, their mummies, must not feed it. Egyptian trust proves to be a trust in the anaesthetic: at a festival to Ares, where many heads are smashed, they claim that no one dies (II.63.3).

---

[14]Cf. Heraclitus frs. 36, 117, 118, 126.

[15]Cf. Strabo IV.3.13 (732): τοῖς θεοῖς οὐδὲν ἀπονείμαντες (οἱ μάγοι) μέρος· τῆς γὰρ ψυχῆς τοῦ ἱερείου δεῖσθαι τὸν θεόν, ἄλλου δὲ οὐδενός; Maximus Tyrius II.4 (ed. Hobein); cf. also Heraclitus fr. 65.

Cambyses sent ambassadors to the long-lived Ethiopians to spy out their affairs, among which was the so-called table of the sun (17–25).[16] Cambyses wished to find out whether "it truly is"; he learned instead a double story; one that those in power put out meat at night which anyone may eat by day; the other, told by the natives, that the earth by itself produced the meat. If the stories are connected, the first would suggest that the heads of state tell the second for the sake of deceiving the people. Something that should be most visible has only stories as explanations. Among the Ethiopians sight and speech come into conflict. "They are said to be the tallest and most beautiful of all men"; and "they say" that the law of royal succession, like all the rest of their laws, differs from all others: they elect the tallest and strongest man for his size to be king. Their customs and nature ought not to be disputable at all but completely manifest. Their corpses "are said" to be prepared in such a manner that they show, in their glasslike coffins "everything visibly like the corpse itself." The Ethiopians, then, who live in the greatest openness, are known only by hearsay: even their appellation "long-lived" might only mean "long-bowed."[17]

When Cambyses' ambassadors lied about their mission, the Ethiopian king told them that they did not tell the truth; and then he examined each of the gifts they had brought. The purple dyed robe impressed him, once he had learned "the truth of its manufacture," and he called both men and cloth deceitful because men conceal the natural color of the cloth and the cloth accepts this imposture; just as he was impressed by the gift of perfume because it concealed the natural smell of the body; and he laughed at the gold necklaces and bracelets Cambyses sent, because they themselves forge gold into chains for their prisoners. Art as adornment, enhancement, or concealment does not exist among the Ethiopians. The sights and smells are taken as they are and remain unaltered by craft. The king, however, was much pleased with the gift of wine—its smell and taste—for it was not artificially produced; and he attributed to its effects the relative longevity the Persians enjoy; for when he learned of the "nature" of wheat—how it was manured—he was not surprised that by eating dung they shortened their life.[18] When the ambassadors expressed their distrust on hearing that the Ethiopians live 120 years or more, they were shown a spring whose waters, on which even wood sinks, made a bather as sleek as olive-oil and as sweet-smelling as violets. At this extreme of

---

[16]Cf. *Odyssey* I.23–26.

[17]Cf. Last, H., *CQ*, 1923, pp. 35ff. Herodotus seems aware of this pun, and could it not be that he also has Heraclitus fr. 48 in mind: the Ethiopians are in name long-lived but in fact long-bowed?

[18]Cf. Strabo XVI.4.26 (784).

the world all sensible things are finer: sight is presented with the most beautiful bodies, touch with the lightest water, smell with sweet-smelling skin or odorless corpses, and hearing with the most wonderful story of how the earth gives forth stewed meat. The only one of the senses that remains unsatisfied is taste. The Persians, like Odysseus with Cyclops, add wine, whose presence of course might have dulled their other perceptions. The Ethiopians' trust in the senses seems to be guaranteed by the lack of artful deception; indeed, they could only trust them on such a condition. And yet, even though they come close to having no customs that are not in accordance with the way things are, they have a double story about the table of the sun. Even at the pure extremes, the problem of speech and lying persists (cf. Plato *Phaedo* 111b1–c3).

It is not accidental that Herodotus makes us reflect, by the absence of wine among the Ethiopians, on the sense of taste; for it raises in the following way the question of custom and law. The public and open character of the Ethiopians might indicate that everything is open; that there are no restrictions on what can be seen or done; or that here, at the extreme, the distinction between the humanly possible and forbidden would be exactly drawn. Such a distinction might be thought to hinge on incest and cannibalism (cf. Aristotle *Pol.* 1253a35–37). Cambyses became so angry at the Ethiopians' reply that he set off against them without adequate provisions; and when he got to the sandy wastes, some of his soldiers "did a dreadful thing: they chose one man out of ten and ate him"; and only then did Cambyses, "in fear of cannibalism," turn back. Cambyses, who broke among many other customs of Persia and Egypt the prohibition against incest, somehow felt that to taste human flesh lies beyond the permissible; even he, the king who can do anything, must not overstep it. To find out why he put the boundary here, we must look at the customs he violated without fear (27–38). He certainly was not afraid that he himself would be eaten.[19]

We can now reformulate the role Cambyses has in Book II as follows. To be guilty means to be the cause of some crime, and a crime is a violation of some law. Those who obey the law are innocent; they do not have to be found out; they are not responsible for anything. The trustworthiness of the lawful has the same character as that of the familiar: neither has to be explained, i.e., neither has to be assigned a cause for being what it is. Any violation of the law or the familiar at once prompts men to look for those guilty, to look for causes.[20] Only a violation is regarded as a problem, while the horizon within

---

[19]Cf. Seneca *de ira* III.xx.4.

[20]$\alpha\check{\iota}\tau\iota o\varsigma$ in Book I always refers to the guilt of men or gods (it occurs only in the first half: 1.1; 2.1; 4.1; 45.2; 76.2; 87.3; 91.4), whereas in Book II always to natural causes (20.2,3; 25.5; 26.1; 108.3), and with one exception (52.7) the same holds true for Book III (12.2,3,4bis, 108.4); but in Book IV

which the violation occurred remains unproblematic. It is held to be 'ground-less.' True thinking begins, however, when even the field of the unviolated, the familiar, becomes problematic. Herodotus uses Cambyses to reveal how problematic the familiar is. As Cambyses shows by his deeds and speech that law may be no more self-evident than crime, he points to the wider problem of πίστις itself: the problem of discovering a *logos* that rises above and yet preserves the distinction between the familiar and the unfamiliar. It is a problem that still turns on the body and the soul.

Upon his return to Memphis from his Ethiopian expedition, Cambyses found all Egypt rejoicing; he suspected the Egyptians were pleased with his ill-fortune, but soon heard that the god Apis, a calf marked with certain signs, had appeared among them. His disbelief made him kill as liars the priests whom he first asked; but when other priests also asserted the god's epiphany, Cambyses had the calf brought in and "wishing to strike the belly hit the thigh; he then laughingly said to the priests: 'Oh evil people (heads), do your gods prove to be so full of blood and flesh and feeling of steel? This god is surely worthy of the Egyptians.'" Cambyses kills an Egyptian god; he does not believe that the gods are made of flesh and blood, or that they can be wounded. The divine or sacred is not something tangible, nor can it be domesticated (χειροήθης, 28.1). Cambyses does more, however, than kill and show up the contradiction in an Egyptian god. He reminds us of Diomedes' wounding of Ares and Aphrodite, and the strange remark of Dione that Ares would have perished unless Hermes had saved him (*Iliad* V.330–339; 385–391; 855–863). The Greek gods, as made by Homer, are shown to hold a middle position between the completely corporeal gods of Egypt and the bodiless gods of Persia. The Egyptians gods bleed blood, the Greek gods ichor, "for they do not eat bread or drink wine, and therefore they are bloodless and called immortal" (*Iliad*. V.341ss.).[21] Indeed, the Greek gods are like the Ethiopians who do not eat bread or drink wine but bathe in a spring whose water is lighter than ordinary water and which makes the bather sleek (cf. *Odyssey* VI.226–231). "If this water," Herodotus says. "is truly as they say it is, it would be for this reason that the Ethiopians are long-lived" (23.3). At any rate, it is among the Ethiopians that the Greek gods are entertained with banquets (*Iliad* I.423), and not far from them lie what the Greeks call the "Islands of the Blessed" (26.1).

Cambyses opened the ancient tombs at Memphis, laughed at the statues of Hephaestus, entered the sanctuary of the Cabeiri and burnt in jest their statues.

---

there are two natural causes (30.1; 43.6) and four that refer to men (49.4; 140.1; 200.1; 202.1); consider VIII.129.2.

[21]Cf. Leumann, M., *Homerische Wörter* (Basel, 1950), 124–127.

Divine things are as inimitable as they are non-corporeal. Cambyses, more-over, carried over this non-corporeality of the divine into human life; he ignored even there the claims of the body. He did not hesitate to have his own brother killed because he dreamt that Smerdis touched the sky with his head: a dream carried more conviction than any familiarity he might have had of his brother's ways. He married and then killed his sister; but his desire waited for a law to justify it, and he killed her for what she said. In a perverse way, true and false speech determined everything he did: deeds had little effect on him. He wanted to know what the Persians said of him; and when Praxaspes said that they blamed him for his love of wine, he became angry at their double dealing; for previously they had praised him to his face, and he could not bear the contradiction. Although he was pleased that Croesus was saved from his sudden anger, he put to death his servants who told him that he was dead.

Cambyses' insistence on telling the truth compelled him to translate it into action; he wanted everything to be open and manifest, including the heart. In order to prove that the Persians were liars in saying that he was mad, he shot at Praxaspes' son an arrow which, striking the middle of the boy's heart, proved, he thought, that he was sane. The sanity of his mind ($\sigma\omega\phi\rho\rho\nu\acute{\epsilon}\epsilon\iota\nu$) was tested by the steadiness of his hand; he confounded, in short, the soul with the body and believed that they were interchangeable. His zeal on behalf of truth made him forget the ineradicable privacy of the body, something that cannot be reduced to the terms true and false. He did not realize that it is something to be respected and trusted without reason; that its demands are only grounded in its mute presence; and that it belongs, finally, to the realm of the sacred. Epilepsy, which "some call the sacred disease," he is said to have had since birth; and Herodotus thinks it is "not unlikely" that a greatly diseased body renders the mind unsound (33).[22] Cambyses, in his attempt to obey only his reason, turned out to have neglected the bodily cause of his madness.

To prove Cambyses' madness in laughing at sacred and lawful things, Herodotus tells how Darius once asked some Greeks for how much money they would be willing to eat their dead fathers; they said that they would do it on no account; Darius then asked some Indians, who do eat their parents, while these same Greeks were present, for what money they would choose to burn their dead fathers; "they shouted aloud and bade him be silent." Two things immediately strike us: the Indians are not present to bear the Greek ans-wer, and the Greeks do not shout when they reply.[23] The Greeks, though they are unwilling to change their customs, listen in silence to the proposal; the

---

[22]Cf. Heraclitus fr. 46.

[23]Cf. I.8.3; VII.18.1; 211.3; IX.59.2; *Iliad* III.1–9; IV.422–438; Benar-dete, S., *Hermes* 91, 1963, 5–12.

Indians cannot even bear hearing Darius, let alone the answer of the Greeks. If "custom is king of all," it does not imply that all customs are equally preferable; the custom of the Indians, which denies the privacy of the body, has deafened them to speech. Far from cannibalism removing the last trace of the secret, it closes the mind to any other custom: the insistence on the commonness of the body leads to an extreme provincialism. Darius put the question in terms of the body, stressed by the offer of money; he did not raise the question of the soul.[24] If customs deal exclusively with the body, there can be no agreement among them; the familiar would blind each of us to anything strange; for in the privacy of the body is rooted our partiality. We could as little reject the customary as jump out of our own skin. But if customs have an effect on the soul, if they either allow or forbid the impartiality of λόγος to arise, then it becomes uncertain whether they cannot be ranked. To abide by the customary would not cripple us, if it left the soul free. It might be the king, without being the tyrant, of all men.[25]

Herodotus next turns to the tyrants of Samos and Corinth (37–60).[26] A tyrant usurps his authority; he destroys the foundation of legitimate government; he no longer puts any trust in the law but in his own power. He might he expected, then, to show the greatest independence from custom, and to be as free from its restraints as any man could hope for. Polycrates was successful in everything he undertook, and his prosperity was proclaimed throughout Ionia and Greece. Amasis, with whom he had formed a personal alliance, wrote to him that his present good fortune disturbed him, "knowing how jealous the divine is," and advised him to throw away what he valued most and would especially grieve his soul to lose. Polycrates accepted this advice and decided that an emerald ring, made by the artist Theodorus a generation previously, would if lost most upset his soul. He tossed it into the sea, where a large and beautiful fish swallowed it; which a poor fisherman later caught and presented to Polycrates as only worthy of him and his rule. Upon getting his ring back, Polycrates thought it was a divine event; he wrote to Amasis to explain what had happened, who at once dissolved his friendship with him, lest Polycrates' future fall pain his soul. Polycrates was so successful that all his bodily wants were satisfied and only in his soul could he suffer. To bring that suffering about, so that he could imitate the usual uncertainty of fortune, he deliberately lost something he prized: he sacrificed a lifeless and soulless thing to grieve his soul. A work of art he supposed would remedy his excessive happiness; a man-made object, designedly lost, would prove a bul-

---

[24]Consider I.195.2; cf. pp. 26–7 *supra*.

[25]Cf. Plato *Protagoras* 336d2ss.

[26]Cf. Immerwahr, H. R., *CJ*, 52, 1956, pp. 312–322.

wark against change; it would master that which is thought to be artless and unconquerable. The ring was recovered in a beautiful fish, as though the beautiful by nature and by art were somehow allied; but the ring is meant to be preserved; it is a memorial intended to endure for many generations. Polycrates tried to transfer that power to himself, in the same way that Croesus sacrificed to the gods in order to preserve their favor. The ring's χάρις, by propitiating divine jealousy, would magically turn Polycrates himself into a work of art.[27] The trust in art is the tyrannical replacement for the trust in the customary. The tyrant tries to wipe out the memory of the old things with innovations, but he puts them on a different basis, his own fame. He tries to replace the embodied customs with a name, which, attached to artifacts, might survive him; and he sometimes succeeds (cf. I.25.2; V.67–68). Herodotus justifies his extended Samian account by an appeal to the three greatest of Greek monuments, all of which were built on Samos (60.).[28]

The Samian-Corinthian episodes appear to be digressions from the main narrative, inserted into it because of a temporal conjunction between Cambyses' invasion of Egypt and the Spartans' of Samos. And yet this coincidence deepens Herodotus' Persian λόγος. The destruction of the primacy of the body through Cambyses' tyrannical actions in Egypt and Persia led to the discovery of the soul. Cambyses' madness which was due to a bodily defect is now replaced by Polycrates' attempt to control his material fortune through his soul; and the Samian-Corinthian episodes are dominated by the natural πάθη of the soul. Polycrates used to rob friend and enemy alike, "for he said that he would more gratify a friend by returning what he had taken than if he had never taken it at all" (39.4); the Samian exiles who obtained the aid of Sparta said that the Spartans helped them in order to return a favor, while the Spartans said that they wished to take vengeance (47); the Corinthians in turn went against Samos out of resentment (48.1–2); the Samians perpetuated by custom the indignation they once had felt (48.3); the seventeen-year old son of Periander refused to speak to his father as soon as he learned of his mother's murder (50.3); and the Aeginetans enslaved the Samian settlers in Crete because they bore them a grudge (59.4). These πάθη are primarily favor or gratitude (χάρις) and jealousy (φθόνος), honor (τιμή), and vengeance (τιμωρίη). They are the passions associated with the gods. The problem of the gods as corporeal beings is replaced by the problem of the gods as beings with souls. The tyrant, whose mainspring of action is jealousy (80.3–4; V.92ζ–η), opens a way into the understanding of the divine.

Whether the soul and the divine as themes somehow depend on Greece, which so accidentally entered Herodotus' *Inquiries*, must be left unanswered

---

[27]Cf. *Odyssey* VII.91–94 with 257; see also VI.232–235.
[28]Cf. 57.2; II.35.1; 148.1–3.

for the moment as we turn again to Persia. The partial articulation of the soul here suggests that a more complete articulation would be possible, were the chance event that partly revealed it—the tyrannical departure from the customary—followed up by a total revolution in political life. The very breakdown of the ordinary, accepted and trusted might bring to light the extremes of political life—ways of life that would entail different understandings of the soul; for the possible kinds of regimes would have to be thought through in order to decide which one should fill the gap. This kind of clarity and openness about political things the conspiracy of the seven against the false Smerdis prepares (61–79). The heart of this story is the complete destruction of trust.

Cambyses had left in Sousa the magus Patizeithes in charge of his household affairs; who, knowing that few were aware of the death of Cambyses' brother Smerdis, set up his own brother in his stead; this brother looked most like the dead man and had the same name Smerdis. The two main props of ordinary trust by which one identifies things are cut away: appearance and name. Nature and convention seem to have conspired together to make uncertain everything one takes ordinarily for granted; just as the dream of Cambyses that warned him of his brother's ambition proves to have been about another Smerdis; and the oracle that predicted Cambyses' death in Agbatana turns out to have meant another city of the same name in Syria.[29] The trust in sight and in hearing breaks down; the public world assumes the appearance of a dream. Even when Cambyses informs his advisers of the deception, they do not believe him; for they "know" that he wanted to slander his brother, as they "know" that Smerdis the son of Cyrus was king; for Praxaspes, whom Cambyses most trusted and honored, vehemently denied that he had killed him.[30] Among the Persians knowledge and trust almost merge. In such circumstances the truth is discovered, and the singleness of things preserved, by touch. Otanes' daughter Phaedymia feels in the dark for the ears of Smerdis, and when she cannot find them, her father knows that the false Smerdis, whose ears Cyrus had cut off "on a serious charge," has usurped the throne. The sense of touch, however, no matter how persuasive it might be for Phaedymia, cannot convince Otanes directly; he must trust to the speech of his daughter; just as the three men Otanes tells, selecting those whom he was "most disposed

---

[29]Cf. II.98.2; V.60; IX. 95; Plato *Politicus* 257d1–258a3.

[30]Herodotus often uses ἐπίσταμαι to mean "have the conviction (falsely)," clearly connecting it with πίστις (cf. Plato *Cratylus* 437a2–b2), in the book at 36.5; 61.1; 66.3; 67.1; 139.3; but uniquely at 61.1 οἶδα has the same sense; Book III and VII have the most (ἐξ)επίσταμαι, 25 and 24 respectively. πίστις occurs nine times out of fifteen here; πιστός five out of 28 (six in I and VIII); and πιθανός three of seven.

to trust," must accept as true what he says; and each of them, in turn, in getting a fellow-conspirator, must choose the most trustworthy. The six Persians then take on Darius as the seventh, "exchanging words and pledges" (λόγοι καὶ πίστις) (71.1; cf. 74.2; VII.145.1). How unreliable these pledges can be the sequel shows, where Intaphrenes loses his life because he believed that Darius' servants were lying when they told him the king was with his wife, the one condition the seven established to limit their free access to Darius (84.2; 118). Moreover, Darius now makes a speech that declares the difference between true and false speech to be based on nothing at all. Far from telling a lie being "most shameful," as Persian law asserts, Darius says that both the liar and the man who tells the truth do so for the sake of gain; "and if neither were going to profit, the truthful man would prove a liar and the liar truthful" (72.2–5; cf. I.96–97; VIII.132.2). Darius himself shows that he follows this rule, for he later tricks his rivals for the kingship in what appears to be the most open of contests; and his trick gives rise to, for the first time, a double account among the Persians (85–87; cf. 105.1,2). No longer can the Persians be trusted to tell the truth for its own sake. Conspiracy necessarily brings along with it a break with custom. The Persian denial, however, that a son ever killed his own mother or father set a limit to disinterested truth-telling among the Persians (I.137.2). Their denial of matricide and patricide contains within itself the germ of Darius' statement; for the law, which determines who is legitimate or not and hence what is true or false, compels the Persians to declare what is of advantage for the preservation of the law. Darius merely brings out the truth behind the truth-telling of the Persians. It would seem that νόμος is inevitably bound up with falsehood.[31]

While the conspirators were deliberating how they should kill the magi, the magi had decided to include Praxaspes in their own deception, since they thought he would resent enough Cambyses' murder of his son to lie about the false Smerdis' genealogy. Praxaspes, "regarded as the most trustworthy among the Persians," and caught in his own often-repeated lie that the son of Cyrus still lived pledged and swore (πίστις καὶ ὅρκια) to tell no one the truth. He got up on the wall of the city to tell all the assembled Persians this lie; but instead he "willingly" forgot what he had promised the magi and revealed the truth, "saying that previously he had concealed it (for it was not safe to speak), but now a *necessity* had overcome him to tell"; and then, after cursing the Persians if they would not revolt, he threw himself from the wall and was killed. "Willy-nilly" Praxaspes told the truth. The truthful man and the liar do not always aim at the same thing by different means; the necessity of the truth itself proves ultimately to be stronger than the fear of death. Trust in the truth,

---

[31]Cf. Xenophon *Cyropaedeia* I.vi.27–34.

the true λόγος, demands the highest kind of courage (cf. VII.139.1). It should not surprise us, then, to find Herodotus asserting that, after the conspirators had succeeded in killing the magi, they deliberated about regimes, and "speeches were spoken, unbelievable to some of the Greeks, but nevertheless they were spoken" (80.1.; cf. VI.43.3).[32] Herodotus asks his readers to believe that this episode took place; he asks us to trust his own *logos* (cf. II.123.1; VII.152.3). Our willingness to believe, like the Persians' willingness to speak, once the pressure of the customary has been removed, merges with the necessity that the truth about political things at some time come to light. What connects 'theoretically' the destruction of priestly authority with the free discussion of regimes turns out to have in Persia a factual connection as well. This coincidence between the necessity of λόγος and the chance of events is the highest praise that Herodotus can bestow on the truth-telling Persians. Only in Persia does λόγος completely shine through ἔργον.

Although the significance of these speeches becomes more evident in the later books, as we see particular examples of democracy and monarchy at work, we should summarize here what each proposes before we consider what importance they have for the third book itself. Each of the Persians, in proposing the establishment of either democracy, oligarchy, or monarchy (and in criticizing the corrupted forms of each), appeals to some considerations that the others neglect (80.2–87). Otanes relies on the "middle" character of democracy, Megabyzus on the beautiful, and Darius on the best. Their language corresponds to their choice. Otanes never says that democracy is best, nor that it makes use of the best people, but he implies that it is good and pleasant. It is a low but solid good. Its advantages lie in three things. All its deliberations are referred to the public where it would be unlikely that anything except the ordinary and usual would be passed. Its officers are responsible and elected by lot, so that the innate envy and insolence of men can be kept in cheek. And third it has the "most beautiful name, equality before the law, and does none of those things a monarch does"; but Otanes is silent about what democracy does do (cf. V.78).[33]

Now Megabyzus appeals to two things in defense of oligarchy, the beautiful and the best; he alone of the three uses a simile (the demos are "like a torrent") and a verb of knowing (γινώσκειν); but he never refers to the law.[34]

---

[32]See further Strauss, L., *Natural Right and History* (Chicago, 1953), p. 85.

[33]See further pp. 144–146 *infra*.

[34]When Plato's Socrates compares what the moneymaker, the man of honor, and the philosopher (to which the three parts of the soul correspond) would say about their own lives, he has the man of honor alone use a metaphor (*Republic* 581c8–e4).

He claims that the people do nothing knowingly, who have never been instructed in or seen for themselves anything beautiful or noble of their own. What he means by this, two remarks of Gobryas, who invited him into the conspiracy, illustrate. In support of Darius' insistence on their acting at once, Gobryas had asked. "When shall we have a more beautiful opportunity to recover the kingdom, or, should we fail, to die?" And during the confusion of their actual struggle with the magi, Gobryas came to grips with one of them in the dark; and when Darius, who rushed in, sword in hand, hesitated to strike, lest he might hit Gobryas, Gobryas had said: "Push the sword, then, through us both." The beautiful is nothing visible; it does not need light to be seen; the grand speech, supported by the grand deed, are its only components. Megabyzus' own son also put into action what his father said. Zopyrus cut off his nose and ears, shaved off his hair and had himself whipped in order to capture Babylon (150-160). "The most beautiful name for the ugliest deed," as Darius called it when he first saw Zopyrus and heard what he said, proved later to be the most beautiful deed as well. Not for twenty-one Babylons—more than his whole kingdom—would Darius have wished his mutilation. The Persians' neglect of the visible shape leads to a deeper grasp of the beautiful: it is the deeds of the soul that alone impress them (cf. VII.180-181; 238.2).

Darius speaks last in favor of monarchy.[35] He tries to show that it alone is stable because the other two regimes tend to be corrupted into it. Even though some might admit with Darius that "nothing would appear better than the one best man," he further assumes that the inevitability of monarchy coincides with the excellence of the monarch, for he equates the best with the strongest (ἄριστον with κράτιστον). The way the conspirators decide to choose their king indicates the falseness of this equation. They rely on chance as much as the democrat Otanes: the rider of the first horse that whinnies will be king. The inevitable is the accidental, and the accidental is the best. Darius' groom then easily turns that accidental event into a certainty: he trusts to a stallion's memory and sense of smell. Darius, then, destroys the basis on which the conspirators had acted—their mutual trust in each other's word—and he relies instead on one of the senses, which works so naturally that it had to be believed, especially after thunder and lightning occurred out of a clear sky, "as though by a covenant." His trick confirms that the accidental, or at least the artful accident, agrees with the inevitable.

These three speeches can be thought of as the most theoretical speeches in Herodotus. They present the possible kinds of regimes and their corruptions

---

[35]Darius alone of the three speakers uses verbs of revealing (φαίνω, διαδείκνυμι, θωμάζομαι, δηλόω), and Herodotus introduces his speech with ἀπεδείκνυτο γνώμην, whereas the other two are said to γνώμην ἐσφέρειν; cf. I.99; all this openness is meant to underline his secret intentions.

without any regard to local conditions. They consider the nature of each regime as such, in light of the nature of man as man (his soul), in making their several claims to superiority. They go most deeply into the nature of man as a political animal. They lay the basis, I believe, for Herodotus' undertaking a parallel inquiry: the nature of man as man both in himself and within the context of the whole. He is given the opportunity to do so by one of Darius' first acts after he became king. Darius divided the Persian empire into twenty satrapies and imposed on each a yearly tribute (89). These satrapies, with the notable exception of India, contain nothing extraordinary. There are, however, certain tribes that dwell at the extremes of the empire who bring only gifts, and at these extremes certain extraordinary things raise the question whether or not the ordinary things with which we are familiar are adequate for understanding the nature of things (97–117). This question may be said to be the theoretical counterpart to that which cannibalism had raised before, which questioned our right to accept the so-called norms of life as the norms. The destruction of trust which Cambyses began now compels Herodotus to reestablish trust on a new basis, a basis that can comprehend the extremes and the center in a single account. Herodotus must show that the extremes are still susceptible to the same understanding as the center, that the looks of things in which we put our trust are the same from one end of the earth to the other. He must show that the "nature which consists in the looks" (φύσις ἰδέης) of something is everywhere the same (II.71). Herodotus, one might say, classifies the unclassified parts of the Persian empire. He proves to be a better shopkeeper than Darius.[36]

Herodotus tells us that the Ethiopians, among whom are said to be the tallest and most beautiful men, ejaculate black semen and are black themselves (101). Not only does color make no difference to their being the most beautiful, but their black semen, which only the Indians at the other extreme have, does not prevent them from being men. The εἶδος of men goes deeper than his skin. Although the nature of men remains the same whether they are tall or short, ugly or beautiful, white or black, hard or soft skulled.[37] Herodotus is not prepared to admit that one-eyed men exist, who "have the rest of their nature (φύσις) like that of other men" (116.2).[38] What does this denial mean? We are at once reminded of Hesiod's description of the Cyclopes: "They were

---

[36]Cf. Xenophon *Oeconomicus* viii–ix.

[37]12; II.32.6; IV.23.2; 43.4; cf. 108.1; 109.1; VI.61.3; Heraclitus frs. 82, 83.

[38]For εἶδος as class-character see I.94.3; 203.2; VI.100.1; 119.2, and for the pre-Socratic use of εἶδος see Taylor, A. E., *Varia Socratica* (Oxford, 1911), Chapter V.

in other respects like the gods, but a single eye was placed in the middle of their forehead" (*Theogony* 142 ss.).[39] The gods are beings who do not form a class in the same way as other beings do. The Cyclopes can be gods without being two-eyed, while it is impossible, according to Herodotus, for one-eyed men to be men. Hesiod's phrase "in other respects like the gods" closely resembles Herodotus' "the rest of their nature like that of other men," with one difference: Hesiod does not use the word φύσις. The gods apparently lack a φύσις, for to have the same φύσις would mean that like generates like, and not all the gods are alike. The gods, however, do they alone lack a φύσις, or do other beings lack it as well, and does only the provincialism of the 'normal' and customary prevent us from taking them into account? The importance of the extremes for Herodotus partly turns on this question. Even if ants are found larger than foxes but smaller than dogs in India, they still make their homes of sand "in the same way as do the ants in Greece, and they also look most like them in shape (εἶδος)" (102.2); just as at another extreme, in Arabia, the winged creatures that dwell about the cassia "most resemble bats" (110); and there also two kinds of sheep, broad and long-tailed, live "which are nowhere else," but they are still sheep (113). Herodotus sees no reason to deny changes in size if they do not affect the look of the animal. It would be natural for the extremes, where the climate is either excessively cold or hot, to produce these changes. That cattle in Scythia grow no horns, while sheep in Libya are almost born with them, accords with the nature of these regions (IV.29). Herodotus can even assert that the camel has two thighs and two knees in each of its hind legs, and that its genitals face backwards, because he thinks these peculiarities explain why horses cannot bear their εἶδος and smell, while at the same time they do not destroy the limits of the possible; limits that must exist if there is to be a nature to each class of things (103; I.80.4; VII.87; cf. IV.129.1–2; 183.2–3).

Herodotus' further understanding of εἶδος in the sense of φύσις can be discovered, if we consider together two passages, one that concludes this section on the extremes, and the other that describes the Thessalian plain in the seventh book; two passages whose likeness to one another can only be regarded as intentional, especially since the plain described here is otherwise completely unknown and geographically impossible (117; VII.128–130). This plain in Asia is locked in on all sides with a mountain range περικεκλημένον ὄρει πάντοθεν); and five chasms through it once distributed the water of a great river to five tribes that dwelt nearby, until the Persians conquered them and shut down the channels, turning the former plain into a sea; whereupon the five tribes were deprived of water during the summer "for in winter god rains

---

[39]Cf. II.46.2; IV.25.1; 191.4.

for them as for other people"; and only by persuading the Persian king with lamentations, does each tribe in turn, according to its need, obtain the opening of the sluice-gate, which is shut again as soon as "the earth drinks its fill." The Thessalian plain, on the other hand, is said to have been in ancient times a lake, "so locked in was it on all sides with very tall mountains" (five in number); and there are five rivers which "collect their water in this plain from the mountains that shut in Thessaly," but before emptying through one channel into the sea, all of them mix their waters together into one river, which goes by the name Peneius, it having made all the others anonymous. In the past, it is said, there was no outlet to the sea, when all of the rivers "had different names though they flowed no less strongly than now"; and the Thessalians say Poseidon made the channel, "speaking reasonably" ($οἰκότα$); "for whoever believes ($νομίζει$) that Poseidon shakes the earth, and that the crevices made by the earthquake are the works of this god, would say, on seeing this plain, Poseidon made it; for the separating of the mountains is, as it was evident to me, the work of an earthquake."

We take up the second passage first. Herodotus himself refrains from saying that Poseidon made the outlet in the mountain; he limits himself to the more cautious assertion that an earthquake caused it. At first sight there appears to be little difference between "earthquake" and "Poseidon"; but the difference appears if one considers that the Thessalians who say that Poseidon did it do not know that he made an earthquake. They miss a step in the phenomena. They go at once from the outlet as it now is to Poseidon its maker, without stopping at the intermediate stage of the earthquake. Poseidon may be the hidden maker of this earthquake, but this earthquake is only one of many earthquakes, which Poseidon may not have made. Earthquakes are earthquakes everywhere. Poseidon is only a Libyan god (II.50.2).[40] Similarly, in the first passage. "god rains" may mean the same as "it rains"; or it may point to the maker of rain separate from raining itself. When Herodotus argues the Egyptian priests' point of view, he says "god rains"; but when he later gives his own account, he says "it rains"; just as there he changes "the god" of his short explanation into "the sun" of his long one.[41] If Herodotus' insistence on sticking to the surface phenomena seems superficial, the case of the River Peneius shows its depths.

Peneius is a name that labels the waters of five rivers; but all their names are recent inventions, while their waters have always flowed with the same strength. "Peneius" has suppressed this collection of rivers and made them one

---

[40]Cf. IV.28.2; 94.4; VI.98.1; VIII.129.3.
[41]II.13.3; 22.3; 24.2; 25.1; cf. III.124.1 with 125.4; IV.94.4; VI.27.1,3; 98.1,3.

in name; but the class is only water or river-water and nothing else. The five river-waters are themselves and not Peneius; and the mountain-range that locks in Thessaly is the five mountains and nothing else. So if water is one of the first things, it is the collection of all waters that must be so called, and not "Oceanus" or "Eridanus," which Herodotus thinks are poets inventions (115.2; II.23; cf. IV.8.2). They are names that look quite like "water," but they lay claim to a distinction between themselves and other waters that Herodotus does not wish to make. We can now gather why Herodotus fails to mention the Titaresius as one of the Peneius' tributaries, even though its importance and fame far exceed that of the rivulet Onochonus, which he does mention. Its fame stems from its description in the Homeric Catalogue of Ships. The host that Gouneus led "cultivated the fields about the lovely Titaresius, which casts its fair-flowing water into the Peneius, but it does not mix together with the silver-swirling Peneius, but it flows above it like oil, for it is an efflux of the dread water of the Styx" (*Iliad* II.751.755).[42] While, for Herodotus, if the Titaresius is water it must mix with the Peneius, and if it does not, it is not water but something else, Homer claims that a river can be of water without being miscible with other waters; just as Hesiod had allowed the Cyclopes to be gods without being two-eyed. Thus the poets see or invent a genealogy of monsters (i.e., beings that are not the same as their parents), where Herodotus sees and articulates a geography of natural kinds.

Herodotus connects these passages with the problem of the extremes in the following way. The mountain range that locks in Thessaly makes Thessaly the hollow plain it is; and the range that encloses the lake in Asia makes the lake what it is. Neither the lake nor the plain could exist apart from these ranges; they are not independent of one another. They do not belong to a different dimension. Herodotus says, therefore, in the sentence prior to the passage on the Asian lake: "The extremes lock in and enclose the rest of the earth (περικληίουσαι καὶ ἐντὸς ἀπέργουσαι), and seem to have what we think are the most beautiful and rarest things" (116.3). The extremes shut in the whole earth; they comprehend all the varieties and kinds of things, while they themselves produce the most extraordinary kinds; but these speciously look as if they have no connection with the ordinary varieties. Their rarity and supposedly greater beauty suggest that they are the models and types for things better known; but in fact they merely belong to the collection itself. For like the range of mountains, which only differ in height from the plain they enclose, the extreme kinds differ from the usual ones only in degree—they

---

[42]Lucan does not fail to give his version of these lines in a passage copied in all other respects from Herodotus, VII.375–380 (see Housman, *ad loc.*, p. 374).

have the same εἶδος. One-eyed men's habitation of an extreme is as much
excluded as Oceanus' encirclement of the earth, which is neither the "father"
of other rivers nor a "first" in any way. All the waters together make up
water, just as all men together make up men. They can generate from one
another. Herodotus casts doubt on the "light" water among the Ethiopians for
the same reason that he doubts the existence of one-eyed men. It would be
water whose properties were not those of water, but as different from it as
divine ichor from blood. To assert, then, the existence of one-eyed men is to
separate "men" from "men being two-eyed"; to make the nature of men lie
outside the men themselves; and to confound something superficial like color
with something as fundamental as sight.

If this interpretation is correct, then Herodotus wished to stress here the
sameness among members of each natural class—in their appearance—
everywhere on the earth. He wished to exclude the monstrous and
'supernatural.' There is, however, a difficulty in his stressing the uniformity in
the εἶδος of each class. εἶδος does not only mean the average look of things but
their best looks; it sometimes has the meaning in Herodotus, as in Homer, of
"beauty" or "comeliness."[43] It is the standard as well as the common measure
of each class: we too say that this dog is a more perfect specimen of its kind
than that one. And in this sense the extremes of the earth do seem to produce
the standards; they produce what "we think are the most beautiful things." The
Ethiopians are the tallest and the most beautiful men. The Ethiopians could be
taken for the standard of human excellence were bodily perfection the only
criterion; but men also have souls, and the Ethiopians might not have the most
perfect souls. Whatever conditions in Ethiopia allow for bodily perfection may
make the virtues of the soul impossible: cannibalism seems to flourish at the
extremes (99). A tension might exist between the excellence of the extremes
and the excellence of the center: "The extremes of the inhabited earth somehow have obtained the most beautiful things, just as Greece has obtained the
most beautifully moderated climate" (106.1). The most inhabitable part of the
earth, humanly speaking, does not contain the finest things (in appearance),
while virtue, on the other hand, might more easily arise in Greece under mod-
erate conditions than under extreme ones. Virtue might be incompatible with
the most excellent εἶδος. The question of human excellence reveals a lack of
uniformity within the class of men which goes deeper than differences in size
or looks. Human excellence and the human simply as a class-characteristic
might stand radically opposed to each other. They might be at war with each
other. Thus the opposition between the excellence of the body and that of the
soul leads Herodotus to consider, in general, opposites and contrarieties within

---

[43]I.8.1; 199.5; VI.127.4; VIII.105.1; 113.3.

classes to be as fundamental as the classes themselves. It leads him to consider war to be as fundamental as peace.

Winged snakes would make Arabia uninhabitable, as lions, hares, and vipers would make other countries so, were it not that "the providence of the divine somehow being, as it is likely, wise," arranges that all animals cowardly at heart (ψυχήν) be prolific, and all wild and noxious beasts be unprolific (108.2). This ecological balance works in two ways: one way keeps down the population of the always-pregnant hare because "every beast, bird, and man" hunts it; and the other way keeps down the population of lions because the cub tears the womb of its mother, so that she can bear only once in a lifetime. The strife between lioness and cub is extended among winged snakes and vipers to all members of the family: the female at the moment of impregnation seizes the neck of the male and does not let go before she has swallowed him; but her own offspring "revenge the male" by eating their way through her womb. If these snakes, whose "nature" is their power of reproduction, were not kept in check, Arabia would become unfit for human habitation. They are kept in check by divine providence, a providence that proves to be war itself: war of species against species (hare against other beasts and men) and war among the members of the same species (lion, snake, and viper). Nature is composed both of generation and destruction; the war between them constitutes providence, whose wisdom consists in preventing the complete triumph of either opposite. It is the same wisdom the Egyptians showed in defeating the natural propensity of female cats not to generate a second time: they killed the first litter (II.66).

In this war among the animals Herodotus pointed to its human advantage, and we are forced to wonder whether he saw the Persian Wars in the same way. It might have to be seen in its divine advantage, so that the war among the animals would be for men's good as the war among men would be for the gods'. The wise providence that makes the earth habitable for men may have, humanly speaking, a malevolent side. Divine jealousy may have dictated the Persian Wars: Herodotus says that providence is wise; he does not say that it is good. Otanes had said that a tyrant, even though he enjoys all goods, still remains jealous of his subjects—"jealousy is innate (ἐμφύεται) from the beginning in a human being"—, a remark that, as has been often noted, applies equally well to the divine.[44] A tyrant is jealous because he is insecure; he cannot be (ἄφθονος) or generous without undermining his rule. His rule depends on his destroying the best and supporting the worst of his subjects. If, then, the divine as tyrant resembles the human tyrant, the Persian Wars would reveal not only the instability but the necessary instability of the human as human

[44]I.32.1; III.40.2; VII.10ε; 46.4.

excellence. They would reveal the precariousness of human excellence in its war with the human simply and with the divine. The divine may guarantee the existence without guaranteeing the excellence of men.

The Persians believe that they are in every respect by far the best of all men, and that those nearest to them share in virtue in the second degree, and so on proportionately until the extremes, whose inhabitants they hold of least account (I.134.2–3; cf. 134.1). This progressive decline away from the supposed center Herodotus playfully employs in his description of the extremes. Since the Persians believe that contiguity with themselves imparts to others their own excellence, he has made the conspiracy of the seven depend on the sense of touch (the true and false Smerdis differed only in a pair of ears), and then assigned as predominant to each of the extremes one of the other four senses: Ethiopia is most famous for the beauty of its people (sight); Arabia for its incense (smell); India for the cannibalism or vegetarianism of its tribes (taste); and Europe for the fabulous stories about its treasures (hearing). This contrast between the extremes, where the objects of sense are finest, and Persia, where the most theoretical speeches in all of Herodotus occurred, but where the lowest of the senses touched off the conspiracy which occasioned those speeches, suggests that the very excellence of the Persians, their trust in λόγος, is not free from defects. To show the misapplication of λόγος, Herodotus now tells how Intaphrenes, Polycrates, and Oroetes met their death (118–128).[45]

Intaphrenes died because he did not believe what Darius' porter and usher told him, convinced perhaps by Darius' own argument that everyone lies or tells the truth for his own advantage; but his eldest son and his wife's brother were saved because the reasons his wife used were pleasing to Darius; reasons that were based on the superiority of names and the unimportance of affection. A blind trust in λόγος overcomes all bodily feeling. Oroetes, in turn, wanted to destroy Polycrates, who had neither harmed nor insulted him, and whom he had never seen, for one of two causes, either of which the reader, Herodotus says, may believe (122.1).[46] The majority say that he desired this "unholy thing," because Mitrobates had compared him unfavorably with Polycrates,

---

[45]The plan of Book III one might say resembles the capital letter lambda: the peak is contained within paragraphs 80–117, where the extremes of polity and of the earth are discussed (they are the most theoretical); whereas paragraphs 1–79 lead up to the peak and paragraphs 118—end lead down and away from it. Book III easily divides into thirteen sections: 1–9; 10–16; 17–26; 27–38; 39–60; 61–79; 80–87; 88–96; 97–117; 118–128; 129–138; 139–149; 150–160.

[46]Cf. 30.3; 32.1; V.45.2.

while fewer say that when he sent a herald to ask Polycrates for some money, Polycrates made no answer but turned himself to the wall. Speech or silence, then, occasioned Polycrates' death. The reader may choose to believe either because each amounts to the same thing: the desire for honor and good repute. Oroetes enticed Polycrates by the promise of enough money to carry out his project of ruling over Ionia and the islands. He held out that promise in a letter which informed Polycrates that, if he distrusted him, he could send whomever he most trusted. Polycrates then sent his secretary to look at the money: a man who writes is trusted to see. The secretary was in fact fooled by the surface of things, for Oroetes showed his chests filled with stones but lightly covered with gold coins; and he, reporting what he had seen, convinced Polycrates, even though prophets, friends, and his daughter warned him (cf. 56.2: 136.1; V.21.2). Polycrates died in a manner "not worthy of relation" and "unworthy of himself and his own proud thoughts." The tyrant with the greatest show (μεγαλοπρεπείη) was destroyed by the most superficial of tricks; and the surface of his body, as his daughter saw in a dream, was washed whenever it rained and anointed with its own moisture whenever the sun shone. The body takes an unexpected revenge on speech.

Oroetes' own death came about in a more farcical way. His success with Polycrates swelled him up to commit other outrages, until Darius put a stop to them. He called together the most notable Persians (λογιμώτατοι), asked one of them to avenge the death of Mitrobates and other Persians, and told him to kill Oroetes by guile (σοφίη), "for where there is need of guile, force has no function (ἔργον)" (127.2).[47] Thirty Persians responded to his request, and Bagaeus was chosen by lot. Bagaeus wrote up many letters, sealed them with Darius' seal, and then came into the presence of Oroetes, who was surrounded by bodyguards. The first few letters, which Bagaeus handed to the secretary to read, concerned various matters; and when Bagaeus observed that the bodyguards "reverenced the letters greatly and to a still greater extent what the letters said," he handed another letter to the secretary who obediently read it aloud: "Persians, King Darius forbids you to protect Oroetes." The bodyguards at once dropped their spears; and Bagaeus, encouraged by their response, handed over the last letter to be read: "King Darius orders the Persians in Sardis to kill Oroetes." The bodyguards at once drew their swords and killed him. The guards who are stationed to protect Oroetes' body trust rather to the spoken word; just as Polycrates trusted a letter and a secretary; and Oroetes sought revenge because of a word or a silence (cf. I.125.2). We have seen before how the destruction of trust in the body and customs led to the liberation of λόγος, but now we can see the destruction of a comical trust in

---

[47]Cf. 65.6; 72.2; 134.6; 157.3.

λόγος and the vindication of the body. This vindication, however, does not return us to where we were before. A new element enters: Greece. We are next told stories about the doctor Democedes (129–138).

Darius one day jumped from a horse and so violently twisted his foot that the ankle-bone came out of its socket; he called in some Egyptian doctors whom he customarily thought to be the best; they twisted and forced his foot so much that they made it worse, until he learned that Democedes was among the booty brought from Sardis at the time of Oroetes' death. Democedes employed Greek medicines, and by applying gentle means after violent ones, he soon made Darius well again. The Egyptian doctors know only force. Democedes knows how to use both force and gentleness together; he has an art that combines compulsion with persuasion. Darius had said to the Persians that "where there is need of wisdom, force has no function"; but the Greek Democedes combines them in practice. The τέχνη of Democedes does not suffer from the excesses of either Persian σοφίη or Egyptian βίη. It is art and not deceit, art and not violence.[48] His skill, moreover, is not confined to medicine; he gains great wealth by a witty remark that pleases Darius, and he persuades him to save the Egyptian doctors who failed to cure him, as well as to free from slavery an Elian soothsayer (130.4–5; 132.2). He knows how to affect both body and soul (cf. 137.5).

Soon after Democedes cured Darius, he was called upon to cure his wife Atossa. Sickness and disease seem to be rampant among the Persians: the eye-ailment of Cyrus, with which the book opened; the epilepsy of Cambyses; the disjointed foot of Darius; the cancerous growth of Atossa; and, to anticipate a little, the genital disorder of Otanes; to which can be added the sickness of Maeandrius and the madness of his brother.[49] The body is not very good security in Persia. Atossa now shows to Democedes the disease on her breast, which she had been ashamed of and had hidden as long as she could; but its spreading compelled her to trust Democedes, whose art lets him see the ugly dispassionately, while Gyges almost paid with his life for seeing the beautiful. Once she is healed, she does Democedes a favor in return; who instructs her to tell Darius that it is proper for a young man to display some great deed, "since white the body is growing, the mind grows along with it, and while it grows old so does the mind." Thus a doctor thinks: mind and body are attuned to one another; and Atossa easily persuades Darius with it: she speaks to him in bed.

---

[48]Cf. *Iliad* XI.830, 846; XV.393ss.: only here λόγοι; *Odyssey* IV.220–234; XIX.455–458.

[49]1.1; 33; 129.1; 133.1; 143.2; 145.1; 149 (cf. I.108.1). νοῦσος and νοσέω together (12 times out of 41) and θάνατος (14 times out of 53) occur more often here than in any other book; cf. ἀκέομαι 16.6; (ἐξ)ιῶμαι 54.5; 132.1,2; 134.1,5.

Democedes' art of persuasion is not shared equally by others. The Persians cannot persuade the Crotonians to give back Democedes, though they threaten them with the power of Darius while they are being beaten; nor can the Cnidians in obedience to Darius persuade the Tarentines to let Gillus return (he had bought the Persian spies out of slavery); for "they were unable to apply any force." Democedes' private art, with its successful combination of force and persuasion, collapses in the public sphere, where favors and words, if unbacked by power, are ineffective or disastrous. So we may judge from the next story Herodotus tells, the capture of Samos (139–149).

At the time of Cambyses' invasion of Egypt, three kinds of Greeks came to Egypt, "some, as is likely, for trade, some to fight, and a few, too, as spectators of the land itself" (139.1; cf. 39.1; 120.1). Unlike the Persians who accompanied Democedes back to Italy, or those whom Cambyses sent to the Ethiopians, these Greeks do not come to spy for the sake of future conquest, but merely to look for the sake of looking. It is the artless counterpart to Democedes' detachment in looking at Atossa's disease. Syloson was one of these spectators, and in accordance with his disinterested observing he gave to Darius, who was in Egypt as a bodyguard to Cambyses, the red cloak he wore. This free gift, however, this pure example of χάρις, destroys Samos. Darius, once king, recognizes his obligation to Syloson, who wishes to be established in his brother Polycrates' tyranny. While the gratitude of Atossa returns Democedes to Croton without any ill effects for its people (his father's unbearable temper had compelled him to leave), the gratitude of Darius, though it may privately be just, proves to be the harshest necessity for the Samians. Maeandrius, who received the tyranny from Polycrates, "wanted to be the justest of men though he could not." He offered to the Samians, in almost the same spirit as Syloson offered the cloak to Darius, to step down from his rule and establish a democracy: but he added two conditions that were fatal to his generosity; he thought it just to take six talents of Polycrates' money, and to obtain the priesthood of Zeus Eleutherius for himself and his descendants; whereupon one of the leading citizens rebuked him for his base birth, which made Maeandrius think that someone else would seize the tyranny if he relinquished it. An idle word, spoken in indignation, compelled Maeandrius to change his mind; he seized all the important citizens, and upon his falling sick his brother Lycaretus, who wanted the tyranny for himself, killed them. The Samians' resentment and Lycaretus' desire for tyranny combined now with Maeandrius' own jealousy to wipe out Samos. His mad brother Charileos persuaded him to attack the unsuspecting Persians, who had brought back Syloson without a struggle. He envied the ease of Syloson's return, and knowing that his own safety was secured, he has slaughtered all the Persians of most account; but their general Otanes, the one who was in favor of democracy, though he remembered Darius' commands to leave Samos intact, forgot and killed everyone, man and child, in and outside the sanctuaries (147.1; cf. 79.1). We may recall Praxaspes, who willingly forgot what he had promised the magi and told the truth at the expense of his own life. That generosity was compelled by the Persian belief in the inseparability of truth and justice; but now Otanes' immediate sense of wrong overrode his obedience to his orders; just as Maeandrius' second thoughts outweighed his desire to be just and forced him to resort to deceit. Only if one is willing to die can the truth be publicly maintained. Envy in the case of Maeandrius, and the sight of bodily injury in that of Otanes, compel them both to forego the truth. The immediate sensation triumphs over every other consideration. Otanes does not resettle Samos until he has a dream and becomes diseased in his private parts. When his body betrays him, Otanes remembers to be just.

The trust in the senses and reason, the trust in the body and soul, and the trust in deeds and words, have come to light as the triple theme of the third book. It tried to distinguish the necessary trust we must give to the senses, the body and deeds from the freedom and grace inherent in reason, the soul and words. This made it at once the most radical book and the book most concerned with the irreducible. The Persians supplied the link, for they trusted λόγος in the way we must trust the senses: as trust and not knowledge. While the Egyptians had confounded speech with language, λόγος with γλῶσσα, the Persians confounded λόγος as speech with λόγος as reason. Their trust in it, in its double character, Herodotus has made use of as a foil in his examination of sensible things, as sensible things in turn have supplied the contrast needed to examine that Persian trust. Their trust in honor and speech at the expense of the body culminates, as we have already said, in the last section, where Zopyrus mutilates himself in order to capture Babylon. But Herodotus' last sentence in this book makes us realize that he has not yet finished presenting all the parts of his own *logos*. There he informs us that Zopyrus' grandson, also called Zopyrus, deserted to Athens. One Zopyrus pretended to desert, two generations later another Zopyrus in fact deserts. A seeming that was almost undetectable is replaced by what is no seeming at all. Thus the question of seeming and likeness, which had already appeared with the double Smerdis, is likely to dominate the fourth book.

The third book was especially concerned with true and false speech; and whenever we speak of the difference between true and false we think at first that we can substitute for it that of "real" and "unreal"; but on reflection we know that "unreal" things sometimes show up the truth better than real things, for example, a play of Sophocles' or a dialogue of Plato's; and we have seen that the same holds true for the stories Herodotus tells. Herodotus does not introduce speeches with, "so-and-so said something like this," as Thucydides does, but he simply says, "So-and-so said this," although he does not expect anyone to believe that he knows exactly what was said a hundred years before he lived. He does not directly justify this poetic way of speaking, but he does let us divine a justification for it in his account of Scythia and Libya, where the problem of imitation gives the book its theme. It will indicate how we are to understand Herodotus as historian and as poet.[50]

---

[50]Cf. Mülder, D., *Die Ilias u. ihre Quellen* (Berlin, 1910), pp. 42ff.

IV. SCYTHIA AND LIBYA

Everyone knows that the fourth book owes much to the second on Egypt: "Also these (the Scythians) avoid extremely the adoption of foreign customs"; an "also" that can only refer to the Egyptians, about whom the same is said, though they are slightly less strict in its observance (76.1: II.91.1; cf. 79.1). Not only the Scythians but the Libyans as well fail to use swine in sacrifice, one of the many indications that the Libyan section belongs to the fourth book (63; 186.1; II.47.1).[1] Sameness or similarity of customs forms but a part of the parallelism. It too falls into four main parts. Paragraphs 1.2–31 concern the Scythians' origins and the tribes of Europe, 32–83 their customs and beliefs, 83–144 the history of Darius' invasion, and 145–205 the origins of Cyrene and the tribes of Libya. That the book is in some way a doublet should not blind us to its divergence from Book II; and in trying to keep in mind both these aspects, the plan of Herodotus' *Inquiries* will for the first time clearly emerge: how its progressive and digressive character, its temporal and geographical elements, belong essentially together in a single *logos*. This book will supply Herodotus with the last way of understanding he regards as necessary before he turns to the Persian Wars themselves. Here the λόγοι of observation come to an end, in Book V the λόγος of action take over.

When the Scythians return to their land, after a brief reign in Asia, they find that the sons of their blind slaves, born from their own women, come out to fight them (1.2–4). Repulsed at first, one of their number suggests a ruse: to ride against them with whips instead of swords and bows, so that they will realize they are resisting their masters, who armed with swords had not shown themselves superior either in birth or in valor. The ruse is successful. The sons of slaves are "thunderstruck at the event, forget the battle, and flee." They at once recognize the whip as a sign of their slavery and equate it with their

---

[1]Cf. the phrases λέγω δὲ τὰ λέγουσι αὐτοὶ Αἰγύπτιοι (II.50.1) and λέγω δὲ τὰ λέγουσι αὐτοὶ Λίβυες (187.3; cf. 173); and further note that Herodotus uses φημί of his own assertions only in II and IV, three times in each (II.49.2bis; 49.3; IV.45.4; 81.2; 180.4).

prospective punishment. They do not see the horsemen as unarmed horsemen but as masters; not what they are but what they are interpreted to be overpowers them. It is no wonder that they are said to be born from blind slaves. Their blindness, as though they inherited their fathers' defect, seems to be shared equally by their masters, who might not have thought that they would fool them unless they were fooled themselves. They too might have assumed that a sign is equivalent to that of which it is a sign; that the emblems of power and power itself are interchangeable; and that the difference between masters and slaves is not taught or learned but naturally is known. These Scythian assumptions are similar to those that underlie the first story Herodotus tells, a story that seems at first so perplexing.

"The Scythians make all their slaves blind for the sake of the milk they drink" (2.1). It is then explained how they milk their mares, and how the slaves are employed in stirring the milk; after which Herodotus repeats himself—"for the sake of this everyone the Scythians capture they make blind"— but he adds: "for they are not agricultural but nomads" (2.2). If the slaves saw the horses and knew that they could not only escape on them but nourish themselves with their milk, the Scythians would have been unable to have any slaves at all. But even if this suffices to explain the blinding—it is Herodotus' own explanation—it fails to account for what the Scythians fancy as the connection between it and milking, which Herodotus first proposes to explain. It has been suspected that some misunderstood Scythian word lies behind this story; but though I believe it turns on a word, Homer holds the key to it. In the *Iliad* there are four instances, and in the *Odyssey* one, of the phrase νυκτὸς ἀμολγῷ, which apparently means "in the dead or dark of night."[2] All the ancient lexicographers and scholiasts derive ἀμολγός from ἀμελγειν "to milk." I suggest that Herodotus has made the same derivation and gone one step further. If "at the milking-time of night" can come to mean "at the dead of night," then the verb "to milk" can stand for "to make dark" or "to blind." The Scythians would have confused two words, so that to account for one practice they fell back on another which only a sameness in sound related. One might rightly object that these are Scythians and not Greeks who are supposed to be speaking; but we can counter that Herodotus writes in Greek for Greeks who, aware of the Homeric phrase, would realize that Herodotus intimates that the Scythians resorted to the same kind of etymology in their own language (cf. II.52.1 with I.57.2); and that he connects somehow Greek poetry with the Scythians: in the first few paragraphs that follow Herodotus mentions or refers to Aristeas, Hesiod, and Homer.

Every time that the phrase νυκτὸς ἀμολγῷ occurs in the *Iliad* it is in a simile, and the single occurrence in the *Odyssey* appears after a dream which

---

[2]*Iliad* XI.173; XV.324; XXII.28, 317; *Odyssey* IV.841; see further *Iliad*

Athena sent to Penelope: "Her heart was warmed, so vivid the dream had come upon her in the dead of night." Similes are fabricated images, just as this dream is an image that Athena made: "she made an image (εἴδωλον) whose shape resembled" Penelope's sister. The Scythians, on the other hand, in interpreting a whip as domination, confounded the sign with the object of that sign; and they would now have taken a similarity for a causal connection. An image would have replaced its original. What the Greeks keep separate, what is and what is made, the Scythians regard as one. They are 'natural' poets. They say that one cannot travel north of their land because the air and earth are full of feathers which shut out the sight; but Herodotus understands that they mean snow: "for snow is like feathers" (7.3; 31; cf. II. 131.; V.10). Aeschylus has the phrase "white-feathered snow" (*Prom.* 993), but the Scythians drop the noun and hypostatize the adjective. A likeness has usurped the place of the original, and the original has disappeared. In the same way, then, that the whip replaces the power and feathers snow, the true reason for the blinding of slaves has yielded to a verbal resemblance. Some blind people who dwell above Scythia an Aristophanic scholiast calls the Μολγοί ("Blind"), and he says that Herodotus mentions them. Although he is mistaken about the word's meaning in Aristophanes, and this tribe's name does not appear in our text of Herodotus, there is something fitting that a comedy should have helped to preserve a corrupted form of Herodotus' own comic invention.[3] Not only does Herodotus prove as playful here as in other books, but here and nowhere else he laughs: he laughs at map-makers, those who make images of the earth (36.2).

If our explanation is correct, we can at once understand why the fourth book follows and departs from the second in its plan. There the first episode concerned Psammetichus' experiment to find out who were the oldest people; and when he learnt that the word "bekos" was Phrygian, he awarded primacy to them, for he failed to notice the resemblance between the bleating of goats and this word. The Scythian story also proposes to explain something; it too turns on a word; but far from failing to notice a resemblance, the Scythians observed a resemblance and then forgot which was the original and which the copy; and unlike Psammetichus, whose experiment dealt with speech, the Scythian story deals with sight. If the Egyptians are deaf to a tonal similarity, the Scythians are blind to the difference between hearing and seeing. If the Egyptians mistake natural for conventional speech, and hence the oldest for the first things, they are at least aware that the first things, if found to be theirs,

---

XIII.1-6; Schol. AT at *Iliad* XI.173; Hesychius; Suda; Eustathius; *EM*; *EG* s.v.; cf. Bolling, G., *AJP*, 1958, pp. 165-172.

[3]Schol. in Aristoph. *Equites* 963: μολγὸν γενέσθαι· Φαεινός μολγὸν ἀντὶ τοῦ τυφλόν. Ἡρόδοτος δὲ ἱστορεῖ τοὺς Μολγοὺς τούτους ἐπάνω τῆς Σκυθίας

would justify their way of life; but the Scythians merely compare one word with another within their own language, utterly indifferent as they are to the first things. The Scythians, we should not be surprised to learn, believe themselves to be the youngest of all races (5.1).[4] Herodotus had added to the Egyptian tale of Psammetichus the Greek version, which said that Psammetichus cut out the tongues of the women among whom the children grew up. Herodotus labelled this version as foolish because it made any interpretation impossible: in the midst of silent women the children would never have spoken at all. Here, however, the shoe is on the other foot. The Scythian tale gains its explanation from the Greeks, from Homer in fact, a blind poet. The fabulous in the Greek variant stood in the way of any understanding of Psammetichus' experiment; but now Greek poetry and imagery alone allowed us any access to the Scythians. The Egyptians retained something more fundamental than the Greeks, who had lost it through its poetic reworking; but the Scythians have gone one step further than the Greek poets; they understand everything metaphorically and hence no longer metaphorically, so that only the Greek poets can restore the distinction between them. Not accidentally Herodotus, on the first page, describes the bone blow-pipes which the Scythians use to milk mares as "most similar to flute-pipes." Only by poetic likeness can Scythia be understood.[5]

In the first part there are two sections; paragraphs 5–15 concern the origins of the Scythians, 16–31 the tribes who occupy Europe. We recall that the two sections of part one in Book II concerned first the land and then the river of Egypt, which were related to one another as product to power, or ἔργον to γινόμενον, εἶδος to δύναμις. The continual action of the Nile had given Egypt its shape. Herodotus had started with the visible earth, shown why it looked the way it did, and then reasoned about the sources and power of the Nile. Here he does the opposite. The origins come first, then the earth; but this reversal does not only reflect the topsy-turviness of Egypt, so that a reversed order can be followed elsewhere, but also the differences between Egypt and Scythia. To discover the Scythians' origins is not as important as to discover the original elements, earth and water. The Egyptians' claim to be the

---

εἶναι; cf. 20.1.

[4] See Pompeius Trogus II.1.

[5] Words of sameness, resemblance, and equality in II and IV occur with the following frequencies. οἶκα: II, 8; IV, 9 (out of 63); παρόμοιος: II, 1; IV, 2 (nowhere else); ὅμοιος: II, 18; IV, 13 (out of 60); εἰκάζω: II, 4; IV, 5 (out of 20); εἰκών: II, 8; IV, 8 (out of 13); παραπλήσιος: II, 3; IV, 5 (out of 24); προσείκελος: II, 1; IV, 2 (out of 4); ἐμφερής: II, 6; IV, 2 (out of 9); προσφερής: II, 1; IV, 1 (out of 3); πρσεμφερέστατος: IV, 1 (nowhere else); ἴσος: II, 11; IV, 10 (out of 45).

first men had compelled Herodotus to uncover the truly first things; but the
Scythians claim no special rank for themselves: they are not the first of all men
but the youngest of all tribes. It is a primacy in novelty, not in antiquity. They
are so recent that one cannot go back to the sources they might have misunderstood; there seem to be no sources except their own imagination. Herodotus
must stick as close to the surface as they try to do before he can uncover something deeper. As their origins. then, replace the Nile-waters, so the geographical location of tribes replaces the Egyptian soil.

Four different versions about the Scythians are presented: one Scythian,
one Greek, one common to both Greeks and barbarians, and one by Aristeas;
just as to account for the Nile's inverted power four explanations were also
given: all were Greek, three presented by those who wished to be "renowned
for their wisdom." and the last by Herodotus (5-13; II.20-27). In each set of
four one is ostensibly poetic; in Egypt, that Oceanus supplies the waters of the
Nile—Homer calls it "back-flowing"; in Scythia, that the Arimaspi expelled
the Issedones, who expelled the Scythians, who expelled the Cimmerians—a
forward flowing, one might say—so that the Scythians thus came to occupy
their present site. Even this highly poetic tale, Herodotus says, disagrees with
the Scythian account; in fact it agrees quite well with the account he does
accept. Whereas Oceanus as cause Herodotus rejected as soon as he stated it,
he now uses poetry to support his own view. A Greek poet "possessed by
Apollo" makes more sense than the Scythians (cf. 13.2; VI.52.1).

The Scythians say that four golden objects once fell from the sky—plow,
yoke, battle-axe, and drinking-bowl—, and that they burst into flames at the
approach of the two older sons of Targitaus, but when the youngest, Kolaxais,
approached, the fire was quenched and he was able to take them home;
whereupon his two brothers handed over the entire kingdom to him. Since they
believe themselves to be the youngest of tribes, they assign to the youngest the
honor of their founding. They refuse to identify the oldest with the first things;
they equate them instead with the most recent. They remember a thousand
years of their history, in which time the Greeks say Dionysus, Heracles, and
Pan were born (II.145.4). They do not genealogize their gods from the time
when they first heard about them—that Herodotus thinks the Greeks do; but
they genealogize themselves from the very beginnings. They are in a way more
consistent than either the Greeks or Egyptians. In separating their being men
from their being Scythians, their claim to a particular providence does not
stand or fall with their antiquity; and in uniting themselves so closely with the
gods—Targitaus was the son of Zeus and Borysthenes' daughter—they do not
make the gods younger than men. Their success, however, in maintaining a
self-consistency depends on a failure to recognize the distinction between art
and nature. The signs from the sky are ποιήματα, made things; the gods are
believed to have made, perhaps for the first time, what men make for them-

selves. Unlike the Egyptians, whose inventions—statues, altars, temples—are human, the Scythians attribute to the gods the making of human implements. Just as they do not see the snow but only its simile (feathers), they do not see the artificial as artificial, but think it has the same status as generation. In the Greek story of the Scythians' origin, generation, even if monstrous, prevails: the bow, belt, and drinking-bowl of Heracles are not divine, and the test to discover who should rule depends on the natural strength of the youngest son. Heracles tells, in direct discourse—there is no speaking in the Scythian story—how he is to be chosen. The mother of Heracles' sons does not have to interpret any sign; but a sign in the Scythian story immediately persuades the two brothers to recognize the youngest as king: they know at once that the quenching of the burning gold is a sign. The reverse of not seeing an image as an image is to see what may not be a sign as a sign. These two mistakes run through the Scythian and Libyan accounts. They let Herodotus discover the true meaning of εἰκασία.

If the Scythians substitute making for generation, the Pontine Greeks substitute imitation for it. Whereas the Scythians make a complete one-to-one substitution, the Greeks employ only a small part of making, the making of a poet. Heracles' wandering with the cattle of Geryon and his mating with a half-snake woman have as their sources, not a direct revelation from the sky, but Hesiod's *Theogony* (287-305).[6] They relate with some distortions what they have learnt from a poet. Poetic origins are the origins whose obscurity is made visible in words: "They say in speech (λόγῳ) that Oceanus begins from the rising of the sun and flows about the whole earth, but they do not demonstrate it in fact (ἔργῳ)" (8.2). The beginnings are found in a poet, to whom the Muses had said: "We know how to say many lies that are like the truth, and we know, whenever we wish, to announce the truth." Poetic imitation is part concealment and part revelation, but the poet never tells how they are to be distinguished. Herodotus must try to interpret the Muses' words if he is ever to penetrate to the λόγος that might underlie all μῦθοι: the two times he uses μῦθος, it implies falsehood (II.23; 45.1; cf. 121δ3).[7]

Aristeas is said to have died in a fuller's shop in Proconnessus, from whence he disappeared, but he was soon to be seen walking toward Cyzicus,

---

[6]The Hesiodic Echidna lives among the Arimi, a name that resembles the "Arimaspi" of Aristeas, 13.1; 27; III.116.1; and Chrysaor ("Gold-sword") born from Medusa has the name of the ποίημα dropped from the sky in the Scythian version (cf. Hesiod *Th.* 283).

[7]Cf. Plutarch *de gloria Atheniensium* 4 (348A–B). Nothing more sharply distinguishes Herodotus from Hecataeus (to judge by the fragments) than Hecataeus' using μυθεῖται for what he himself says and λόγοι for the Greek stories he believes absurd; *FGH*, I, fr. 1.

only to reappear in Proconnessus seven years later and write his poem *Arimaspea* (of which perhaps not a genuine line remains); he then disappeared a second time but showed up again in Metapontum in Italy 240 years later to command them to build an altar to Apollo and a statue of himself: and Delphi later confirmed this command to obey "the apparition of the man." Appearance and disappearance, φάσμα and ἀφάνισις, are the privilege of a poet: not only can he conceal or lay bare in speech but in fact. He can do what the gods are supposed to do. Herodotus had said in the second book: "He who spoke about Oceanus, by referring his myth to the invisible (ἀφανές), cannot be refuted: for I do not know of any river Oceanus, but Homer or some previous poet invented the name and transferred it to poetry" (II.23; cf. III.115.2). Aristeas does more than Homer: he can make himself disappear and reappear. He is a more spectacular Arion. Not merely the transference of a name into poetry to make it appear, and thereby the reference to something unseen, but his own body he can hide or show at his will. If Homer and Hesiod made the Greek theogony, Aristeas makes himself part of it. As a follower of Apollo he is a crow, which Hesiod says lives 108 times longer than the oldest man (fr.171R[2]). When the Phoenicians raped the two Egyptian priestesses, and one of them came to Dodona, the Greeks likened her to a black pigeon because she was dark and spoke a barbaric tongue: but as soon as they understood her they built an oracular shrine of Zeus (II.54–57).[8] Not a priestess but a poet commanded the Metapontines to build an altar to Apollo; not a priestess of a god who refuses to reveal himself and is shown with a ram's head (Zeus Ammon). but a poet possessed by a god whom the Greeks sculpture in a completely human shape; not a likeness to a bird but a bird itself appeared. Herodotus had been able to interpret the Dodonan tale in the light of what the Egyptians said; by comparison he had discovered that the black pigeon was a poetic rendering of a straight-forward story; but now no external source exists by which Aristeas could be made human again. The poet himself has become self-sufficient and as irrefutable as Oceanus. Just as original and copy have become one and the same, so poet and poem are now inseparable. If poetry sometimes confers on those it praises immortal fame, it now almost grants Aristeas immortality itself.

Herodotus, checked by both Greeks and Scythians in their separate versions from giving any rational account, discovers that the common story (ξυνὸς λόγος) shared by Greeks and barbarians alike offers a way out. Their agreement (ὁμολογία) not only is purged of all fabulous elements, but it agrees with the visible remains of the Cimmerians found in Scythia, and with the evident fact of their invasion of Media (11–12). Just as the agreement between

---

[8]Cf. p. 49 *supra*.

Egyptians and non-Egyptians had made the later history of Egypt more certain than the independent testimony of the Egyptians alone (II.147.1; 154.4),[9] so now Greeks and barbarians together come closest to the truth. The diversity of their customs guarantees the truth in the sameness of their *logos*.

Seventeen tribes are known to inhabit Europe; others whose existence some affirm Herodotus does not believe in (16-27; cf. 45-1, 5:III.115.2). "No one knows accurately what is beyond," he says, "for I am unable to learn from anyone who was an eyewitness and claims that he knows." Repeatedly he now says, "as far as we know," and it is almost entirely the knowledge of hearsay. "We" occurs more often here than in any other book, and it once means "we Greeks" (27).[10] His ignorance about the land parallels his former ignorance about the course and sources of the Nile: "From no one else was I able to learn anything, having come as an eyewitness up to the city of Elephantine, but beyond this inquiring by hearsay" (II.29.1; cf. 19.3; 31). Whereas in Egypt the land was known but the river and its power unknown or obscure, here the opposite is true: except for the source of the Borysthenes, those of all other European rivers are known, but much of the land is uninhabited and consequently unknown (53.5; II.28.1).[11] The rivers do not show any inverse power, but the land does: "If you pour water on the earth you will not make mud, but if you light a fire you will make mud." The waters of the Nile built up Egypt out of the silt it carried; here warmth turns the earth to water, as cold turns water to ice. Water and earth are not related as fluid and solid, for each can assume the appearance of the other; but they constitute together, as in Egypt, the two main principles of Scythia. Sun and sky determine in both regions the appearance each will have: metamorphosis in no way changes their nature.

During the winter it hardly ever rains but snows, and in the summer it never stops raining, contrary to what happens in other regions; for the extreme cold would turn all rain to ice and snow, and the slight warmth of summer melts any snow that falls (28.2-4; 50.2-4; cf. 94.4; 184.2). These features seem so constant to the Scythians that any departure is taken as a sign. The frozen earth appears so solid that an earthquake is thought a miracle, and

---

[9]Cf. pp. 63-64 *supra*.

[10]Cf. 180.2; III.111.2; 115.1,2; 116.3; V.49.6; 88.1; also p. 35 *supra* and Chap. II, fn 15. In line with the difference between II and IV, though each book has eight instances of ἀτρεκέως (or other cognate forms), in II only three are Herodotus' and four the Egyptians', while in IV all are Herodotus'.

[11]Out of 61 instances of γινώσκω seventeen occur in IV, none in the Libyan section; II, with the next highest number, has eight; and of 152 οἶδα, IV has 27; III, 21; II, 23; I, 22.

thunder so infrequent in winter that they marvel at its miraculous occurrence. The Scythians do not see snow and rain as aspects of the same water, nor summer and winter as belonging to the same sky. They do not connect the thunder that might arise in winter with that which happens so often in summer; any more than the Egyptian priests believed that the Nile depends on rain, which made them equally disparage the Greeks' reliance on "god's raining" and count a slight drizzle in Thebes as "the greatest apparition" (II.13.3–14.1; III.10.3; cf. II.121.1). Now Herodotus connects the Scythians' transformation of a natural into a miraculous event with their failure to see an image as an image in the following way. After describing their weather, he mentions as one of its consequences that asses and mules cannot survive the cold, nor do cattle grow horns; and he uses a line of Homer's as witness, which implies that in Libya sheep almost have horns at birth. Herodotus infers that the heat there hastens growth, as the cold here checks it. He then adds a digression—"for my *logos* has sought additions from the beginning"—about Elis, where "no evident cause" (i.e., neither extreme cold nor any other climatic peculiarity) explains why mules are unable to be born; but the natives say that "a certain curse" prevents it. And he resumes his account of Scythia by saying that they have likened snow to feathers. If we summarize this sequence, it looks like this: a) Scythian miracles; b) Homeric witness; c) Elian digression and curse; d) Scythian imagery. The Scythians are shown to replace snow with a simile, and thunder and earthquakes with signs: they are the same kind of mistake. Herodotus employs poetry to bolster his argument about hot and cold, just as, inversely, he discovers the fact behind the Scythians' natural poetry. The snow explains why the regions north of Scythia are uninhabitable, but the Homeric line offers only a description: Herodotus himself must add the cause. He must liken Scythia to Libya by inversion, even as he must remove the likeness from the Scythians' belief. He becomes a "true" poet. He replaces both the divine and the imagistic with his own understanding. In the same way that an oracle bears his judgment witness in Egypt, Homer bears witness here.[12] This alliance between poetry and the divine, which appear separately in Scythia as two kinds of weather, comes out most clearly in Greece. Aristeas, Homer, Hesiod, and the Delians are alone in testifying to the existence of the Hyperboreans (32–35; cf. 13.1).[13]

---

[12] 29: μαρτυρέει δέ μοι τῇ γνώμῃ καὶ Ὁμήρου ἔπος ἐν Ὀδυσσείῃ ἔχον ὧδε; II.18.1: μαρτυρέει δέ μοι τῇ γνώμῃ...καὶ τὸ Ἄμμωνος χρηστήριον γενόμενον.

[13] 32–35; cf. 13.1. Paragraphs 32–35 are the first section of part II; part I ends with the words (cf. II.120.5): ταῦτα μέν νυν τὰ λέγεται μακρότατα εἴρηται; and part II, section one ends: καὶ ταῦτα μὲν Ὑπερβορέων πέρι εἰρήσθω (36.1; cf. 15.4; II.34.2; 76.3); section two ends: ταῦτα μέν νυν ἐπὶ

Neither the Issedones nor the Scythians know anything about the Hyperboreans; but Homer and Hesiod have made up their name "Beyond-the-North"; just as the Greeks translated the Scythian word "Arimaspi" into "one-eyed." Invention supplants translation. And if Homer did not write the epic poem *Epigoni*, the Hyperboreans would prove to be a fabricated name in a spurious poem (cf. II.117). We would be two removes from the possibly true. A lie transmitted under the protection of a famous name would duplicate Aristeas' disappearance. His own incorporation into the realms of his poetry parallels the attribution to Homer of another's handiwork; for to fake the authorship of verses that are false makes Homer himself poetic. If the testimony of the gravest poet is suspect, the Delians can offer nothing better than signs. That sacred offerings are brought to Delos, which resemble those Herodotus knows Thracian and Paeonian women sacrifice to Artemis, he does not wish to deny; nor that Delian girls twine some of their hair about a spindle and place it at a tomb, and boys twine theirs about a green shoot and add to the same tomb. These ceremonies prove nothing about their origin (cf. II.122.2). To link them to the Hyperboreans the Delians say that the Hyperboreans hand the offerings to the Scythians, who have them handed on from tribe to tribe until they reach Delos. Spatial transmission, then, is the sacred counterpart to poetic invention. What the poets do figuratively, placing the Hyperboreans beyond anyone's knowledge, the Delians do literally. They rely on distance, as the poets on imagination, to lend them credence. Their further assertion, however, that two Hyperborean girls once came with Apollo and Artemis themselves seems to depend entirely on a poet: Olen composed ancient hymns in which their names appear. If geographical obscurity suffices to explain sacred offerings, a poet must still be invoked to prove the bodily presence of gods.[14] Memory and her daughters the Muses seem to be not only inseparable but indistinguishable.

τοσοῦτον εἰρήσθω· τοῖσι γὰρ νομιζομένοισι αὐτῶν χρησόμεθα (45.5); section three opens with the last of the rivers (58); and section four opens: τὰ μὲν δὴ μέγιστα οὕτω σφι εὔπορά ἐστι (59.1); section five begins at 76.1 and ends thus: τοῦτο μέν νυν τοιοῦτόν ἐστι, ἀναβήσομαι δὲ ἐς τὸν κατ' ἀρχὰς ἦια λέξων λόγον (82; the reference is to 1.1). Part III, section one ends: Δαρεῖος μὲν ταῦτα εἴπας ἐς τὸ πρόσω ἠπείγετο (98.3); section two ends: ἡ μέν νυν γῆ αὕτη ἐστι μέγαθος τοσαύτη; section three ends with the history of the Amazons (117); section four ends: ταῦτα μὲν νυν ἐπὶ σμικρόν τι ἐφέροντο τοῦ πολέμου (129.3); and the fifth ends at 144.3. Part IV naturally falls into two sections: 145–167 and 168–199 (ταῦτα μέν νυν επὶ τοσοῦτον εἰρήσθω (cf. 15.4), and 200–205 go back to section one of Part IV. See Chapter II, fn 25.

[14]Cf. 27 with 35.3; (see 110.1). For the meaning of αὐτός compare the difference between τῷ μάλιστα λεγομένῳ αὐτὸν πρόσκειμαι (11.1); οἶδα

When Darius came to the Bosporus on his way against the Scythians, he had set up two stelae, one in Assyrian, the other in Greek, commemorating all the tribes hc led; but the Byzantines transported these stones to build an altar of Artemis Orthosia, except for one stone that was left behind at the temple of Dionysus (87; cf. II.106.4). Darius' attempt to make himself remembered fails. His secular monuments are transferred to a divine use. They are reworked for the sake of remembering the gods in the inverse way that Homer had reworked the profane history of Egypt in order to make a Greek theogony.[15] Mandrocles, the Samian architect of the bridge which yoked the Bosporus, avoided the fate of Darius' stelae by dedicating his own memorial to Hera (88; cf. 91;III.60). He painted a picture that portrays "the entire yoking of the Bosporus, King Darius seated on his throne, and his army's crossing": and he inscribed four lines of verse that explain who he was and what he did. Not the bridge but the image of the bridge survives. The sacred precincts of the Heraeum preserve the poetic and pictorial signs of his work. The sign outlasts the original: so each soldier in Darius' army placed one stone at a designated spot, and thus great hills of stone were left behind (92). But these memorials are completely silent; they do not tell who made them: for unlike Mandrocles' they do not imitate the original: they are mere tokens of something that once happened. They immortalize that army in the vaguest and most shapeless way. These stones stand at the opposite pole from the literal immortality the Getae achieve (93–96).[16] Every fourth year they send a man, chosen by lot, to Salmoxis, the only god they believe exists. He is thrown up in the air, and spears pierce him as he comes down; and if he dies they believe their god is gracious: if he lives they accuse the messenger himself of being bad, and they send another who reports to Salmoxis what the Getae need. This kind of death is not thought of as perishing but as a way of disappearing into another realm. The Pontine Greeks believe Salmoxis was a slave of Pythagoras, who learnt from him how to feign immortality. Salmoxis entertained the Getae munificently and taught them that they and their descendants would never die but always have every kind of good; but in the meantime he built an underground chamber into which he disappeared for three years, and then in the fourth year reappeared after they had missed his banquets and mourned for him as dead; "and thus they were convinced by what Salmoxis

---

αὐτὸς τούτοισι τοῖς ἱροῖσι τόδε ποιεύμενον προσφερές (33.4) and αὐτός οἱ ἕπεσθαι ὁ νῦν ἐὼν Ἀριστεύς (15.2; cf. 16.1); ἅμα αὐτοῖσι τοῖσι θεοῖσι ἀπικέσθαι λέγουσι (35.2); cf. 94.3; II. 77.1.

[15]Cf. pp. 49–50 supra.

[16]Cf. II.122–123; V.4–5; Sophocles Electra 59–64; Plato Charmides 156d4–157c6; Pompeius Mela II.18–19.

said." A god is made by longing (cf. II.79; 129.3; 132). Salmoxis learnt the "deeper ways" of the Greeks: he learnt how to deceive. He disappeared as completely as Aristeas; but whereas Aristeas needed poetry to make his disappearance plausible to the Greeks, Salmoxis could rely on the Getae's longing and his own bodily return to hide the deception. Either a literal interpretation of immortality by the Getae, or its superficial imitation by Salmoxis in the Greek version, replaces the poetic devices that Darius, Mandrocles, and Aristeas were forced to employ. Imagery and poetry replace in Scythia and Thrace historical memory: Herodotus believes that Salmons lived many years before Pythagoras. That Salmoxis was a man who pretended to be immortal, Herodotus neither believes nor disbelieves; he cannot distinguish between a native god and a clever man who assumed a divine role. He dismisses both alternatives with the phrase by which he had dismissed in Book II the epic *Cypria* which contradicted the *Iliad* (96.2; II.117).[17] Homer and the pseudo-Homeric *Cypria* have the same status as Salmoxis in the two versions; for the lines in the *Iliad* contradict the rest of the poem—they imply that Helen was in Egypt and not at Troy—so that Herodotus can no more decide between the spurious *Cypria* and the Homeric mistake than between a fraudulent Salmoxis and a genuine god. (The Homeric mistake occurs in a passage where the gods are explicitly said to be absent.) The greater decency of the version Homer preferred to tell can be trusted as much as the native story of the Getae; and, inversely, the consistency of the *Cypria* with the *Iliad* testifies to Homer's authorship as much as the doctrine of Salmoxis shows his Pythagoreanism. In the world of fancy the genuine and the spurious seem to collapse into one.

The Scythians' failure to see a likeness as a likeness indicates that Herodotus himself can, and he shows this ability by making a map of the earth (36–45).[18] To read a map requires that one know what a map is: that it is not self-contained as sensible things are. Sensible things do not have to be "read." A horse is a horse, but a map is a map of something other than itself. One must know in some way the something before one can understand its map. Herodotus laughs at the maps of others because they are self-contained; they make Oceanus flow around a circular earth "as though it were made by a compass." The earth is not the unmade original from which one copies, but it becomes a fabricated object that is only duplicated in these maps. The absence of the Hypernotians shows, however, that the map-makers refute themselves. If they make the whole earth circular, this imposed symmetry demands that men live as far south as they claim men live to the north. To geometrize the

---

[17]Cf. pp. 46–7 *supra*. With IV.96.1 compare Plutarch *Camillus* 6.6.
[18]Cf. Strabo I.3.3 (48–49); VII.3.1 (295); Aristotle *Meteor.* 362b12–14.

earth but not its inhabitants seems as inconsistent to Herodotus as for the Ionians to believe that Egypt is only the Delta, but that three continents make up the whole earth (II.15–16). Just as the Ionians must either say that there are four parts to the earth, or retract their belief about Egypt, so the map-makers must either postulate Hypernotians to correspond to the Hyperboreans, or retract their belief in the earth's circularity. Since lack of evidence allowed them to use fictions, they should have rounded out their account. They should have invented Hypernotians to justify the circularity of the southern half, just as they invented Hyperboreans and Abaris' journey to justify that of the northern half. As Herodotus could detect a baser story because Homer nodded, so he now detects the error in previous maps, because they failed to conceal their fabrication behind a homogeneous and self-contained facade. The anomalous position of the Hyperboreans, like Homer's nodding, suggests that every making must betray itself; or, more exactly, that the imagination always has its source outside itself. There cannot be an image that is not, in however distorted a way, an image of something.

Herodotus thinks that the earth is one, upon which at some unknown date some unknown persons imposed three feminine names. These names are not original, for previously Asia, Libya, and Europe were anonymous (39.1; 42.1; 45).[19] Only by convention (νόμῳ) does Asia cease at the Nile, and the River Phasis or Tanais divide Asia from Europe. Herodotus wishes to stress the arbitrary character of the conventional divisions, for they obscure the sameness that runs through the whole earth. His perspective is so distant that Greece does not even receive a single mention. It is a pin-point, as it were, in the whole.[20] Human beings inhabit the same earth, even if as races and tribes they show great differences.[21] The map suppresses all local variants which thereby lose their importance. By gathering together in a few pages the known world, Herodotus shows his indifference to every convention. His laughter at inferior maps is without malice and truly Homeric.[22]

When Herodotus comes to particular places, however, he does not preserve his detachment. In order to make clear what kind of shape the Crimea has, where the Taurians live, he likens it to Cape Sunium in Attica; but lest that indicate too great a provinciality, he likens it to the heel of Italy, adding: "Though I mention these two there are many other similar places, I say, which the Crimea resembles" (99.4–5; cf. II.10.1, 3). He admits that to compare Sunium with the Crimea is to compare small with large; but size should not

---

[19]Cf. 198. 1–2; II.52.1; see I.202.4.
[20]Cf. Aristophanes *Nubes* 206–217; consider V.49.1; 50.2.
[21]Cf. pp. 86–89 *supra*.
[22]Cf. III.37.2–3; *Iliad* I.599ss.

blind us to similarity: the action of the Nile is found on a smaller scale else-where. Similarity goes so deep into the nature of things, Herodotus believes, that he is willing to chart the course of the Nile from the Danube's (48–50; II.33–34). The Danube is the largest river known, for it collects the waters of seventeen other rivers; but neither any other river nor spring contributes to the Nile, so that "one-to-one" it surpasses the Danube. Nevertheless their near equality justifies the one being taken as the model for the other. If Herodotus' map is folded lengthwise across the middle of the Mediterranean, the course of the Danube would match the unknown part of the Nile's, just as its known part lines up longitudinally with the mouth of the Danube. Europe and Libya are mirror-images of one another. Neither is original nor copy. Only Herodotus' knowledge of the Danube gives it a priority over the Nile, just as the reader's familiarity with Attica or Italy made them suitable comparisons for the Crimea. Having once suggested the similarity between Libya and Europe, each becomes the copy of the other. They are duplicates within the horizon of a single earth. Herodotus' conjecture that a reversal of the sun's course would make the Danube act as the Nile (each of which has five natural mouths) would also convert Europe into Egypt and Egypt into Europe. Convertibility, however, does not mean sameness. Their differences seem attributable to that between the recent and the ancient, on the one hand, and cold and heat, on the other; but in spite of these opposites, they fundamentally belong together. The fourth book's resemblance to the second turns out to have a natural base: reflection and doubleness are characteristic of nature itself. Herodotus only imitated its doubleness.

If The second and fourth books differ from and resemble each other, the third book's place in Herodotus' plan becomes clear. It concerned Persia, but the Persians claim all Asia and its tribes as their own (I.4.4; IX.116.3). Asia geographically holds the middle position between Europe and Libya, and Herodotus preserved that position in his *Inquiries*. The three major divisions of the earth find their reflection in the three parts of Herodotus' own *logos*, whose unity seems guaranteed by the unity of the earth. Although Persian, Scythian-Libyan, and Egyptian customs are different, they nevertheless belong together: each allows Herodotus to discover one aspect of the true *logos*. Their several ways of looking at things are distortions, because each ignores the other two and carries to an extreme its own understanding. The partiality of each makes each claim the whole; but the whole is composed of these parts without itself being partial. Herodotus objects to the conventional triplicity of the earth because it is conventional; it ignores Egypt and separates Europe from Libya, whereas Egypt, though geographically part of Libya, belongs by itself because of its distinct *logos*; and whereas Europe and Libya are geographically distinct, they belong together because of their same *logos*.[23]

There is a true triplicity, for three λόγοι constitute it, and not three names. Egypt led Herodotus to the discovery of the doubleness of things, Persia to that of λόγος itself, and now Europe and Libya reveal another kind of doubleness, which, though present in Egypt, is found most purely here. To label Scythia naive and barbaric and Egypt sophisticated and civilized, imprecise though it is, does indicate on what lines Herodotus will try to draw the distinction.

Egyptian customs could not be traced back directly to the earth and water that were the two components of Egypt's nature. They paralleled, without being the same as, that nature. The Egyptians' partial grasp of it explained their apparent imitation. The Scythians, however, imitate the nature of their land without understanding. They parrot rather than imitate. Thus a closer connection holds between what nature and customs exhibit. They do, one might say, what nature itself does. Their land has as many rivers as Egypt has canals (47.1; cf. II.108.2–4). What Sesostris compelled to be done in Egypt occurs naturally in Scythia. Nothing man-made interferes with the seeing of its original condition, a condition that is an ally of the one Scythian custom Herodotus admires. "The Scythian race has discovered most wisely one thing that is the greatest (most important) of all human things which we know" (46; cf. 124.2; 127). It consists in having no settled abode but always travelling with one's home, so that no enemy can destroy their non-existent cities. They are as masterful as Aristeas at the art of disappearance. They can be at home anywhere; but they buy this self-sufficiency at an enormous price: nothing else that they do is admirable. Their way of life copies the rivers: they are always in motion. They imitate so perfectly the constant flow of water they cannot have any of the wisdom that comes with rest. Whatever requires memory—that is, all learning—escapes them: they believe themselves to be the youngest of tribes.[24] If the Egyptians look more to the stable earth, and hence "exercise their memory the most and are by far the most versed in history of all men," but consequently forget their land's slow emergence out of the Nile; the Scythians look exclusively to water, taking the earth as much for granted as the

---

[23]Cf. *Geogr. Gr. Min.* (ed. Mueller), II, p. 495: οἱ παλαιοὶ τήν τε Λιβύην καὶ τὴν Εὐρώπην, ὥσπερ μίαν οὖσαν, συναμφοτέρας ἐκάλουν ἑνὶ καὶ μόνῳ τῷ τῆς Εὐρώπης ὀνόματι; Lucan IX.411–417; *Geogr. Lat. Min.* (ed. Ries), pp. 71ss.; Sallust *Iug.* 17.3; Orosius I.2.1 (the references are from Housman's ed. of Lucan).

[24]Cf. Aristotle *de memoria* 450a30-b7. For puns on 'remaining' and 'memory' (μένω and μνήμη) see Aeschylus *Agamemnon* 154ss.; *Eumenides* 381ss.; *Prometheus V.* 788ss.; Plato *Meno* 71c8; Eustathius *Comment. ad H. Il.* 963, 5 on XIII.836.

Egyptians the Nile. Their greatest god is Hestia ("Stationary") and every earthquake they believe a miracle (28.3; 59.1).[25] Their forgetfulness shows up in the different reports Herodotus has heard about their number: they are either very many or very few (81).[26] Even the attempt of a Scythian king to number them ends in failure. He commanded every Scythian to bring one bronze arrowhead, from which their number should be knowable; but the king decided to make a memorial out of them and had them melted down into one huge cauldron. Once the arrowheads have flowed together and lost their distinctness, the original number cannot be determined. Darius' order, on the other hand, that each of his men bring one stone, from which huge hills are formed, does furnish exact knowledge of his army's size: Herodotus knows that cavalry and foot were numbered at seventy ten-thousands (87.1:92: cf. 98).

The nomadic way of life among the Scythians literally renders the flow of rivers. Equalities and not proportions as in Egypt dominate. In Egypt geometry and the fourth proportional were discovered (II.109). And Egyptian customs were found to correspond analogically to the nature of water and earth; but in Scythia a perfect symmetry between them prevails. The Danube always flows in summer and winter equal to itself (48.1; 50). Its volume of water may become "slightly greater than its own nature during the winter"; but the rains and melting snow in the summer cancel out that excess, so that "a balance is struck." This equality of the river is repeated in the shape of the region the Scythians occupy. It is an exact square, each side being four thousand stades long. Not only are square sanctuaries built to Ares and square tombs for their kings, but some animals have square faces (62.1: 71.1: 109.2). The one-to-one correspondence between nature and custom is so strictly maintained that the seventeen tributaries of the Danube are echoed in the first list of seventeen tribes, and the eight major rivers besides the Danube are echoed in the eight tribes whose help the Scythians seek when Darius sets out to invade them (17-26; 47.2-58; 102-117). These identities are, in a sense, not to be taken seriously, but they do point to one cause of the difference between Egypt and Scythia. Egypt has a single river without tributaries, and one people occupies its whole north-south course; but this apparent unity produced the greatest variety and diversity of customs and monuments, which made it impossible to discover a simple relation between them. The great length of time had almost wiped out their simple beginnings. In Scythia the opposite is found. A great number and variety of rivers has led to an equally great number of tribes, each with its own set of customs that differ, even if only in the color

---

[25] Cf. Plato *Phaedrus* 247a1ss.; *Cratylus* 401b8-e1.
[26] Cf. I.202.1; also I.50.3-51.2.

of dress, from Scythian norms.[27] It is as though Egypt was refracted into its simpler elements in Scythia, so that Egyptian complexity becomes simplicity here, each tribe reflecting only one facet, as it were, of Egypt; but these facets, by their very isolation from one another, are pushed to extremes. Each assumes a character that represents more sharply something Egyptian. Two examples will suffice.[28]

"The Neuri seem to be magicians"; once a year each becomes a wolf for a few days and then is restored to his original state; but at a festival in Egypt two wolves are said to lead a blindfolded priest to the temple of Demeter (105; II.122.3-123). If both events are unbelievable, the one in Scythia exceeds all bounds. Animals and men at least remain distinct, even if they live together, in Egypt. That the invisible soul enters various animals over a period of three thousand years, until it reenters the human body, now becomes a yearly occurrence, without any distinction between body and soul. Metempsychosis turns into metamorphosis. And of what Homer sings—Circe turned men into wolves—or uses in similes—Achaeans and Trojans are likened to wolves—is transformed into fact.[29] The sacred in Egypt becomes the ordinary in Scythia and the poetic in Greece.

In Egypt men and women had reversed a number of their customary roles, a reversal that narrowed the apparently natural gap between them;[30] but in some European tribes nature or custom has made the gap entirely disappear. Both male and female among the Argippaei are born equally bald; the Issedones "are said to be especially just and their women to have equal power with men in ruling"; the Scythians have a group of soothsayers who are hermaphrodites (ἀνδρόγυνοι); the testicles of certain animals are useful for curing diseases of the womb; and the women among the Sauromatae, who were originally Amazons, hunt, go to war, and wear the same clothing as men.[31] The loss of sexual difference depends on something more fundamental: the disappearance of the distinction between the public and the private. Either there are communal marriages as among the Agathyrsi, "so that they might be brothers of one another and all being relations might lack both envy and hatred"; or there is cannibalism as among the Androphagi and Issedones; or

---

[27]Observe how Scythia becomes the standard: κατὰ ταὐτὰ Σκύθῃσι ἐπασκέουσι (17.1); ἔθνος ἐὸν ἴδιον καὶ οὐδαμῶς Σκυθικόν (18.3); ἄλλο ἔθνος καὶ οὐ Σκυθικόν (20.2); cf. 22.1; 23.2; 105.1; 106; 107; but 26.2; 104; 108.2.

[28]See further 23.5 and II.113.2; 62 and II.63; 67 and II.83; 71-73 and II.86-88; 82 and II.91.3.

[29]Odyssey X.210-219; see also Iliad IV.471ss; XI.72ss.; XVI.156-163.

[30]Cf. pp. 41-43 supra.

[31]23.2; 26.2; 67.2 (cf. I.105.4); 109.2-117; cf. 9.1.

both together as among the Massagetae.[32] The body, which seems naturally to belong to each, is made to belong to all; for the demand for symmetry and likeness not only reduces the sexes to one but all other differences as well. As the Neuri see no difference between wolves and men which would prevent them from being both, so the Androphagi see none between men and other kinds of meat. But they must still distinguish most sharply between themselves and other men. The Taurians sacrifice only enemies to Iphigeneia, as do the Scythians to Ares, nor do the Androphagi eat themselves. Thus an extreme provincialism accompanies an extreme reductionism. The figurative, when blind, goes hand in hand with the literal. The Scythians' customs illustrate both (59-75).

The Scythians do not have statues of their gods, not because they believe the gods are not of human shape, but because they do not see an image as an image; indeed, their gods are indistinguishable except by name, for they sacrifice to all of them (except Ares) in the same manner. A name or a sign suffices to keep them separate: a sword is the statue of Ares. A sign replaces the god, just as a whip convinced the offspring of slaves that they were still slaves. Metaphorical identity, however, is balanced by literal identity. A Scythian warrior must show the head of an enemy before he can share in the booty; and he strings each head on his bridle, so that the exact number of his killings can be known. Since a living hand can hold arrows, the dead hand of an enemy is used to cover his quiver; since a living head is filled with blood, a skull becomes a drinking cup; since the skin protects the body, the skin of a slain enemy is sewn into a cloak; and since the living man rides horseback, they sometimes stretch the human skin on a wooden frame and carry it around on a horse. Men themselves replace statues. The gilded skull of his father each of the Issedones "uses as a statue," performing great yearly rites "just as the Greeks" (26). Thus the literal leads to a kind of self-sufficiency. Their avoidance of all alien customs is but part of this. In spite of the evidence the Scythians adduce that Darius intends to enslave all of them, five of eight tribes refuse to believe it, because they think the Persians are right to take revenge (118-119). Their sense of self-sufficiency prevents them from making any concerted effort. It makes them rely entirely on themselves. In thunderstorms the Getae threaten the same god they beg for blessings, "believing there to be no other god except their own" (94.4; 109.1). The preference for their own blinds them to the better. The Chalcedonians must have been blind, the Persian Megabazus said, if they did not see that the site of Byzantium, which was unoccupied at the time they settled across from it, was fairer than theirs: it

---

[32]26.1; 104; 106; I.216.2-3; cf. 65. 76.6; IV.80.3-5; see pp. 77-80 *supra*; Plato *Republic* 462b4-e3.

took seventeen years for others to settle there (144; cf. 158.2). Among the Scythians a sacrificial animal is choked to death and then skinned, its own bones being used for fuel; and if they have no cauldrons, its own stomach is used instead, so that, as Herodotus puts it, "a bull stews itself." The reflexive and the reflective belong together. In one kind of divination they set together and separate many rods, and in another they twine and untwine the inner bark of the linden tree around their own fingers. They are completely independent of anything external to themselves, an independence that leads, in turn, to duplication. If a man has slain very many men, he is not given a double portion of wine, but two cups from which he drinks at the same time; and their kings are buried with their whole retinue, making the after-life an exact duplicate of this. If the king falls sick, three soothsayers are called in to say who swore falsely by the royal hearth: the health of the king is affected by the words of another; and if six other soothsayers agree with the first three, the man stands convicted and is killed: the death of one man is supposed to restore the life of another. These Scythian mistakes of taking the other for the same seem to be based on what sometimes naturally happens. Hemp grows there that is "most similar to the flax-plant," and the Thracians make garments of it, "most like linen ones." "Nor would anyone, who is not very familiar with it, be able to distinguish flax from hemp; and whoever has not yet seen hemp, will think the garment is of linen."

To confuse the other with the same works both for and against the Scythians. Their king sends Darius a bird, a mouse, a frog, and five arrows, and commands him to interpret what they mean (131–132). Darius believes that they indicate surrender, which was usually shown by the presentation of earth and water. He likens the mouse to the earth because it lives there and eats the same food as man; and he likens the frog to water for the same kind of reason; while the bird ("it most resembles a horse") and the arrows show that the Scythians hand over their power. Darius, then, sees these objects as signs of something else; but Gobryas realizes that they are not meant as signs but literally. "Unless you become birds and fly up to heaven, Persians, or unless you become mice and descend under the earth, or become frogs and jump into lakes, you will not return home, being struck by these arrows." They did not stand for other things but for themselves, metamorphosis and not likeness. Darius could wish that he had as many Megabazuses as there are seeds in a pomegranate; but he did not imagine that a simile could be transformed into that of which it is a simile (143; cf. III.32; 160.1). The Scythians, on the other hand, so often take the sign as sufficient in itself that they are easily deceived. Gobryas is able to spirit away Darius' army by lighting fires at night and leaving asses tied to stakes, to which sight and sound the Scythians have become so accustomed that they believe the Persians are still in camp (134–135; cf. VIII.19.2). The Scythians' credulity makes them trust the Ionian tyrants twice, not suspecting that the self-interest of the tyrants might not coincide with their own, or that the tyrants are not the same as the Ionians, whom they call the worst men but the best slaves (136–142). And for the same kind of reason they fail to find the Persians: they think the Persians are the same as themselves. Having destroyed the pasturage and caved in the wells, they looked for the Persians where they knew they would find new pasturage and water; but the Persians, in ignorance of the country, kept to their former route and escaped. They mistake what they themselves do for what the Persians would do. They do not know how to put two and two together.

It would be a mistake on our part, however, to deny to the Scythians every kind of intelligence; and lest we forget that a minimum of understanding necessarily belongs to man as man, Herodotus tells the story of the Amazons (110–117). The Greeks had conquered the Amazons at the battle of Thermodon, and all that were captured alive they took with them on board ship; but the Amazons surprised and killed them, and not knowing how to sail were carried by wave and wind to the shores of Lake Maeotis; there they pillaged the countryside and fought a tribe of Scythians, who thought they were young men until some were slain; the Scythians then made a guess as to how many they were and sent off an equal number of youths to imitate whatever they did. When the Amazons scattered "by ones and twos" to relieve themselves, the young men did likewise; and one of the women allowed herself to be seduced; but since they were unable to understand one another, she "signified with her hand that on the next day he should return to the same place and bring another, *indicating two,* and that she herself would bring another." Men always know how to count; they always know how to put one and one together. The Scythian imagination that tends to make everything that is different the same cannot fail to see this kind of other. Knowledge of two is not only more fundamental than any art, but even than the awareness of any sexual difference. The Amazons look like men even at close range, and after their marriage to the Scythians, they continue to do the same things as men. Even if they learn the Scythian language poorly and commit solecisms, they know how to convey at once the number two. That the number of Scythians is unknown—Herodotus does not know whether they are very many or very few—concerns their forgetfulness and not their ability to count. 'Aristotle' remarks that the Thracians only count to four, because like children they cannot remember any more, nor do they have any need of larger figures.[33] Perhaps it is not accidental, then, that only in Book IV does Herodotus refer to Pythagoras himself, "not the weakest wise man among the Greeks" (95.2; cf. II.81.2).

---

[33] Aristotle *Problemata* 911a1–4; cf. Plato *Epinomis* 978b7–e5.

The forgetfulness of the Scythians does not prevent them from strictly observing their own customs; and Herodotus tells two stories to show how they punish any infraction (76–82). Anacharsis left Scythia to travel; he both observed other men and displayed his own wisdom; and on his way home he saw at Cyzicus a magnificent festival of the mother of the gods; he vowed to that goddess that, if he returned safe and sound, he would sacrifice in the same way as he saw the Cyzicans were doing; but while he was fulfilling his vow, the king of Scythia shot him dead. Anacharsis becomes corrupted: he forgets his own gods. In thanksgiving for the preservation of his life, he fails to preserve Scythian customs. The memory of what is his own falls away at the sight of an alien festival, dedicated to a goddess whose rites are orgiastic. He adopts a worship that makes one forget oneself. His lack of sobriety in forgetting his own seems to be occasioned by the very spectacle he watches. What the Greeks say about Anacharsis is absurd precisely because they make him praise Spartan sobriety; and the Spartans are the very ones who attributed Cleomenes' madness to his learning to drink undiluted wine from the Scythians, and who disagree with all the Greeks who attributed his madness to some god (VI.84; cf. IV.75.2). The second story which Herodotus tells strengthens this interpretation. Scyles learnt the Greek tongue and letters from his mother; and even after becoming king he preferred Greek ways to Scythian; and he desired to be initiated into the cult of the Bacchic Dionysus. "The Scythians reproach the Greeks for Bacchic frenzy; for they deny the propriety of their *inventing* a god who drives men mad" (79.3). They reproach the Greeks for attributing to a god what wine does naturally; but we must not forget that the Scythian imagination is always intoxicated. Scythian forgetfulness resembles that induced by wine; and Anacharsis and Scyles merely replace one kind of forgetting with another. Both forget their own customs only to practice cults that make them forget themselves; but the Scythians take their revenge by not remembering Anacharsis. In this atmosphere of forgetting Herodotus playfully tries to remind the reader of what he has said. Not eight lines after he has described how Anacharsis died, he says: "But the man was destroyed just as was said previously"; and not six lines after his mention of Scyles' home: "of which a little while before this I made mention" ($\mu\nu\acute{\eta}\mu\eta\nu$ $\epsilon\hat{\iota}\chi o\nu$) (77.2; 79.2).[34] Herodotus' fear of forgetfulness applies even to the dead; he reminds Anacharsis of who killed him: "Let him know that he died at the hands of his brother." Even in Hades, it would seem, a Scythian might forget his own murderer (cf. 46.1).

---

[34]Cf. 81.2 (a reference to 52.3); 16.1 (a reminder of Aristeas the poet whose name occurs three lines before); 44.2 (to 42.2); 129.2 (to 28.4); 156.3 (to 153); 181.2 (to II.42.4); see further V.35.3 (to 35.2); VI.15.1 (to 8.1); VIII.88.3 (to 87.4); 119 (to 117.2).

We have noticed before that the quadruplicate division of Book IV resembles that of Book II; and we have tried to show to the reader how the five sections in its second and third parts could be interlaced in the same way as those of Parts II and III in Book II. In Egypt these parts dealt with Egyptian customs and history, while here they dealt with Scythia in its many disguises and the history of Darius' invasion. Paragraphs 32–35 were about the Hyperboreans, whose poetical existence brought us to see their counterpart in the first section of Part II (83–98), where the ways of making oneself immortal—from the literal Getae to the poetical Mandrocles—were taken up. Paragraphs 36–45 gave an outline map of the earth, whereas its corresponding section (99–101) described the Crimea and how it could be likened to many other peninsulas. Paragraphs 46–58 listed the eight major rivers of Europe, which seemed to bear on Herodotus' describing the customs of eight tribes in the third section of the third part (102–117). The fourth and fifth sections gave in turn an account of Scythian customs (59–75), and how the Scythians punished any violation of them (76–82); while paragraphs 118–129 showed the success of Scythian customs against Darius and 130–144 their failure. Earth and water dominate Parts II and III here just as they did in Book II but they dominate them in a different way. Earth and water there guided Herodotus' *logos* in a way that could only be called metaphorical: the stationary and the moving in Egyptian customs and history were traced to earth and water as the ultimate sources for these characteristics. Here, however, earth and water acted in Scythia in a way at once more literal and more poetic. The Scythians by their newness were both closer to these sources and farther away from them. They both mimicked and ignored these sources. We had suggested in Chapter II that this book might help us to answer the following question: How did Herodotus think earth and water in Egypt generated likenesses to themselves throughout her customs and history? I think the reader will see that Book IV only partially answers this question. Herodotus apparently thinks that the symmetry of the earth, suggested by the parallel courses of the Nile and Danube, guaranteed the power of earth and water to induce self-likenesses in thought; but he seems to have neglected to ask, even if we should grant this power to them, how a λόγος such as διάνοια or εἰκασία can arise from what is not a λόγος itself. A disproportion still exists between his account and that of which it is an account, and nothing in his *Inquiries* is adequate to remove it. Only in Book III, his Persian account, can a closer connection be found between Persian customs and Herodotus' own λόγος, for he does not there try altogether to reduce speech and reason to what is neither speech nor reason.

Herodotus has shown so far the correct and incorrect use of εἰκασία against the background of Scythia; and since it would be vain to repeat all of it when he comes to Libya, he merely sketches in enough so as to convince us that Libya and Scythia parallel each other. They are not, however, exactly

alike. There are things in Libya that can complete his *logos*. We are reminded
of the promise he had made to explain fully later the reason why Aprias came
to a bad end (145–167; II.161.3).[35] The reference occurs in the fourth part of
Book II, and it is now answered in the fourth part here. The longer answer
turns out to depend on the history of Cyrene's beginnings; but unlike the
Scythians' origins the number of variant accounts is less, although the agreement is not so great as Herodotus had found to exist in the later history of
Egypt.[36] Cyrene is a Greek city in a non-Greek land; its history is the first
account of something Greek (since Book I) that does not entirely look like a
digression. In presenting the three ways of his *logos*, Greece has not been
prominent; for it did not offer any but derivative principles. Its gods came
from either Egypt or Libya, except for six whose names they learnt from the
Pelasgians, a barbaric people (II.50; I.57; cf. IV.18O; 189). How the Greeks
understand the first things does not differ fundamentally from the barbarian
ways of understanding; but they are more difficult to discover in Greece, perhaps not only because of the derivative character of its customs but of its
nature as well. There was no evident cause at hand to explain why Elis could
not produce mules (30; cf. VIII.25–26). Herodotus deliberately digressed to
wonder about Elis' lack of mules. Greece would appear to be nothing more
than a digression from or an addition to the nature of things. And yet half of
his *Inquiries* is devoted to Greece and its war against the Persians. There
would seem to be a disproportion between the importance Greece has in
Herodotus and its importance for the understanding of the whole. How
Herodotus justifies this apparent disproportion will concern us later; but the
example of Cyrene will to some extent show how the Greeks depart from and
yet depend on barbarian principles.

Herodotus first indicates how closely Libya, Egypt, Scythia, and Greece
are joined. The ancestors of Cyrene's founders were descendants of Jason's
companions, who sailed to Colchis, originally an Egyptian colony on the east-
ern shore of the Black Sea; and the third generation from these Argonauts were
expelled from Lemnos by the very same Pelasgians who later abducted
Athenian women from Brauron, where a cult of Artemis-Iphigeneia was practiced, just as among the Taurians in the Crimea; and Jason is said to have been
carried off course to Libya.[37] Cyrene is the melting-pot of Egyptian, Libyan,

[35]Note that a Persian is now called Amasis (167.1); cf. II.182.1.
[36]Cf. pp. 63–64 *supra*.
[37]103; 145.2; 179; II.103–104.2; VI.138; VII.193.2; cf. Euripides *IT*
1462–1467, and the *Notice* of Grégoire), H., (ed. Budé), pp. 88–96. The
Median story should also be recalled: Medea of Colchis gave them their name
(VII.62.1); as well as that Theras is a descendant of Cadmus who searched for
Europa (147.4).

and Scythian things. Its founding suggests the Scythian account of their origins. They said that golden objects fell from heaven, which flashed fire when the two older brothers of Kolaxais approached them, but Kolaxais himself was able to take them home. To these celestial ποιήματα there here correspond the oracular verses of Delphi which, in both the Theran and Cyrenaic versions, prompted the sending of a colony to Libya. Scythian 'poetry' only signified its meaning through mute objects; Greek poetry is articulate and spoken: but both kinds of poetry are connected with founding. A founder and a poet make something that was not there before; and though they make different things, the example of Homer and Hesiod, who made the theogony for the Greeks, shows their intimate connection.[38]

Oracles sometimes speak enigmatically. Whereas the Therans and Cyrenaeans say that Battus received his name from his stammering and lisping, Herodotus believes he was given this name after he came to Libya, and that the oracle addressed him proleptically as Battus, the Libyan word for king. This lack of agreement about a name between Herodotus and the Therans and Cyrenaeans, as well as their own disagreement about the rest of Battus' history, seems to imitate his name: they do not hold the same speech about a man whose speech was impaired. And yet the Cyrenaeans and Herodotus agree that the name means something; but while Herodotus thinks it refers to the words of an oracle and the honor he later obtained, they think it stands for a deed. Herodotus merely translates the name and keeps it on the level of language, but the Cyrenaeans transform it into a fact. He sees metonymy where they see metaphor. They do with names what the Scythians did with signs. The Greek counterpart to the Scythian replacement of things with signs is their identification of words with deeds (cf. V.1; VI.63.3; 98.3). Many of the names in this section indicate the role which their bearers play in the story. Theras ("Hunter") leads a colony into Kalliste ("Most-beautiful"). where the descendants of a Phoenician Poekilus ("Many hued") live; but his son prefers to remain in Sparta, and Theras says "he will leave him as a sheep among wolves," a phrase that prevails so much over his original name that he is remembered only as Oeolykus ("Sheep-wolf"). We have only to recall the Neuri who became wolves once a year to see the difference in Greek and Scythian 'poetry.' Oeolykus' son was Aegeus ("Goat"). Battus ("Stutterer") was the son of Polymnestus ("Much-remembering") of the Minyan family Euphemides ("Auspicious"). Etearchus ("True-ruler") had a daughter Phronime ("Prudence"), whose stepmother became "in fact a stepmother" to her; but Themison ("Righteous") proved doubly righteous in discharging the oath he had sworn and in saving Phronime. The Libyans brought the Greeks to

---

[38]Cf. Plato *Republic* 378e7–379a4.

a place which was called the spring of Apollo, as though the name Cyrene (Κυρήνη was derived from the word for spring (κρήνη).[39] Several generations after the founding of Cyrene, when its king limped and was not sound of foot (ἀρτίπους)—a sign of tyrannical ambitions[40]—, the Pythian oracle bade them procure a reformer (καταρτιστήρ) from Mantinea ("Prophecy"). The Mantineans sent their most notable citizen Demonax ("Leader-of-the people"), who took away all the power from the king and gave it to the people. In the next generation Arcesilaus, whose mother was Pheretime ("Bearer-of honor"), demanded back the offices and honors of his ancestors; and when he was defeated in civil strife, his mother fled to Cyprian Salamis, where she was received by its ruler Euelthon ("Well-come"), who gave her everything rather than the army she craved; but when she did finally exact vengeance for the death of her son only to die a horrible death, her name then came to mean "Bearer-of-punishment." Now all these examples of omen-nomen may be called a kind of popular poetry; for poetry in the strict sense of verses also occurs—not only the oracles printed as such, but even the one that Herodotus inserts into his prose retains echoes of dactylic rhythm (163.2-3).[41] This prose oracle is a series of metaphors, one of which has not yet been clarified: the only clue is a Homeric simile.

Cyrene resembles Scythia in one other respect. It is composed of Greeks who have left their homeland and hence forgotten their own. Not far from Cyrene dwell the Lotus-eaters, whose food, Odysseus says, made three of his men forget their return; and Herodotus says an oracle predicts that the Spartans will one day settle an island nearby (177-178; cf. 179.3). Even without flowing rivers to imitate, Libya has the same character as Scythia. Its dryness and heat do not prevent its inhabitants from being like the Scythian and non-Scythian tribes (168-199). Twenty-four tribes, many of them nomadic, are mentioned. Most of them dwell along the coast or not far inland; and the rest

---

[39]But cf. Chamoux, F., *Cyrène sous la monarchie des Battiades* (Paris, 1952), pp. 126ff.

[40]Cf. V.92β1; Xenophon *Hellenica* III.iii.3; consider Oedipus.

[41]Herodotus himself sometimes writes metrically and uses poetic phrases; cf. 150.2: ἄγων ἀπὸ τῆς πόλιος ἑκατόμβην (the last word recurs only at 179.1); 150.3; 155.3; poetic words or phrases are: πῦρ αἴθω (145.4; the verb recurs only at 61.2); φυτεύω (145.3); βαρὺς ἀείρεσθαι (150.2); μῆχος (151.2; also at II.181.4); ἀμήτωρ (154.1); μαχλοσύνη (154.2; cf. 180). Note that πῦρ αἴθω is said by the Spartans, while Herodotus uses πῦρ ἀνακαίω (145.2); and while the Minyans say that the "sons of the heroes" (an epic phrase) of the Argo "planted" them, Herodotus says that they were the grandchildren of "the mariners of the Argo" (145.2).

live around hills of salt, placed at ten-day intervals from one another on a ridge of sand, which stretches from Thebes to the Atlas mountains. Such a linear symmetry does not differ in kind from the square country that the Scythians occupy; but sameness and likeness are perhaps even more prominent here. The first tribe, the Adyrmachidae, "use mostly Egyptian customs, but wear the same dress as the rest of the Libyans": the second, the Giligamae, "use customs similar to others"; and the Asbystae, who "imitate most of the Cyrenaeans' customs," are soon followed by the Bakales, who "use the same customs as themselves." The Bakales do not imitate the Cyrenaeans directly but at one remove. They resemble Aryandes, the Persian general, who agreed to give Pheretime an army; she pretended that her son had died because of his medism, and he pretended, as Herodotus thinks, that he was helping her for that reason, "but the expedition was sent to subjugate the Libyans," (165.3–167). Aryandes was later killed because "he made himself the equal of Darius"; for he "imitated" Darius in producing silver coinage as pure as the gold coinage Darius had wished to leave behind as a unique memorial of himself; but he was killed on the trumped-up charge of sedition. Pretext on top of pretext occasions Libya's conquest, and pretext on top of imitation Aryandes' death. The capture of Barka comes about through a similar kind of double deception (200–201). During the siege the Persians build tunnels under its walls, but a blacksmith discovers them by listening to the echo they throw back when struck, while the solid parts of the earth are "dumb." The Persians then resort to speech; they dig a ditch during the night and cover it with boards and a layer of earth; they come to an agreement with the citizens and swear that as long as that plot of ground stays the way it is, their oath will remain. The Barkans trust an oath that depends on the earth's stability just after they have discovered its hollowness. It does not occur to them to carry out the same test again; a false oath is more undetectable than an unspoken deception. They believe in an oath more than in echoes. They are like the Scythians who missed the Persians because they trusted the Ionian tyrants twice, and believed that the Persians were the same as themselves.

If square-faced animals in Scythia imitate the square land, a more extravagant imitation is found here. The Makae shave all round their heads but let a top-knot (λόφος) grow long in the middle; and in their land there is a hill (λόφος) thick with trees, while elsewhere it is bare; this crest is called the Graces', to whose locks of hair Homer once likens those of Euphorbus (175; *Iliad* XVII.51; cf. III.8.3). A custom that embodies a topographical peculiarity, whose name recalls a simile of Homer's, might well be thought the strangest mixture of the literal and figurative. The Machlyes go further. They hold a yearly festival, where their daughters, divided into two groups, fight one another with sticks and stones; and if any die they call them "false-virgins." They distinguish the true from the false by metaphor: the true virgin is inviolate or unwounded, hence the survivors are true virgins. The festival is in honor of an "indigenous goddess whom we call Athena"; and before the battle they adorn the most beautiful girl with Corinthian helmet and Greek armor, and carry her on a chariot around Lake Tritonis. Athena's epithet in Homer and Hesiod, "Tritogeneia," does not alone prompt Herodotus to compare the two goddesses, but Pisistratus' trick as well of dressing up in full armor a beautiful woman, whom he had carried on a cart through the city of Athens (180; I.60).[42] A deception in Greece is a festival in Libya. The Machlyes imitate Athena in one other way. "They say Athena is the daughter of Poseidon and Lake Tritonis, but blaming her father for something, she gave herself to Zeus, and Zeus made her his own daughter." Now this assertion is translated into custom, for their women are held in common, and in the third month, when a baby's features are fully formed, the men come together, "and to whomever of the men the baby resembles, it is believed to be his child." They would know Athena's true parentage in the same way that they know who is the father of each. Likeness among themselves finds its parallel among the gods.

The Nasamones also illustrate the mixture of the literal and the imagistic, which reveals as well two sources of the belief in gods, avenging justice and the ancestral (172.3).[43] They swear by those men who were said to have been the best and most just, grasping their tombs as they do so—bodily contact guarantees their oath; and they prophesy by sleeping on the tombs of their ancestors, and whatever dream comes then they use. Signs (σήματα) or images are trusted because they occur when they are near the tombs (σήματα) of their ancestors. Their own dreams are not their own but divine by contiguity; their body on these occasions becomes alien. So they hold their women in common, and every bride sleeps on the first night with all the guests, a practice that recurs—slightly altered in each—among the Adyrmachidae, Gindanes, Machlyes, and Ausees.[44] The body is common and not private: the Atarantes are the "only anonymous men of which we know" (184.1).[45] No one has his own name but all share in the common name of the tribe. They wipe out the difference between one man and another as effectively as those Scythian tribes who eat their fathers. While the Scythians achieve community more by cannibalism than by common marriage, there are no Libyan tribes which are cannibal, though so many hold women in common. They are not as "savage" as the Scythians. Although the Zauekes' women drive the chariots to war, they do

---

[42] πανοπλίη occurs only in these two passages.
[43] Cf. 190; Pomponius Mela I.46; also *Iliad* XXIII.326, 331.
[44] 166.2; 172.2; 176; 180.5.
[45] Cf. *Odyssey* VIII.552-554.

not fight and kill like the Sauramatian women; nor are the Garamantes (or Gamphasantes), who possess no weapons, considered sacred, which allows the Argippaei to be unarmed.[46] Libya and Scythia, then, share the same view of the body's commonness, and perhaps only the intense heat of Libya, which fosters rapid growth, favors the community of women rather than of flesh. The body, in any case, overrides all considerations of the soul. The Ethiopian troglodytes, who live underground, speak a language "unlike any other, but jibber like bats," a simile Homer had used of souls in Hades; and the Atlantes are said to eat nothing alive (ἔμψυχον), nor to see any dreams (183.4; 184.4; *Odyssey* XXIV.6-9).[47] Since they eat nothing with a soul, they do not dream: they do not even have that pale copy of the soul.

Having now shown how Scythia and Libya belong together, and what way of understanding they mostly follow, we should indicate how that way differs from and agrees with the Egyptians.[48] In Egypt Herodotus discovered doubleness, in Scythia and Libya images. In Egypt a single thing had to be looked at in two ways because it was composed of two different things; in Scythia and Libya a single thing had been multiplied again and again, so that its doubleness was the result of a likeness and not of an original two. similarity has no end to the number of copies it can make—the Crimea is like Attica, Italy, and many other places—; but Egyptian doubleness is not reproducible. It is a co-presence of two things in one and the same thing. Earth and water, for example, belong together in Egypt, which the Egyptians somehow preserve in their customs; but the Scythians are aware of water but not of earth, and the Libyans of earth and sand but not of water. Hence Book IV presents two countries and not one as Book II; for what holds together in Egypt becomes separated into Libya and Scythia. There the image almost replaces the original completely—everything takes on a made look; in Egypt the original persists along with its copy—something natural could more readily be found in Egyptian stories. Amasis sees more than Anacharsis. Amasis is able to combine sobriety and drunkenness; Anacharsis must forego one to discover the other. And yet Scythia is hardly touched by human works, while Egypt's almost rival the works of nature. Libya's and Scythia's lack of monuments not only allows

---

[46] 23.5; 116.2-117; 193.

[47] Cf. *Iliad* XXIII.100ss.; see IV.190.

[48] Cf. Hippocrates *de aer., aq., loc.* 18: περὶ δὲ τῶν λοιπῶν Σκυθέων τῆς μορφῆς, ὅτι αὐτοὶ αὐτοῖσι ἐοίκασι καὶ οὐδαμῶς ἄλλοις, ωὑτὸς λόγος καὶ περὶ τῶν Αἰγυπτίων, πλὴν ὅτι οἱ μὲν ὑπὸ τοῦ θερμοῦ βεβιασμένοι, οἱ δὲ ὑπὸ τοῦ ψυχροῦ (cf. 19). As Books II and IV present the southern and northern parts of the earth, so III brings together the east and west (Ethiopians and Indians); for their similarity see Arrian *Indica* 6.8-9.

their nature to show through more clearly, but their nature seems to affect the inhabitants more directly. Rather than the slow accumulation of customs and beliefs over ten or twenty thousand years, which inevitably makes them lose their original source, the Scythians remember about a thousand years back, and in this time they recall nothing except their 'poetic' origins. The multiplicity contained in a single Egypt is parcelled out among many tribes in Libya and Scythia, each of which retains and transforms a single facet of Egypt. Egypt's failure to reunite the doubleness she found in things becomes Libya's and Scythia's failure to separate the image from the thing imaged. The Egyptians know the statues of the gods do not represent the nature of the gods; the Scythians do not have statues because they cannot see the statue as a statue of something, any more than they can see feathers as an image of snow. Herodotus suggests the difference between them by the different uses he makes of Homer. Homer is a liar in Book II, he is a witness in IV. If he falls short of the Egyptians, he surpasses the Scythians and Libyans in preserving some semblance of the truth. His similes there become facts; in Egypt his poetry as a whole proves to be a copy of facts.[49] He stands between Scythian fancy and Egyptian history. It is a position that Greece itself might be thought to hold, for the Egyptians have no heroes, and the Taurians worship Iphigeneia the daughter of Agamemnon as a goddess (103.2).[50]

---

[49]Book IV's lack of "facticity" is suggested by the rarity of the word πρῆγμα; out of 210 occurrences only five are to be found here; all of them are instructive: 11.2; 46.2; 111.1; 126; 164.1. In spite of the differences of meaning, all five instances of πρῆγμα are occasioned by the pressure of external, foreign, or alien matters; compare the silence of Egypt.

[50]The sameness and difference of Euripides' *Helena* and *Iphigeneia in Tauris*, both of which owe much to Herodotus II and IV, present very vividly the sameness and difference between Books II and IV. For the sameness of their plots see Grégoire's *Notice* to *IT*, p. 85; and for their differences in light of Herodotus consider the following. Helen is in Egypt, an exact replica of herself is at Troy (32–36); Iphigeneia is among the Taurians, an animal replaced her at Aulis (28–30). Helen is doubled in body and image, Iphigeneia remains one and only "opinions" proclaimed her dead (176). Menelaus comes to Egypt with the image of Helen, but when it flies away he sets out to recover the true Helen; Orestes comes to Tauria to recover an image of Artemis that fell from the sky (Helen's image is made out of air and cloud, 584, 705), and he steals it along with Iphigeneia (87ss., 1315ss). Menelaus recognizes Helen by her likeness to herself once he learns that her image has disappeared; Orestes recognizes Iphigeneia by the images she once wove in tapestries and by the mementos of her tomb (814–826). Teucer, when he see Helen, believes her an "imitation" of herself (74); Orestes, when he goes mad, sees cattle as

Homer has appeared in Books II–IV as both Herodotus' authority and opponent; and he has appeared as both for the same reason. The Greeks called Homer "the poet," which means for Herodotus "the Greek poet." He somehow determined what the Greeks thought about war and peace, gods and men, the unjust and the just. As the source of what became the 'Greek tradition,' Herodotus looked to him to find out how the sources of things were understood in that source. He found that Homer had presented a man very much like himself. Odysseus "wandered very far, saw the cities of many human beings and knew their mind." Odysseus has no counterpart among the Trojans, and Achilles is merely the most outstanding hero among many other heroes, both Achaean and Trojan. Odysseus' uniqueness in Homer's poems seems comparable to the uniqueness of Greece, when seen in the light of Egypt, Persia, Scythia, and Libya. His uniqueness in the first Greek poet of whom we know seems to entitle him to be called the first Greek, the first to do what Herodotus presents as his own unique doing, viz., inquiry. Odysseus, however, as the source of something unique, partly stands outside the tradition of which he is the source. To see the tradition itself we should have to look at his offspring, just as Herodotus not only looks at Homer, the source of Greek understanding, but at the tradition which flowed from him, the Greece of his own day. Odysseus' offspring was Telemachus, whose story Homer tells in the first four books of the *Odyssey*, from which I should suggest Herodotus partly obtained his insight into the character of Greece. When Athena, disguised as Mentes, asks Telemachus who his father is, remarking that he looks very much like Odysseus, Telemachus replies: "My mother says that I am his, but I do not know, for no one has ever yet known his own descent" (I.215–216). Telemachus is unsure of his own parentage, but under the prompting of Athena

---

"imitations" which the Furies send (291–294). Helen voices the wish that she could be painted "as a statue is" to make herself uglier (262ss.); Iphigeneia regrets that she is not at home weaving images of Athena and the Titans (222ss.). Helen wishes to preserve her body from reproach, even if her name is infamous (66ss.); Orestes refuses to tell his name so that only his body will be sacrificed (504). Menelaus shows himself as somewhat proud of Troy's destruction (806–808); Orestes does not wish to see even a dream of Troy (518). Helen persuades the prophetic Theonoe (she has another name as well, 10–13) to lie about the presence of Menelaus; Iphigeneia has a dream that she wrongly interprets, likening the pillars of a house, which appear in her dream, to male children (42–58). Although the "excessive piety" of both kings allows the ruse each woman employs to work, a pious Taurian believes that Orestes and Pylades are gods (267–274). And, finally, in the *Helena* two gods (the Dioscuri) appear, in the *IT* Athena.

he does three things that assure him of it. He holds an assembly and visits both
Nestor and Menelaus, the three episodes that make up Books II–IV. At the
assembly, "he sat in the seat of his father and the old men yielded their place;
and among them the hero Egyptius began to speak, who was bent by old age
and knew ten-thousand things" (II.14–16). Telemachus assumes his father's
authority, and the old men of Ithaca immediately recognize his right to do so.
His legitimacy is confirmed in the most ancestral way, and by old men who are
the bearers of the ancestral. He then visits Nestor who confirms his legitimacy
in another way. "No one has ever," he says, "been willing to match himself
against him in counsel, for Odysseus in every kind of guile prevailed by far,
your father, if truly you are his offspring: awe grips me in beholding you.
Your words are quite like his ($\mu\tilde{\upsilon}\theta o\acute{\iota}\ \gamma\varepsilon\ \dot{\varepsilon}o\iota\kappa\acute{o}\tau\varepsilon\varsigma$), nor would you think that a
young man would speak so reasonably ($\tilde{\omega}\delta\varepsilon\ \dot{\varepsilon}o\iota\kappa\acute{o}\tau\alpha$)" (III.120–125). Nestor,
the speaker among the Achaeans, notes the resemblance of Telemachus to
Odysseus in his speech. He gives Telemachus another reason for believing his
mother. Telemachus last visits Menelaus, where he and Helen note another
resemblance. "Shall I lie or tell the truth?" asks Helen. "My heart prompts
me. Never yet I say have I ever seen anyone so like ($\dot{\varepsilon}o\iota\kappa\acute{o}\tau\alpha\ \tilde{\omega}\delta\varepsilon$), neither man
nor woman—awe grips me in beholding him, as he is like the son of great-
hearted Odysseus, Telemachus"; to which Menelaus replies, "So I think too,
my wife, as you liken him; for the feet are like his, his hands, the flash of his
eyes, his head, and his hair on top" (IV.140–150). The proofs of Telemachus'
legitimacy are now complete. He has inherited his father's ancestral authority,
his way of speaking, and his looks. This series cannot fail to remind us of
Egypt, Persia and Scythia-Libya, as Herodotus has described them. Egypt as
the home of the ancestral, Persia of speech, and Scythia-Libya of likeness are
all represented in Telemachus' triple discovery of his legitimacy, which
Herodotus seems to have detected as a parallel to his own procedure of discovering the three sources of Greece.[51] The parallel should not be thought of as

---

[51]Not accidentally the fourth book of the *Odyssey* bears a greater resemblance to Herodotus' IV than do the previous three books to Herodotus' three,
especially in likeness (Odysseus' deception at Troy; Helen's imitation of
voices; Menelaus' disguise of seal-skin' Proteus' metamorphoses; Athena's
sending an image in a dream to Penelope) and in memory-forgetfulness (recol-
lections of Odysseus; Helen's drug; Menelaus' forgetting to sacrifice: the verb
"remember" occurs 11 times, in no other book more than 4); and Herodotus
quotes line 85 at 29. It is also a remarkable coincidence that Lucretius presents
his doctrine in a threefold way, II being devoted to the nature of atoms, III to
the nature of the soul, and IV to that of images; and that V contains his
account of the origin of cities.

more than a parallel. It should not be thought of either as proving anything about Homer's purpose in the *Telemacheia* or as revealing Herodotus' complete intention. Herodotus goes much further in his analysis of the ancestral, speech, and likeness than Homer does, for whom these are only peripheral observations that have become central for Herodotus. He discovered, for example, the triple character of the Homeric gods in these three ways of understanding. Ancestral Egypt led him to see how Homer had abstracted from the ugliness—the sexuality—of Egyptian gods in order to make them beautiful; reasonable Persia compelled him to consider the Homeric gods in light of its cosmic gods; and imagistic Scythia and Libya allowed him to show the poetic and invented side of Greek gods. And yet, even though Herodotus goes much further than Homer in this and other ways, the parallel does suggest that as the *Telemacheia* is a necessary prelude to the story of Odysseus, so the first four books of Herodotus necessarily belong to his inquiries about Greece; and that as the sources from which Telemachus learns of his legitimacy are distinct and yet come together in Odysseus, so the triple understanding of things. which appears in three different kinds of customs, comes together in Greece. It is what we have set out to show in the sequel.

If we have correctly articulated Herodotus' threefold understanding of things, we can now compare it with another scheme of understanding that is much better known. Plato has Socrates present in the sixth book of the *Republic* an image of the world as a divided line (509d1–e5). The line is divided into two main parts, one representing the world of sensible things, the other the world of intellectual things; and each segment of the line is divided again, the first cut representing the world of images, the second that of sensible things themselves, which two cuts together constitute the world of opinion; and in turn the intellectual world has its first cut assigned to mathematical objects (e.g., the equal, the double, and the more and less), and the second and highest cut to the ideas.[52] Socrates calls the first cut εἰκασία, or the seeing of an image as an image, the second he calls πίστις or trust, the third διάνοια, or the understanding of a contradiction as a contradiction, and the fourth νόησις or intellection. Now the fourth book of Herodotus deals with εἰκασία, the third with πίστις, and the second with what I have called διάνοια.[53] But there is no book devoted to νόησις. There is no book devoted to νόησις because there are no νοητά for Herodotus. There are no 'ideas.' This crucial difference between Herodotus and Plato means that the διάνοια which governs

---

[52]Cf. Klein, J., Die griechische Logistik und die Entstehung der modernen Algebra, *Quellen und Studien a. Gesch. d. Math., Astron. u. Phys.* III (1936), pp. 71–79.

[53]See p. 66 *supra*.

Herodotus' understanding of Egypt does not apply as in Plato to the intellectual but to the sensible world. Book II presents the doubleness of things without transcending the realm of sense. How the doubleness in φύσις itself (εἶδος and δύναμις) gave rise to the imperfect understanding of that doubleness by the Egyptians is inexplicable because of the absence of νοητά. Herodotus' failure to see the νοητά illustrates what Plato regards as the fundamental weakness in pre-Socratic philosophy.[54] It is a weakness, however, that should not lead us to denigrate Herodotus' accomplishment. Herodotus attempted to draw aside the veil which νόμος casts over things as they are. Whatever inadequacies exist in Herodotus' attempt are nothing compared to the light he has shed on the seeing of things as they are.

Herodotus places the rest of Pheretime's story at the end of the fourth book (200–205). He indicates thereby that his "barbarian" λόγοι have come to an end, and that his Greek inquiries will begin. These inquiries revolve around Athens and Sparta—how and why they fought against the Persians. War becomes the most important single thing from now on. The deeds of war almost entirely obscure the facts of peace. The leisurely and digressive almost disappear in Herodotus' account. He becomes more orderly under the pressure of events. He is compelled to replace geography with what we call history; but geography does not altogether vanish, just as a temporal sequence continued through the first four books. That a change occurs, however, no one would deny. Herodotus indicates the change by referring to a Carthaginian report, on whose truth he cannot decide, though "anything might be" since he himself saw something similar in Zacynthus—this he says almost at the end of the fourth book; but near the beginning of the fifth he mentions the claim of the Sigynnae that they are a Median colony, saying that he cannot understand how that happened, though "anything might happen in a long enough time" (195.2; V.9.3). A geographical possibility is replaced by a temporal one. It demands a shift from sight to hearsay; or, rather, from a combination of seeing and hearing to hearing alone. We might more generally describe it as the change from λόγοι to ἔργα: theory to practice.[55] It is not wrong but rather vague to say this. Certainly war has played a minor role in I–IV; the customs of men and the nature of things appear more permanent than the battles of Marathon, Thermopylae, Salamis, and Plataea. These battles, which are in a way the foci of Books VI–IX respectively, happen in a political context. How the Greek cities, especially Athens and Sparta, responded to and were affected by them, is Herodotus' main concern. Political things in a narrow sense—cities and

---

[54]See pp. 204–206 *infra*.

[55]That war is to peace as deed is to speech, see *Iliad* II.796ss.; cf. VI. 492ss. with *Odyssey* I.358ss.

citizen—concern him: no longer the customs but the actions of people, which may include, of course, the establishment of laws. To prepare the way, then, for the Persian Wars, as well as to link these wars with what he has said, demands a book devoted to political things proper. It is the function fulfilled by the fifth book.

V. ATHENS

When Croesus asked Solon who he thought was the happiest of men, Solon had "truthfully" answered Tellus; and when he asked who was in second place, he answered Cleobis and Biton (I.30–32). Solon's descriptions indicate why he ranked them as first and second. While Athens was flourishing, Tellus had "beautiful and good" sons, all of whom in turn had children that were still alive; he himself had a modest fortune and met with a "most brilliant end of life"; for in a battle at Eleusis he routed the enemy and died "most beautifully"; and "the Athenians buried him where he fell at public expense and honored him greatly." Cleobis and Biton were Argives, whose livelihood was "adequate," and whose "bodily strength" had won them prizes in athletic contests. A story was told that when their mother had to appear at a festival to Hera, and the oxen to draw her cart were not at hand, they put themselves under the yoke and drew it forty-five stades to the sanctuary; for which they obtained the "best end of life," since "god showed in their case that it is better for a man to die than live." The Argive men "blessed the strength of the youths," the Argive women their mother; who "joyful at their deed and report" prayed to the statue of Hera to grant her sons, who had "honored her greatly," "what is best for a man to obtain." Cleobis and Biton were found dead in the sanctuary; and the Argives made images of them which they dedicated at Delphi, "thinking that they had proved to be the best men."

The first story turns on seeing, the second on hearing. Solon knows about Tellus—Croesus asked him whom he had seen most happy; he only knows a "story" about Cleobis and Biton, whose mother prayed because of the φήμη her sons received Tellus had "beautiful and good" sons; Cleobis and Biton were strong. Tellus had a "most brilliant death"; Cleobis and Biton had the best. Tellus was honored by the city and buried at public expense, for he had fought for the sake of the city. Cleobis and Biton had helped their own mother: nothing is said about who buried them. Tellus lived at a time when Athens was flourishing: nothing is said about Argos' prosperity—its preeminence had been at the time of Io's rape (I.1.2). Tellus dies in a political setting, Cleobis and Biton in a sanctuary. Tellus' death at a ripe age was the most brilliant from a civil point of view, Cleobis' and Biton's from the divine. Tellus freely chose to die, god gave to Cleobis and Biton their end. Tellus lived and died within the human horizon, the horizon of the city. He obtained everything that men regard as desirable. Cleobis and Biton obtained what god thought best for men. The city looks to the beautiful and fine things, the gods to the best (cf. *Homeri et Hes. Cert.* 70–87). The human good and the divine good are not the same. One restricts the ends to visible and tangible goods—money, beautiful children, grandchildren, public honor; the other cares more for non-political and even antipolitical ends; it says that life is not worth living. The difference in the way in which god regards man and man regards himself, as Solon understands it, proves to be that between man as man and man as citizen. Unless death is suffered for the sake of the city, the city cannot rank its own dead higher than life; the dead are buried outside the city. Its preservation and perpetuation must be the concern of the city; by its very existence it has already chosen the beautiful instead of the best. If any people were to choose the best, they could have no city; they would have no public good that could take precedence over the private advantage of a private death. It would exclude the possibility of any common effort, for so extreme a case of private gain could never be diverted into any public channel. Although Herodotus knows no tribes which maintain this view, the Thracians come closest to it in various ways; and in order to pose properly the political problem, he begins the fifth book with them (3.8).[1]

As the Thracians are the largest tribe after the Indians, Herodotus believes that they would be unconquerable and the strongest as well if a single man ruled them or each tribe thought the same as the others; but he believes that can never happen, and hence they must remain weak. Three tribes, whose customs depart from the rest of the Thracians', explain why they cannot unite; for their customs are merely extreme versions of those which the other Thracians have in common. The Getae believe that they can make themselves immortal. Among the Trausi the relatives weep at the birth of each new member of the family, considering "all the human sufferings" he must endure, but at his death they jest and are joyful, "considering that he is released from so many evils and is in perfect happiness." And in the third tribe, who dwell beyond the Crestonaei, the several women of each dead husband compete for the honor of being buried with him, and for those not chosen, "it is the greatest disgrace." Death is not a terror for these tribes; they are perfectly willing to quit this life for the sake of immortality, happiness, or honor. Their excessive courage, far from working in defense of the common, makes them oblivious to the needs of the common, as it reduces the private to so low a level that even the body is only by convention one's own. Among the other

---

[1] See pp. 108–109 *supra*.

Thracians the body is branded to signify noble birth, in the same way that horses are branded to indicate their breed and mark their ownership. They sell their children for export, nor do they prevent their daughters from having any man they choose; but as soon as the girls are married, they strictly guard them: Artemis is one of their gods. Since they do not pay for their children they do not consider them as theirs; but since they pay great sums for their wives, they acquire a price that makes them worth something. Money is the only recognized sign of the common. To be a tiller of the soil is most dishonorable, for he lives from what is his own; but to live from the booty of pillaging is noblest, for he appropriates from others what is not his own. To be idle is also noblest, for pillaging is an occasional occupation. The Thracians cannot be constant. They alternate between sloth and furious activity; they worship Dionysus and Ares. They do not know peace, any more than the Scythians, whose continual wandering has its only advantage in war. Their kings reverence Hermes as well, by whom they swear, for they are like Autolycus, Odysseus' grandfather, who learnt how to steal and swear falsely from Hermes.[2] When Aristagoras allows the Thracians to leave their city under a truce, they destroy him and his army instead (106.2). The common cannot be established where there is no trust, which even the dishonest Aristagoras takes for granted.

The Thracians are free but uncivilized (cf. VII.111). They are like the tribes of Europe (except the Scythians) who, Herodotus says, were the most uneducated and artless of men (IV.46; 95.2). The Scythians are excepted because "they have most wisely found the most important thing in human affairs." They have found how not to have cities and walls. They then can never be enslaved (cf. IV.142). Their freedom is bought at the price of their savagery, for their nomadic existence allows them no leisure for the cultivation of the arts. They are at one pole of human life, while Egypt and Asia are at the other: they are civilized but not free (cf. VIII.136.1). The Greek city alone combines freedom with the arts.[3] What this combination means is shown in the case of justice. The Greek city is neither as just as the Argippaei, who are sacred, unarmed, and never wrong anyone, nor as unjust as the cannibal Androphagi, who resemble the Cyclopes (IV.23.5; 106; *Odyssey* IX.112–115; cf. IV.26.2; 104). Herodotus indicates this mean at the very end of the fourth book, when the horrible death of Pheretime prompts him to remark: "The gods abominate the excessive punishments which human beings exact" (205: cf. II.120.5). The gods of the Greeks allow punishment but not excessive punishment. The gods because of their human shape do not allow human sacrifice,

---

[2]*Odyssey* XIX.394–398.
[3]Cf. Aristotle *Politica* 1327b23–36.

which both the uncivilized Scythians and the civilized Persians practice (IV.71.4; 72.2; VII.114.2; 180). The delicate balance between extremes demands therefore a longer account than the more self-evident nations that surround it.

If the Thracians, then, represent a non-political way of life,[4] the tyrant may be considered to be its representative within a political context. His exclusive concern with his own private advantage and security at the expense of his subjects resembles the Thracians' customs, which look only to each family or tribe. Herodotus' second way, then, of bringing to light the common is to discuss its subversion by tyranny.[5] Given his choice of anything, Coes, "because he was a private man," chose to be tyrant of Mytilene; while Histiaeus, already the tyrant of Miletus, wished to found a city in Thrace (11; cf. 42.2).[6] The desire to become the founder of a city, to combine one's own ambitions with the common good, must be ranked higher than the desire to establish a tyranny. Histiaeus, however, found it impossible to sustain this nobler ambition (23–24). He preferred the private friendship of the king to being a founder, and he later occasioned the ruination of Ionia in order to escape from that preference (35.4). The private finally won out completely over the common: Histiaeus tried to become tyrant of Miletus once more, and when he failed became a pirate (VI.5). Two brothers, who wished to rule over the Paeonians, tried to be founders and tyrants at the same time (12–15). Knowing that the Paeonians would resist any domination in their own land, they enlisted the support of Darius, who ordered his general Megabyzus to bring them over into Asia. The Paeonians' will to resist was broken as soon as they learned that their undefended cities had been captured—an indication of why Herodotus attached such importance to the Scythians' lack of cities. Once the bases of their unified action were lost, they scattered "each group by themselves" and surrendered. The sense of being a whole proved too weak to sustain the loss of their individual cities. How the common can be forgotten, even if it once was necessary to establish a way of life, the lake-dwellers illustrate (16).[7] They dwell on piles that "all the citizens long ago must have setup," but now "by convention" a man sets up three piles for each wife (each has many wives), so that the originally common effort is no longer needed to maintain their separate

---

[4]Cf. Thucydides II.97.6 and Gomme's note ad loc; Aristotle *Politica* 1324b1–12.

[5]τύραννος occurs in V 26 times out of 65; τυραννίς 9 out of 36; and τυραννεύω 8 out of 27.

[6]Cf. also IV.137; 147.3; VII.164.1.

[7]Heliodorus borrows the details for his account of a pirates' stronghold in marshes from here (*Aethiopica* I.5–6).

dwellings. Fish are abundant enough to dispense with any common labor, and since only a single bridge connects them with the mainland, they do not have to band together for mutual defense.

After presenting the anarchy of the Thracians, the illegality of tyrants, and the private way of life among the lake-dwellers, Herodotus turns to the common (17-22).[8] Amyntas surrenders to Darius and entertains seven Persian notables, who when drunk claim that Persian custom allows both concubines and wives to be present at feasts; they insist that Amyntas follow their custom, and Amyntas submits, though he protests that it is contrary to Macedonian usage; but out of fear he even allows the Persians to touch and kiss the women. His son Alexander, however, "because he was young and innocent of suffering," cannot put up with it; he orders his father out of the room, replaces the women with young men, who kill the Persians. Alexander later obtains the silence of Bubares, who conducted the search for the missing ambassadors and their retinue, by paying him great sums of money and marrying his own sister to him. The indignation of a young man successfully defends the law—it is a private defense of the common; but he must sacrifice the private in order to conceal the murders. He opposes to the lust of the Persians his sense of injustice; their illegitimate desire, which even makes them lie about a Persian custom, makes him angry. Against their ἔρως his own θυμός or ὀργή is aroused. Herodotus uses ἔρως in only two senses: sexual desire and the desire for tyranny;[9] In every instance of sexual desire (except one) it is illegitimate: Mycerinus is supposed to have loved his daughter, Cambyses his sister, Ariston the wife of another man, Xerxes the wife of his brother, and later the wife of his son; while Candaules' love of his own wife proved so strong that he broke Lydian custom, which led to his own death and Gyges' tyranny. There is a story told in Book V, for whose truth Herodotus will not vouch, that Pausanias married the daughter of Megabates, having the ἔρως to become tyrant of Greece" (32). Ἔρως, then, designates all private and illegal desires, whether they break the law in a sexual or political way. Alexander must choose between the private and the public; he cannot keep together his own

---

[8]In the so-called gardens of Midas near where Alexander's ancestor founded the Macedonian kingdom (VIII.138.2), Silenus told Midas that it was better not to be born (Plutarch *Consol. ad Apoll.* 115b-e.

[9]Sexual desire: I.8.1bis; II.131.1; III.31.2; VI.62.1; IX.108.1,2; 113.2; desire for tyranny: I.96.2; III.53.4; V.32 (cf. 92 1-3; also I.61.1); see Plato *Republic* 573c7-575a7. Thucydides digresses to narrate the ἐρωτικὴ ξυντυχία of Harmodius and Aristogeiton after Alcibiades is suspected of tyrannical ambitions, and an ἔρως has swooped down on all the Athenians to sail to Sicily (VI.15.3,4; 24.3; 54.1).

feelings for his sister and his wish to maintain the common law. The consequences of his anger compel him to sacrifice his sister. Anger, as the immediate awareness of some wrongdoing, can only be satisfied by the punishment of the wrongdoer; but punishment may also act as a deterrent. Sisamnes was flayed for preferring money to justice, and his skin was stretched over a throne, on which Cambyses made his son sit in judgment, so that he would always be reminded of his father's fate (25). The attraction of private gain—it is a non-political kind of ἔρως (cf. Plato *Lgs.* 870a1-6)—so easily overrides the concern for justice that only the harshest punishment can check it. Otanes not only learns to abide by the common but to despise his father as well. All filial affection must yield to the law, just as Alexander was compelled to give up his sister. In θυμός, then, Herodotus sees the human basis for the maintenance of public justice. That it does not necessarily lead to the maintenance of justice he indicates by beginning this book with the Thracians, whose θυμός is so excessive that it produces anarchy rather than order. And yet he begins with them precisely because of their excessive θυμός, for it sets the underlying theme of Book V: the articulation of the private and the public in light of the distinction between ἔρως and θυμός.[10] Moreover, it now becomes clearer why Herodotus concluded Book IV with the rest of his Cyrenaic story (200-205). The brutal revenge Pheretime exacted lies beyond the civil order. She satisfied a private wrong but gave the Persians an excuse to conquer Libya. The common counted far less than the private. She made the same choke as Harpagus, who to revenge the murder of his son conspired with Cyrus against Astyages, and thus lost the Medes their empire and reduced them to slavery (I.129-130.2). But perhaps nothing more clearly indicates the change from the private to the public than the description of Periander in the first, third, and fifth books.[11] In Book I he warns his fellow-tyrant Thrasybulus of a Delphic oracle (he is one of the seven wise men); in Book III he engages in a private quarrel with his son about the murder of his wife; but now we learn of his cruelty to citizens—Thrasybulus instructed him—and complete shamelessness. Herodotus seems deliberately to have suppressed any consideration of Periander as a tyrant in a political sense before he turned to the question of the common good.

Civil strife is the conflict of private interests, and usually between the rich and the poor.[12] It means that the concern for the κοινόν has disappeared. After Miletus had suffered from civil strife for two generations, the Milesians asked the Parians to reform their city (28-29). They sent their best men who,

---

[10]Cf. Plato *Republic* 435e3–436a3; *Lgs* 731a2–d5.
[11]92ζ1-η5; I.20–24; III.50–53; cf. V.95.2.
[12]30.1; IV.11.2–4; VI.91.1; VII.155.2–156.

observing the economic disorder, asked permission to look at the country-side; and whoever's land was well tilled they wrote down his name, and since these were few they appointed them rulers of the city, "for they thought, they said, that these will take as much care of the public things (τὰ δημόσια) as of their own (τὰ σφέτερα)." To manage a household well does not differ from the management of a city.[13] The same ends, at least in terms of prosperity, apply to both; but that the privately just may coincide with the common good seems to depend on chance. The Naxians escape enslavement because of this chance coincidence (33.2-34). Megabates, the commander of the Persian fleet, punishes a captain (his name means "Puppy") for having left his ship unguarded; and Aristagoras' reply so much enrages him that he warns the Naxians of their danger. Only by accident does the sense of personal injury help a people; often it works against a people's good; for the sense of injustice might be unjustified and politically dangerous. Θυμός looks both to the public and the private good, and the political problem might be said to be to enlist it on the side of the public.[14] Aristagoras' fear of punishment, when he fails to fulfill his promise, and Histiaeus' resentment at being kept a virtual prisoner in Sousa combine to foment the Ionian revolt, whose origin in private matters was bound to make it fail (35-38; VI.10). Its appearance of being for the common good is only an appearance. Aristagoras only in name put down the tyrants in the Ionian cities (37.2).

One further point, however, does emerge from Megabates' action. He is moved to warn the Naxians not so much by what Aristagoras does as by what he says. His anger is aroused by words. Xerxes later tells the Lydian Pythius, whose request angered him, the reason: "Be well assured that θυμός dwells in the ears of men, which if it hears good things fills the body with pleasure, but if it hears the opposite swells up (in rage)" (VII.39.1; cf. VII. 160.1). Anger may be blind; it is not deaf, which perhaps most sharply distinguishes it from ἔρως. It pays some attention to λόγος. Xerxes sees only how speech arouses anger or pleasure, he does not consider how θυμός becomes articulate through speech itself. He knows that it is not deaf; he does not know that it is not mute, which his own speaking demonstrates. When Gorgo, whose name means "Fierce" or "Spirited," at the age of eight or nine heard Aristagoras offering more and more money to her father Cleomenes, she finally spoke: "Father, the stranger corrupts you, unless you take leave" (51; cf. I.85; 47.2). The sense of right and wrong, then, seems to be based on the intimate connection between λόγος and θυμός. Aristotle appeals to human speech as one of the proofs that man is by nature a political animal, and Herodotus would, I think, understand

---

[13]Cf. Aristotle *Politica* 1252a7-16.
[14]On θυμός in Homer see Benardete, S., *Hermes*, 91, 1963, pp. 5-12.

their connection in a similar way; for Aristotle goes on to say: "Now sound indicates the painful and the pleasant, and hence other animals possess it (for so far has their nature come, to have an awareness of pain and pleasure and to indicate them to each other), but speech is for making clear the advantageous and harmful, and consequently the just and unjust; for this is what is peculiarly human vis à vis the other animals, that he alone has an awareness of good and bad, just and unjust, and the rest."[15] Herodotus would attribute this fundamental awareness of the just and unjust to θυμός, whose receptiveness to and use of speech Xerxes affirms and shows. "Anger," Aristotle says again, "seems to listen to λόγος to some extent, but to mishear it, as do hasty servants who run out before they have heard the whole of what one says, and then muddle the order, or as dogs bark if there is but a knock at the door, before looking to see if it is a friend; so anger because of the warmth and hastiness of its nature, though it hears, does not hear an order, and springs to take revenge. For λόγος or imagination makes clear that there has been an insult or a slight, and anger, reasoning as it were that this must be fought against, bolts up straightaway."[16] Whether Herodotus would agree exactly with Aristotle here does not matter as much as his recognition that θυμός not only responds to speech but speaks itself. It not only expresses itself in an act of revenge but in the establishment of laws, the public speeches, as it were, of a city. When one Athenian returned from a disastrous expedition against Aegina, the wives of those who died there "thought it a terrible thing that he alone should be saved"; they stabbed him to death with the pins of their dress, each one asking him all the while where her own husband was; and the Athenians thought no deed more terrible than this, so they passed a law that commanded women to wear Ionian dress, which is not fastened with pins; while the Argives and Aeginetans established a contrary law that pins should be extended half their length (87.2-88; cf. I.82.7-8). Indignation dictates the Athenian law, contemptuous satisfaction the Argive and Aeginetan law. The wish to punish someone or avenge some deed supplies the ground for certain laws, and the wish to honor someone or praise some deed supplies the ground for others. In the same root word are gathered together retribution (τίσις), punishment

---

[15]*Politica* 1253a7-18; cf. Sophocles *Antigone* 354-356, where the three things man has taught himself (φθέγμα, ἀνεμόεν φρόνημα, ἀστυνόμοι ὀργαί) contrast with the three kinds of animals he overcomes (342-346), witless birds (φρόνημα), dumb fishes (φθέγμα), while θηρῶν ἀγρίων ἔθνη show how great a problem is posed by ἀστυνόμοι ὀργαί.

[16]*EN* 1149a25-b18, partly quoted in Ross' translation; cf. Plato *Timaeus* 70a2-d6; see pp. 69-70, 81 *supra*; Hirzel, R., *Themis, Dike, und Verwandtes*, pp. 416-418.

(τίνομαι), revenge (τιμωρίη) and honor (τιμή), all of which play so important a role in V and later books. If anger is the more obvious side of θυμός, its opposite, the wish to be superior, cannot be ignored. This double character of θυμός, its awareness of good and bad that leads to praise or blame in speech, allows us to call it the political passion.

Aristagoras goes to Sparta and Athens to obtain help. We are instantly reminded of Croesus' inquiry about them in Book I, for Herodotus now begins Athenian and Spartan history again at the moment he had there broken it off (39–48; 55–65; I.56–69.1). Croesus had chosen Sparta, without asking Athens, because of its piety; but now Aristagoras asks both, and Sparta refuses while Athens agrees to help. An oracle had told Croesus to solicit the help of the greatest Greek city; Aristagoras knows by himself to which cities he must appeal. The shift to the common that the Ionian revolt at least pretends to represent seems to entail the rejection of oracular counsel. We can easily observe this shift in the difference between the ways Cyrene and Miletus settled their internal problems. Whereas the Cyrenaeans had asked Delphi how to guard against the tyrannical ambitions which they thought Battus' limp signified (IV.161.2–3),[17] the Milesians now asked the Parians to reform their city already "diseased" with civil strife. The Mantinaeans had sent their "most notable" citizen, the Parians sent their "best" men. Demonax had reserved sanctuaries and priesthoods for Battus; nothing is said about those of Miletus. But Delphi still retains a greater hold over Sparta than over Athens, just as before the Spartans' obedience to oracles pleased Croesus more than Pisistratus' fraudulent use of divine support. Herodotus' digressions on the history of Athens and Sparta before Aristagoras came show the same contrast they possessed in the time of Croesus. This contrast, however, is now presented in terms of the private and the public.

Anaxandrides married the daughter of his own sister, who, pleasing though she was to him, had borne no sons. The Spartan ephors, in fear lest one line of kings die out, ordered him to divorce her and marry another. Anaxandrides refused on grounds that testify to his affection for his wife but show no concern with the needs of Sparta. The ephors then allowed him to have two wives, "acting in a completely un-Spartan way." As a result of this violation of custom, not only did the second wife bear the slightly mad Cleomenes, but the first wife, supposedly barren, now bore Dorieus, who proved to be outstanding in manly virtue (ἀνδραγαθίη). There is a disproportion between what convention demands and nature produces. The legally good king should be the naturally good king; and if the ephors had not compelled

---

[17]καταρτιστήρ at V.28 is surely meant to recall its only other use at IV.161.2.

Anaxandrides to have two wives, this condition would have been fulfilled; or if Anaxandrides had been willing to divorce his first wife, the legal would have been preserved and, the story implies, Cleomenes would not have been mad. As it is, the legal on top of the illegal is preserved, but the naturally better Dorieus is lost. Monarchy rests, then, on the chance coincidence of nature and convention, or of the private and the public. And it is this chance coincidence that oracles seem to work against rather than sanction.

Dorieus becomes so indignant at the injustice of Spartan law, which establishes the first-born as king without any regard for merit, that he leads a colony to Libya. If he cannot be king, he wishes to be a founder. His anger makes him fail to consult the oracles at Delphi or "do any of the customary things." In the third year of his settlement he is expelled from the "most beautiful region" of Libya. He is then advised to consult Delphi about settling in Sicily in accordance with ancient oracles that foretold the colonization of Eryx. Herodotus now gives a double account, the Sybarites saying that he helped Croton, the Crotonians insisting that no alien except a soothsayer aided them. Herodotus leaves it open which story the reader should accept, for one questions the efficacy, the other the goodness of oracles. The Sybarites claim Dorieus established a temple to Athena near Sybaris, and they regard his later death as the greatest witness, for if he had not disobeyed the oracles, he and his army would not have perished. The Crotonians claim, however, that the honors they gave to the Elian soothsayer that he helped Croton, the Crotonians insisting that no alien except a soothsayer, who did not help them with an army, they gave so much, they would have honored Dorieus still more.[18] If we accept the Crotonians' version, that Dorieus did not help them and hence did not disobey the oracles, we cannot explain his failure in Sicily, where the Phoenicians and Egestans defeated him, as we might have explained his failure in Libya by his disregard of oracles and customary rites. He would have failed twice because of purely human considerations. If, however, we accept the Sybarites' version, that Doricus helped Croton and hence suffered defeat because he disregarded oracles, we are confronted with the two stories that immediately follow, which hardly warrant a belief in the goodness of the divine. Euryleon, the lone survivor from Dorieus' expedition, attempted to become tyrant of Selinus, and after ruling for a short time was killed at the altar of Zeus Agoraeus, which he had sought as a refuge (cf. 71). Zeus Agoraeus would appear not to take care of his suppliants; to which we might object that as the guardian of popular assemblies a tyrant was most fittingly

---

[18]The Sybarites call Telys a king, the Crotonians a tyrant; cf. 190.1: ἔλεξαν οἱ τύραννοι τῆς Κύπρου with 110: διέτασσον οἱ βασιλέες τῶν Κυπρίων.

killed at his altar. We would thus assume that the gods only look to the common good and never favor its enemies. In the second story, however, we learn that Philippus followed Dorieus "with his own trireme and at his own expense"; and upon his death the Egestans propitiated him as a hero because of his beauty, "being the most beautiful Greek of his time." That beauty should even find favor in the eyes of the enemy while the manly excellence of Dorieus fails speaks against the belief in the gods' partiality for the common good. The gods who as beautiful themselves support the beautiful are incompatible with the gods as the defenders of justice. The public enterprise of Dorieus finds less support in the divine than the private undertaking of Philippus, whose personal beauty suffices to make him a hero; just as later the tallness of the Persian Artachaeas, and perhaps the beautiful burial Xerxes gives him, makes him a hero at Acanthus, for an oracle commands it (VIII.117). Oracles seem indifferent to the common good. Not only do the Amathusians sacrifice to Onesilus as hero, even though he besieged them, but the Athenians only enlist the support of Sparta against the Pisistratids by bribing the oracle at Delphi, "for the Spartans think the commands of a god more important than the obligations of men" (63.2; 114). Only when the oracle of Delphi lies does it back freedom against tyranny.

Kings and tyrants have dreams that can be interpreted: it is hardly possible that a dream come to all the citizens. Dreams belong to the private world of sleep. "There is one common order for those who are awake," Heraclitus says, "but everyone when asleep turns away to his own" (Fr. 89). Herodotus brings out the same point by juxtaposing the dream Hipparchus had the night before his death and the importation of the Phoenician alphabet into Greece by the ancestors of Harmodius and Anstogeiton (55–61). Hipparchus' dream was "rather vivid"—a tall and beautiful man appeared to him—but the verses he spoke were "enigmatic" one line urged him to endure "intolerable" sufferings, the other warned him that no one unjust will not pay retribution. Hipparchus consulted dream-interpreters, but either on their advice or on his own went through with the procession in which he was killed. He could have hardly worked out that the first line referred to himself and the second to his brother Hippias, who for four years thereafter was harsher than he had been before. The dream is necessarily obscure; it is not publicly knowable; it has a different status from the inscriptions Herodotus himself has seen written in "Cadmean letters." Even if he cannot tell whether the Scaeus who dedicated a tripod might not have been someone else with the same name as the son of Hippocoon—a remark that obviously applies to the other two inscriptions as well (cf. 65.4, II.98.2; IX.95)—these inscriptions are still public and open. Not what the verses mean, as in the case of Hipparchus' dream, but whose they are can be disputed. Herodotus' knowledge increases once the public domain is entered: διδασκάλια, sciences and arts, are brought in along with letters. He can disagree with the Gephyraei, who claim to have been originally from Eretria, and he can explain why the Ionians still call paper "skins." The alphabet, like the map Aristagoras uses to persuade Cleomenes, adds a certainty that was lacking before, when Herodotus could not understand how the Sigynnae could have been originally Medes, or how *sigynnae* could come to mean shopkeepers (9.3). If Doneus had left an inscription at the temple of Athena, which the Sybarites put forward as one of their proofs that he aided Croton, Herodotus would not have been forced to leave it open whether they or the Crotonians were correct. As soon as these is writing, the possibility of exact knowledge arises: of the past and of the laws. No longer 'dumb' custom that is only remembered and practiced, but laws that are articulate and decided upon. This digression, then, on the origin of the Greek alphabet calls to our attention the importance of writing for the politically common: Herodotus had to refute a clan's genealogy in order to connect the slaying of tyrants with the introduction of letters. Moreover, the alphabet not only allows for private dedications—Herodotus records here a tripod for Amphitryon's vengeance, Scaeus' boxing, and Laodamus' monarchy—but for the first time an inscription is dedicated by a whole city: "the sons of the Athenians" gave a tithe to Athena on defeating the Boeotians and Chalcideans (77.4).[19] Freedom—the Thracians of Europe—and the arts—the Phoenicians of Asia—come together in Athens.

We can see how closely the sacred and private things are related, if we consider that the Gephyraei, whose ancestors introduced the alphabet into Greece, were excluded from "a few things not worth mentioning" when the Athenians admitted them as citizens (57.2). These unimportant things were undoubtedly certain sacred rites, just as the Gephyraei maintained certain sacred rites in which no Athenian can share. Athens, as a political entity, is not founded on the sacred; indeed, Athenian democracy becomes powerful precisely because of its abandonment of divine sanctions. That a tension exists in Athens between the divine and the civil becomes clear much later,[20] but

---

[19]Cf. Justinian *Inst.* I. Tit. II.10: *et non ineleganter in duas species ius civile distributum videtur; nam origo eius ab institutis duarum civitatum, Athenarum scilicet et Lacedaemonis, fluxisse videtur. in his enim civitatibus ita agi solitum erat, ut Lacedaemonii quidem magis ea quae pro legibus observarent, memoriae mandarent; Athenienses vero ea quae in legibus scripta comprehendissent, custodirent;* also Andocides *de mysteriis* 85–87; Plutarch *Lycurgus* 13.1–3.

[20]Cf. VIII.143.2–144; IX. 7; and the phrase οὔτε ἡ πόλις οὔτε τὰ ἱρά (VI.25.2; cf. 32; 96) with οὔτε τὰ ἱρὰ οὔτε τὰ ἴδια (VI.9.3.; cf. 13.2; VIII.109.3).

Herodotus is now more concerned with its purely political actions: the over-throw of the Pisistratids and the establishment of democracy (63–71; cf. VI.131.1). Unlike the sacred things that are not worth mentioning, Herodotus thinks he must tell all that the Athenians, "once free, did or suffered worthy of narration."

The Spartans would not have succeeded in expelling the Pisistratids, had not an "evil coincidence" occurred; their children were captured as they were being sent outside the country. "Their affairs were disordered" and they agreed to depart on condition that their children be returned on payment of a certain amount of money. The private interests of tyranny make it depend entirely on private things (cf. I.61.1–2). With the loss of successors disappears the possibility of its preservation. The family is its only legitimate support, for it looks rather to foreign help—the Pisistratids urge both Darius' and Xerxes' invasion—and to its own foreign origins than to anything native: Pisistratus was named for the son of the Homeric Nestor. A poetic name (i.e. not only alien but invented) belongs to the same region as the tricks of Pisistratus, who dressed up a woman as the goddess Athena. That private names now have less significance, once the common is established, the names Isagoras ("Equality-of-speech"), who attempts to become tyrant of Athens, and Aristagoras ("Best-in-speech"), the son of Molpagoras ("Song-speech"), who aims at tyranny under the cloak of freedom, suggest; whereas Aetion ("Eagle"), the father of the tyrant Cypselus ("Box") and the husband of Labda (the letter lambda to signify her limp), had a name that an oracle predicted would prove significant. And yet names can be invented for the sake of democracy as well. Herodotus brings this out by contrasting the different aims to which Clisthenes the Athenian and his maternal grandfather (another Clisthenes), the tyrant of Sicyon, put the power of names. Being at war with the Argives the tyrant Clisthenes first stopped the Homeric poems from being recited, for they celebrated Argos and the Argives so much; second, he wiped out the cult of the native hero Adrastus and replaced him with the Theban Melanippus, giving to him all of Adrastus' former honors except the tragic choruses, which he assigned to Dionysus, a god also connected with Thebes; and third, he changed the names of the Sicyonian tribes, which were the same as the Argive, and contemptuously called them after the pig, ass, and porker, except for his own tribe, whom he called "Rulers-of-the-people." These names had so great an effect that it took sixty years after his death before the Sicyonians recovered their pride and gave themselves more appropriate names. Clisthenes the Athenian, on the other hand, enlarges the number of tribes from four to ten, removes their Ionian names, and replaces them with the names of native heroes, except for the one he calls after Ajax of Salamis. While the tyrant gives meaningful names, the democrat gives names that have a local rather than an etymological significance; and while the tyrant attempts to alienate the people from themselves, the democrat imposes on them a stronger sense of belonging to Athens. Not poetry and choruses but only names suffice to differentiate the people of Attica from other Ionians and give them a separate identity (cf. 3). The change of names, then, serves a double function: to break all ties with any other city and enlarge the power of the Athenian people, since they would now all belong to equally native tribes, over against the claims some might have had of nobler birth.[21] This double function tends toward a single end: the conquest of other cities. "Equality of speech makes clear not only in one respect but in every way that it is a weighty thing ($\chi\rho\hat{\eta}\mu\alpha$ $\sigma\pi\sigma\upsilon\delta\alpha\hat{\iota}\sigma\nu$), if the Athenians under a tyranny were not better in war than any of their neighbors, but once rid of tyrants proved by far to be the first. This makes it clear that they were willingly base as long as they were held down, working as though for a master, but when they became free, each one was eager to work for himself" (78; cf. 97.2; III.80.6). Once the common master has been removed, everyone strives for mastery, but in common they strive for mastery over the enemy (cf. 66; VIII.79.3). "The most beautiful name— equality before the law," which Otanes had given as the first reason for choosing democracy, becomes, in Herodotus' own view, the excellence of equality of speech. Thus Clisthenes, by equalizing the share which each Athenian had in the names of indigenous heroes, made it possible for each one to be eager to work for himself. Community of speech and name permitted everyone to work for his own advantage. Private acquisition and public aggrandizement in war seem to go hand in hand (cf. VI.109.3). Themistocles perhaps best exemplifies the good and bad aspects of this pairing (VIII.4.2-5; 109.5-110; 112.3). While Aristagoras cannot convince Cleomenes to succor the Ionians, because of his Spartan lack of daring, nor bribe him, because of the chance remark of a child, he does persuade the Athenians. It is easier to hoax thirty thousand than one, if the thirty thousand believe they will share in the booty of a common enterprise (97.2). What now distinguishes Athens from Sparta and her allies is its unanimity. The triple-pronged attack that Cleomenes launches— Peloponnesian, Boeotian, and Chalcidean forces invade Attica at three separate points—fails both on the common and private levels (74-77), while Athenian success is based on the coincidence of public and private interest. Cleomenes gathers a Spartan army together without explaining his reasons. His sense of being outraged "in words and deeds" compels him to punish the Athenian

---

[21]Cf. I.143.2-3; 146.2; 147-148; Aristotle *Ath. Pol.* XXI.4: $\kappa\alpha\grave{\iota}$ $\delta\eta\mu\acute{o}\tau\alpha\varsigma$ $\grave{\epsilon}\pi o\acute{\iota}\eta\sigma\epsilon\nu$ ($K\lambda\epsilon\iota\sigma\theta\acute{\epsilon}\nu\eta\varsigma$) $\grave{\alpha}\lambda\lambda\acute{\eta}\lambda\omega\nu$ $\tau o\grave{\upsilon}\varsigma$ $o\grave{\iota}\kappa o\hat{\upsilon}\nu\tau\alpha\varsigma$ $\grave{\epsilon}\nu$ $\grave{\epsilon}\kappa\acute{\alpha}\sigma\tau\omega$ $\tau\hat{\omega}\nu$ $\delta\acute{\eta}\mu\omega\nu$, $\acute{\iota}\nu\alpha$ $\mu\grave{\eta}$ $\pi\alpha\tau\rho\acute{o}\theta\epsilon\nu$ $\pi\rho o\sigma\alpha\gamma o\rho\epsilon\acute{\upsilon}o\nu\tau\epsilon\varsigma$ $\grave{\epsilon}\xi\epsilon\lambda\acute{\epsilon}\gamma\chi\omega\sigma\iota\nu$ $\tau o\grave{\upsilon}\varsigma$ $\nu\epsilon o\pi o\lambda\acute{\iota}\tau\alpha\varsigma$, $\grave{\alpha}\lambda\lambda\grave{\alpha}$ $\tau\hat{\omega}\nu$ $\delta\acute{\eta}\mu\omega\nu$ $\grave{\alpha}\nu\alpha\gamma o\rho\epsilon\acute{\upsilon}\omega\sigma\iota\nu\cdot$ $\acute{o}\theta\epsilon\nu$ $\kappa\alpha\grave{\iota}$ $\kappa\alpha\lambda o\hat{\upsilon}\sigma\iota\nu$ $\grave{A}\theta\eta\nu\alpha\hat{\iota}o\iota$ $\sigma\phi\hat{\alpha}\varsigma$ $\alpha\grave{\upsilon}\tau o\grave{\upsilon}\varsigma$ $\tau\hat{\omega}\nu$ $\delta\acute{\eta}\mu\omega\nu$.

people, but the Corinthians soon depart on the grounds that it is unjust, and
later Demaratus the other king of Sparta dissents, clearly not out of a sense of
its injustice (he later advises the Aeginetans falsely and unjustly) (VI.50;
61.1), but out of his own indifference to Cleomenes' private vengeance.

Another characteristic of Athens' post-Pisistratean wars is their lack of a
sacred element; for in the very transformation of Athens into a democracy the
sacred was pushed aside as irrelevant. That the Alcmeonids and their partisans
were guilty of Cylon's murder, while he who had "preened" for tyranny was a
suppliant at Athena's statue, so that "they were named the accursed,"
Cleomenes used as a pretext to set up Isagoras as tyrant; but when the
Athenians "thinking the same" drove Isagoras out again, the Alcmeonids were
at once recalled without any regard to their nominal pollution, whereas the
tyrant Pisistratus partly had not wanted children from the daughter of an
Alcmeonid because of this same pollution (I.61.1). One can even say that after
Clisthenes' reforms the ἴδιον-κοινόν replaces the ὅσιον-κοινόν as the binding
force in their wars. That this change has not yet occurred in the other Greek
cities, and that the sacred influences them now as much as it once did Athens,
the examples of Thebes, Aegina, and Sparta show (79–91; cf. I.26.2). While
the Athenians made an expedition against the Chalcideans as soon as they
decided that they wanted to punish them (77.1), the Thebans, in wanting to
take revenge on Athens, first sent to Delphi, and the oracle advised them to
seek those "nearest" to them as allies. They decided that the nearest were the
Aeginetans, for Thebe and Aegina were said to be daughters of Asopus, and
they requested the aid of the Aeacidae, i.e. the statues of these heroes. The
Athenians overwhelmingly defeated them, since the Thebans now dispensed
with their usual allies; and the Thebans returned the statues and asked for men,
which the Aeginetans sent, "puffed up by great prosperity and remembering
with resentment an ancient hatred against Athens" (81.2). Aegina's resentment
had its origins in the sacred, which Herodotus describes in detail (82–88).
Apart from the major importance that oracles, the sacred and the divine assume
in this story, is the importance of women. Two statues of goddesses are
involved, which the Aeginetans stole and propitiated with sacrifices and
choruses of women that reviled the native women; and when only one man
returned home from the Athenians' expedition against Aegina, the wives of
those lost put him to death on their own (cf. IX.5). An ancient story contains
the last reference to women in Book V, except for the speech of Socles who
mentions the mother of Cypselus, the wife of Periander, and the shamed
women of Corinth. Women hardly appear in Athens from now on, though they
are still influential at Sparta. It is indicative, moreover, of the change at
Athens from considerations of the private to devotion to the public that when
the Athenian women pricked to death the sole survivor from Aegina they each
asked where her own husband was, but when they heard that Lycidas had been

stoned to death for proposing an accommodation with the Persians, they went
on their own to Lycidas' house and stoned to death his wife and children; and
whereas the Athenians had thought that their former action was "more terrible
than the calamity" and legislated against its recurrence, they apparently
approved the slaughter of Lycidas' wife and children (87.2: IX.5.3). Even the
women of Athens become public-spirited. But in general it still holds that men
become more prominent as the purely political begins to dominate. The word
"woman" occurs twice as often in the first four as in the last four books, and
more strikingly the ratio of "men" to "human beings" is by far the highest in
this book.[22] The disappearance of women as a factor in political affairs
accompanies the slighter influence of the sacred. The Athenians became
indignant on learning that an oracle advised them to abstain from attacking
Aegina for thirty years, and they proposed to disobey it when a chance event
prevented them. Oracles now remain the preserve of Hippias who threatens the
Corinthians and Spartans with them (90.2: 93.2; cf. VII.6.3-5). They lose as
much ground as poetry does. Pisistratus had justified the war against Mytilene
by appealing to the *Iliad*, and when Alcaeus lost his shield in one of the
battles, he felt no shame in writing a poem about it, just as Solon often praised
in verse the tyrant of Cyprus (94–95; 113.2). The luxury of the private, when
it stands opposed to the common, becomes forbidden: Simonides praised the
athlete Eualkides, who died at Ephesus fighting against the Persians (102.3).
Not only private generosity within the city but the favor of one city to another
becomes less important. Of the four times Sparta invaded Attica, twice they
came for war, and "twice for the good of the Athenian populace": but when
they learned that spurious oracles urged them to drive out the Pisistratids, they
regretted the violation of their friendship with them, for they found Athens
ungrateful and feared her growing power. Their generosity has proved to be
not in their own interest, and they were only prevented from invading again by
the speech of Socles (92). His speech, by painting the evils of tyranny, made
Sparta's allies ignore the threats of Hippias. which were based on his
"accurate" knowledge of oracles (93.2). A speech freely spoken overrides
oracles. It is the first political speech in Herodotus, the first addressed to an

---

[22]The ratios of ἀνήρ to ἄνθρωπος are as follows: I, 94:54; II, 59:63 (cf.
Chap. II, fn 26); III, 105:36; IV, 92:44; V, 83:9; VI, 62:12; VII, 130:49,
VIII, 74:20; IX, 67:19; and consider VII.8γ3. Book V is the only book where
'Egypt' and 'Egyptian' is never mentioned. γυνή, apart from the phrase
παῖδες καὶ γυναῖκες and the like, occurs rarely in Thucydides; consider
I.136.3; II.4.4; 29.3; 45.2; III.104.5; VI.56.1. Note how the establishment of
the Areopagus follows upon Athena's denial of equal right for women (hence
the superiority, politically, of θυμός to ἔρως); *Eumenides* 736-740.

assembly that advocates the just at the expense of self-interest.

In the course of his speech Socles raises the political problem in an acute form. Periander once asked Thrasybulus how he could "most safely" establish his rule and manage Corinth "most beautifully." In answer Thrasybulus brought Periander's messenger to a wheat field, where he began to cut down every outstanding ear until he had destroyed "the most beautiful and tallest part of the wheat." Thrasybulus implies that the tyrant cannot combine the safest with the most beautiful, but that to secure safety the beautiful must be sacrificed. Pisistratus changed none of the laws on his first acquiring the tyranny of Athens, "ordering the city beautifully and well"; but he was easily expelled because he was "not deeply rooted," and he only "rooted" his tyranny on the third try, when many mercenaries and much money backed him, and his opponents were either dead or exiled (I.59.1, 6–60.1; 64.1).[23] But the difficult choice that faces the tyrant faces any regime: are the καλόν and the ἀσφαλές compatible? Τὸ ἀσφαλές means both internal and external security, which rests on the excellence of a city's arms and laws. A city must have men good in war (ἀγαθοὶ τὰ πολεμήια), men with a disciplined θυμός (i.e., somewhat harsh), but whether such a condition can ever admit the acquisition of τὰ καλά, which are rather the objects of ἔρως, remains an open question. What characterizes the beautiful, noble, or fine things is their air of being superfluous and unnecessary. It is their unconcern and carelessness that make them desirable and dangerous at the same time. The beautiful and wealthy Hippoclides represents an extreme instance: οὐ φροντὶς Ἱπποκλείδη could be taken as the motto of the irresponsibly beautiful. An oracle warns the Corinthians that the son of Aetion will become a tyrant, and they send ten men to kill him; but by a "divine chance" the baby smiles at the first man assigned to kill him, and "a certain pity" prevents him. Cypselus' smile, a sign of his complete trust and indifference, proves to be disastrous for Corinth. The city cannot afford this smile: τὸ γελοῖον seems incompatible with τὸ σπουδαῖον, and it was τὸ σπουδαῖον that Herodotus had attributed to Athens' equality of speech, which in turn had made the Athenians victorious in war. So too Syloson's "enjoyment of a divine chance" depopulates Samos, for his generosity to Darius, who desired his cloak, obligates the king to return the favor and make him tyrant (III.139.3).[24] Only in the private sphere is the generosity of the καλόν harmless: the Alcmeonids in exile built a temple "more beautiful than specification," but they are later accused of conspiring

---

[23]Cf. Thucydides I.17; VI.54.5–6; 59.2. The proverb χαλεπὰ τὰ καλά was supposed to have been originally said of Periander's change from mildness to savagery; Scholia Plat. ad Crat. 384b; Hipp. Mai. 304e.

[24]Cf. pp. 95–96 supra.

with Persia against Athens (62.3; VI. 115; 121-125.1; cf. I.196.2). The offer that the Cyprian tyrants make—to fight either on land or at sea—appears to be more generous than the Ionians' insistence that they must obey the common; and yet the Ionians defeat the Phoenician fleet, while some of the tyrants prove treacherous, even though they all had willingly revolted (104; 109-113; cf. VII.160.2). And the bravery of Onesilus, who willingly ranges himself against the Persian general, is purely personal; for his Carian esquire explained that death at the hands of someone of equal rank cuts the calamity in half; just as if Cyprian independence were a question of a private duel, and Onesilus should have no concern for his people's safety (cf. 1.2; 8; IX.20-25.1; 48.4). The oligarchical regime that Megabyzus proposed, based as it was on the beautiful (III.81.82),[25] never is shown to exist in Herodotus, unlike democracy and monarchy; and Darius had objected to it on the grounds that, "when many practice virtue for the sake of the common, fierce private hatreds are wont to arise." The common good and the privately beautiful seem inevitably at war with each other.[26]

If we recall Solon's distinction between the political καλόν and the divine ἀγαθόν, we can see that a radical shift has occurred. Solon had attributed to Tellus a perfect union of the private καλά and the public ἀγαθόν, which has now appeared to be uneasily connected, while the problem posed by the divine good has been suppressed. The relation of man to the whole that occupied Herodotus in the first four books seems to have been replaced by a narrower problem. What god had shown to be the best end simply—never to be born—now becomes the patriotic death. "Best" now means "bravest," not in the Thracian way of non-political courage, but in the way the Spartans die at Thermopylae. Herodotus believes that the best advice given to the Carians, when they revolted from Persia, was for them to cross the River Maeander, and "having the river at their backs engage in battle, so that being unable to flee the Carians would be compelled to remain and prove still better than their nature" (118.1).[27] Not simply the natural by itself but the natural under compulsion, so that it might be better than itself, indicates the extent to which Herodotus has contracted his inquiry. No longer earth, water, and sky dominate, but the cities of Athens and Sparta, although Soles now and the Athenians later do not believe there is any difference between the city and the whole.[28] Soles begins his address thus: "Surely the sky will be below the

---

[25]Cf. VII.237.2; p. 84-85 *supra*.

[26]Could Pericles' paradox φιλοκαλοῦμεν μετ᾽ εὐτελείας (II.40.1) allude to this problem? Cf. Wardman, A. E., *CQ*, 1959, pp. 38-42.

[27]Cf. 101.2; II.173; VII.103.4-104; VIII.83.1; 108.3; 109.2; see *Iliad* IV.297-300.

[28]92α1; VIII.143.2; cf. I.98.5-6; 212.3; see further *Iliad* VIII.19-26.

earth and earth above the sky, and human beings will have their province in the sea, and fishes on land, when you, Spartans, are prepared to put down democracies and reestablish tyrannies, than which there is nothing more unjust or more blood-thirsty." Soles assumes that the advantage to Athens of democracy would be advantageous to Sparta, and that the whole and the part are so intimately bound together, that a political revolution would bring about a universal upheaval. That Herodotus does not believe this, should go without saying, but what status political things have in the whole will prove to be the theme of the last four books. The war of Greece against the barbarians will prove to be the war of the part against the whole. Almost all the tribes and people Herodotus described in Books I–IV are marshalled against Greece; and these tribes have been shown to contain all the elements and ways of knowing that he has been able to discover. What Greece peculiarly presents vis à vis this whole, and why a conflict necessarily comes about between it and the whole are questions that Herodotus will answer; but it is important to see first how his own understanding adapts itself to the fifth book's political setting.

Herodotus records two pieces of advice that Hecataeus gave, one at the beginning of the Ionian revolt, the other toward its collapse (36.2–4; 124–125). Hecataeus first advised them not to revolt because of the enormous power of Persia: but unable to convince them he advised them to use the treasures Croesus had dedicated at Branchidae. Whether this advice was the best that could be offered—Herodotus suggests elsewhere that it was not, though changed circumstances might have excluded any better proposal (I.170)—it clearly surpassed the decision the Milesians did make, which was to revolt without adequate preparations but to enlist the support of Athens or Sparta. And yet Hecataeus had been shown up in the second book as believing that he could trace his ancestry in sixteen generations to a god (III. 143). His willingness here to remove the sacred dedications of Croesus contrasts strangely with his vanity in Egypt; while his boldness, in later advising Aristagoras to use a nearby island as a base for the reconquest of Miletus, contrasts favorably with the poor-spiritedness of Aristagoras himself. His courage and political sense far surpass his knowledge of divine things. Herodotus might well follow his judgment about political issues, but he refuses to admit his opinion about man's relation to the gods, or even his opinion about some ancient history: "The Pelasgians were expelled by the Athenians from Attica, either justly or unjustly, for this I cannot tell, except what is said, that Hecataeus the son of Hegesandrus speaking in his writings said that it was unjustly" (VI.137.1). Hecataeus' knowledge of the first things stands far below Herodotus' own, and his knowledge of the old things shows an uncritical acceptance of one tradition, which cannot be admitted when Herodotus knows an equally plausible but contradictory account. But Hecataeus' judgment about political things that he knows at first hand cannot be so easily dismissed. Perhaps the "most useful" plan of Bias and the "good" plan of Thales—two of the seven wise men—are beyond him; but if he had persuaded the Milesians, their chances of success would have improved. Herodotus could have found no greater index of the difference between Books I-IV and VI-IX than Hecataeus as historian and Hecataeus as statesman. Deciding between true and false has a different rank from deciding between good and bad, if Hecataeus can fail at the first and succeed at the second. His practice is better than his theory.

Herodotus indicates throughout Book V how the difference between theory (seeing for its own sake) and practice can be made. The Athenian law that compels women to wear Ionian dress allows Herodotus to distinguish them: "For those observing a true λόγος this kind of dress is not anciently Ionian but Carian, since every kind of ancient Greek dress for women was the same as that which we now call Doric" (88.1).[29] For his narration "Ionian" suffices, but for those who wish to know the barbarian origin of Greek things, he must correct the impression that "Ionian" is something original; just as in the first book he noted that the Corinthian treasury at Delphi is "for one observing a true λόγος not the public property of the Corinthians but of Cypselus the son of Aetion," although whenever it is mentioned again, it is called the Corinthian treasury. The difference between these two sole instances of the phrase "to observe a true λόγος" is also instructive. In Book I it notes the erroneous shift from a private to a public name—so much a part of Book V, while here Herodotus suggests the derivative character of Greek things. Between the exact name "treasury of Cypselus" and the common "treasury of the Corinthians" lies the gap between the first and second parts of Herodotus' *Inquiries*; or, as he indicates in the fifth book, between the more accurate and the correct (54.1; 50.2). Cleomenes asked Aristagoras how long it took from the coast of Asia Minor to Sousa, and Aristagoras, though he could have said anything (the distances on the map he pointed to must have been measured in inches), told him the truth, a journey of three months. Herodotus then takes up the discourse Aristagoras would have made had not Cleomenes cut him off and ordered him out of Sparta; but the truth that the journey takes three months is not the whole truth. "It was correctly said, but if anyone seeks still further what is more accurate than this, this too I shall mention; for one must calculate in addition the journey from Ephesus to Sardis." The more accurate calculation adds three days. Aristagoras might be pardoned for this slight error. From an expedition's point of view or even from a traveler's this difference hardly matters; but from Herodotus' standpoint in Books I-IV—that of θεωρίη—the difference is enormous. Herodotus gave his own map for us to look at in Book IV; Aristagoras shows a map to Cleomenes so that he might desire to conquer

---

[29]Cf. I.14.2; 50.3; IV.162.3; Plutarch *de Pythiae oraculis* 13 (400D-F).

Asia. The smallness of Aristagoras' map is meant to deceive Cleomenes into believing that such a conquest would be easy; but Herodotus described the earth in order to show that it was one. The unity of the earth was meant only to be seen and not stimulate any thought of aggrandizement. As soon, however, as conquest is in question, the accurate must yield to the approximate.

Herodotus pointed out the same kind of difference before. The road from Athens to Elis is "similar in length" to that from the seacoast to Heliopolis: "one would find on calculation the difference to be rather slight," for the Athens-Elis road fails short by fifteen stades from the Egyptian distance (II.7). Such accuracy cannot be expected nor is it found in the last books, where Herodotus must rely on what is said more than on what he himself has seen, counted, or measured.[30] What he knows and others say they know almost become one and the same. The triple agreement here among the descendants of Perdiccas, Herodotus ("I myself actually know that it is so"), and the judges of Olympia, that the Macedonian kings were originally Greek, as though each had a different source of knowledge, marks the end of Herodotus' independence, as it points to his future dependence on others (22; VIII.137-139). No longer will Herodotus be able to be as independent as he was in Egypt, where he distinguished so sharply between his own judgment and what the priests said. The difference between I-IV and VI-IX is like that between the old and the first things, which may be collapsed for the sake of defending a city's way of life, but which Herodotus tried to keep separate in Books II-IV. Unless one considers the change that Book V effects, one may wrongly assign to Herodotus something conditioned by the theme of Books VI-IX; and vice-versa wrongly demand that Herodotus preserve the accuracy of Books I-IV in the second half. The phrase "as far as we know" or the like drops sharply in frequency from twenty-four in I-IV to nine in VI-IX (V has two): Herodotus is no longer at the limits of his knowledge. The restriction of his scope does away with the superlatives that must be so qualified. Not that this restriction makes Herodotus more superficial, but rather he now deals with derivative rather than first things. The Persian Wars will prove to be a surface phenomenon that has its basis in the principles and elements he discovered in the first four books. They will show, as it were, his own λόγος in action.

Another way of stating the difference between the two parts of Herodotus' *Inquiries* would be to see it in the double purpose he sets forth in his proem. His *Inquiries* will prevent what human beings have done (τὰ γενόμενα) from disappearing in time—they will be remembered; but it will

---

[30]Cf. VII.60.1; 185.1; IX.32.2. Out of 51 instances of ἀτρεκές, etc., 19 of 28 in I-IV are Herodotus' own, while 9 of 19 are his in VI-IX.

also prevent great and admirable deeds (ἔργα μεγάλα τε καὶ θωμαστά), shown forth by Greeks and barbarians, from going without fame—they will become celebrated. Herodotus knew he had a unique chance to inquire into the whole range of human customs, a range that would not remain if ever a universal conqueror imposed the customs of his own nation everywhere else. Regarded simply as τὰ γενόμενα of human beings they could guide him to the discovery of a triple λόγος; and the emendation once proposed, τὰ λεγόμενα ἐξ ἀνθρώπων (what human beings have said), only hits the truth in too rash a way; for the first part does turn on λόγοι as the second on ἔργα. But τὰ γενόμενα are the source for Herodotus' own *logos* without being a *logos* themselves; and they concern what men say without being entirely lacking in visible things. The phrase indicates the distant view Herodotus takes in the first four books: Greeks and barbarians are simply human beings, who show in their γενόμενα all the possibilities of human beings. Not so in Books VI–IX. To take a distant view when two nations are at war would be to distort the phenomena. Herodotus must look on the war in the way the warring nations themselves looked on it; for otherwise he would miss the true character of the war. In coming closer to historical events in the last four books, Herodotus does not find, as he could in the customs of Egypt, Persia, Scythia and Libya, universal assertions, which had led him to reflect on their truth and error. Now he has to see much deeper, for the silent ἔργα, the particular battles and day-to-day moves, do not seem to offer up by themselves any universals. They seem to be what they present themselves as being and nothing else: the miraculous victory at Marathon or the magnificent defeat at Thermopylae. It will take all the insights of his triple λόγος to be able to see their λόγος and make them speak.

Herodotus comments as follows on Aristagoras' answer to Cleomenes' question about the journey to Sousa: "Aristagoras, though being in other respects clever and having well hoaxed him, here made a slip; for he ought not to have told him the truth." The truth may be disastrous and a lie the best resort in practical affairs—Themistocles' deceptions come at once to mind—though Herodotus can have hardly written Books I–IV in accordance with this principle. There the truth was the only aim, no matter who suffered from it. Greek provincialism had been shown up for what it was, and its disparagement accompanied the discovery of the first things. Whether Herodotus can afford such a luxury in VI–IX remains to be seen; but we must now consider why he made this comment at all. Nowhere else does he give advice; and yet, unjust though Aristagoras was, he does advise him in retrospect. He gives advice in the way that someone indifferent to the justice or injustice of a cause might do. But everyone knows where Herodotus' sympathies lie. He looks at what Aristagoras ought to have done in a completely non-partisan way, as if it were a distant scene and not the immediate problem of Ionia's freedom. He is looking in the way he looked at Greek maps, at which he once laughed, and one of which Aristagoras now carries. He assumes the indifference a true map would have to the conventional names of Europe, Libya, and Asia. He shows the same indifference when he says that the capture of the Pisistratus' children was "an evil coincidence for them," though it aided the Athenians; and, again, that Clisthenes the Athenian "imitated" Clisthenes the Sicyonian.[31] It was an imitation only if the difference between democracy and tyranny is ignored; only if the different purposes each Clisthenes had are abstracted, and the power of names is alone considered. Herodotus made that abstraction. He made it to point up the change that his *logos* will undergo when he deals with Greek-barbarian things. Book V shows the transition from Herodotus' *logos* about the whole to his *logos* about a war, and he uses the examples of Aristagoras and the two Clisthenes' to indicate their difference: Aristagoras is given advice, democracy is equated with tyranny. Herodotus' indifference in both cases shows how the political problem of combining the beautiful with the safe repeats itself in his own *logos*. The smile of Cypselus and the Corinthians' good were incompatible. Harshness necessarily accompanies the political. Herodotus might have to make the same sacrifice as Periander, who destroyed the beautiful for the sake of the secure. The correct and the accurate are in the same ratio as the ἀσφαλές and the καλόν. What Herodotus added to Aristagoras' answer of three months made his account more accurate, just as the Alcmeonids' substitution of Parian marble for tufa made the temple at Delphi "more beautiful than specification." If the divine is jealous, as a Greek, Egyptian, and Persian believe it is, perhaps the superfluous and generous in both Herodotus' *logos* and men's actions must disappear. Perhaps the safe and good must replace the beautiful.[32] It is this question which we must keep in mind as we read the last four books of Herodotus' *Inquiries*.

---

[31]65.1; 67.1; 69.1; cf. 30.1; 93.1; 97.3 with VI.98.2.

[32]The following frequencies, even without being analyzed, indicate this problem. καλός(ῶς occurs 37 times in I-IV, 9 in V, 19 in VI-IX; εὐειδής 10 times in I-III, twice in V, once in VI and VII; ἀγαθός 46 in I-IV, 8 in V, 41 in VI-IX; ἀμείνων 20 in I-IV, 8 in V, 25 in VI-IX; ἄριστος 37 in I-IV; 6 in V, 53 in VI-IX; εὖ 51 in I-IV, 15 in V, 59 in VI-IX; χρηστός(ῶς) 17 in I-IV, 4 in V, 24 in VI-IX. That the same problem recurs in the whole Herodotus' and his characters' use of θεῖος indicates; either it refers to a kind of χάρις or φθόνος and ἀναγκαίη. For divine χάρις see I.62.4 (cf. III.77.1); 122.3; 126.6 (cf. 209.4); III.42.4; 139.3; IV.152.2; V.92γ3; VI.69.3; VIII.94.2bis; and for divine φθόνος see 1.32.1; 174.4; II.66.3; III.40.2; 108.1; cf. IV.205; VII.10; 46.4; 137.1,2; VIII.109.3; IX.65.2; 100.2; pp.193-4 *infra*.

VI. SPARTA

The Ionian revolt failed. The causes of that failure and its repercussions occupy the first 32 paragraphs of Book VI. When the Persians sent the former tyrants of Ionia to urge each of the cities to desert the alliance, their threats and promises were rejected; for each city thought the Persians negotiated with itself alone. The Ionians did not consult with each other on how they should answer the Persians' demand, but each attended only to its own pleasure, the "taste" each had had of freedom, which made the Milesians refuse to take Histiaeus back as tyrant. The Panionian sanctuary, originally founded as a sign of their pride in being "pure" Ionians (I.141.4-148), gave the appearance without the substance of a common purpose. Though it had been erected in common to Heliconian Poseidon, the common did not extend beyond the sacred festivals that they all shared. Their "stubborn senselessness" (ἀγνωμοσύνη), which Herodotus accuses them of, did not consist in their wishing to be free, but in the way they believed it could be brought about. In rejecting Hecataeus' proposal to finance a large navy from the dedications of Croesus, they had shown their ignorance of the half-truth that money is the sinews of war; and now in disobeying Dionysius, who pointed to the need for the strictest discipline, they showed their preference for slavery with pleasure to freedom with toil. Dionysius promised them victory if they practiced naval maneuvers under his command; but after seven days the unaccustomed exercises so wore them out that they said to one another: "Which god have we transgressed that we take our fill of these evils? So senseless have we become, having sailed straight out of our minds, that we entrusted ourselves to a Phocaean boaster, who contributed three ships" (12.3).[1] The pains the Ionians endure induce them to exaggerate and speak metaphorically. Rather than seeing their pains as the necessary condition for freedom, they see them as justifiable only in the light of some transgression against the gods. Whereas Dionysius had boasted of no divine favor—"if the gods assign equal things (to both sides)"—the Ionians accused him of boasting; and whereas Herodotus thinks

---

[1]Cf. *Iliad* II.671-675.

that they were senseless to reject the Persian offer each on his own, they looked on their only possible hope as folly. After they had said such things, "no one was willing to obey, but as a land army they set up tents on the island and stayed in the shade, and they continued to refuse to embark or go out to sea." They do not see a navy as a navy but as an army; they do not see things as they are but as they wish them to be. They make the same mistake as the Scythians and Libyans had. They do not see what is but the image of what is. They change the sense of Dionysius' preparations by metaphor; and this excess of imagination accompanies, just as it did among the Scythians, an excessive literalness: they see the three ships Dionysius brought and wrongly conclude he is boasting.

Herodotus devoted the fourth book to showing us the nature of εἰκασία; it was the seeing of a likeness as a likeness, which the Scythians and Libyans were blind to, but of which he gave examples in his own map-making and *logos*. His *logos* was concerned with a certain way of seeing and not with acting; but now the change in perspective that Book V has effected dictates a change in his *logos*. No longer will it be concerned with ways of seeing simply but ways of acting as determined by ways of seeing. Greece, as a derivative phenomenon, does not reveal itself as clearly in its land and customs as the rest of the world. To discover its character requires Herodotus to look at what the Greeks do politically, how they respond as citizens of some particular city to particular events. In their practice they reveal their understanding of things. The Ionians' folly here proved to be based on the same kind of error that the Scythians reveled in; but unlike the Scythians they are not simply prone to this one kind of error; rather, the Greeks will be shown to borrow the ways of understanding of Egypt and Persia as well. Herodotus will try to find counterpart of his *logos* in their "great and admirable deeds."

In order to sharpen the Ionians' awareness of their situation, Dionysius had opened his speech thus: "Our affairs, Ionians, are on a razor's edge, either to be free or slaves" (11.2).[2] He hoped to make the alternatives completely exclusive, and hide the possibility which the Samians adopted when they saw the great disorder of the Ionians, to accept the promise that the Persians would burn neither their sanctuaries nor their private goods if they betrayed the alliance (9.3; 13.2; 25.2; cf. VIII.109.3). If the Ionians were to fight at all, they must be made to forget this alternative, which lay between their common freedom and the threat of a harsher slavery. While Dionysius, then, used a metaphor for the Ionians' benefit, and the Ionians used one to hide their foolishness, when they refused to practice naval maneuvers, the Samians resorted to exaggeration to justify their betrayal. In addition to the Ionians'

---

[2]On Dionysius' speech see [Longinus] *de sublimitate* XXII.1-2.

disobedience, what persuaded them was the power of the king, which "seemed to them impossible to overcome, being quite convinced that even if his present naval force were defeated, there would be another five times as strong." Since the fleet of Xerxes numbered only 1200 at Salamis, three thousand ships (the Persians here have 600) seem far beyond Darius' resources. Merely by imagining a quintupling of the Persian fleet, the Samians conceal from themselves their own responsibility. Inversely to the Ionians, who underestimate Dionysius because he commanded only three ships, the Samians excused themselves by multiplying the Persians' power. In both cases there is a failure to see what is before them, a failure to attend to the evident. As a consequence, Herodotus says that he cannot "accurately write down who of the Ionians proved to be base or good men in the naval battle, for they lay the blame on each other" (14.1: cf. 82.1; 124.2; 137.1). What must have been perfectly evident at the time, their mutual recriminations have obscured. All but eleven ships of the Samians are said to have fled; and the Lesbians, "seeing those next to them in flight did the same as the Samians, and most of the Ionians also did the same." The Lesbians and other Ionians do not only see the Samians in flight, they see them as men to be imitated. That there was no necessity to look at them in this way the Chians showed, who "seeing most of their allies betraying did not think it just to be like the base." Most of the Ionians did not see the Samians as traitors, which was obviously what they were, but as an example. A conjecture usurped the fact. When the Chians beached their ships near Ephesus, the Ephesians did not inquire who they were, but since the women were celebrating the *thesmophoria* at night, they "guessed" (καταδόξαντες) from the Chians' being an army that they were thieves. They made the reverse mistake of the Ionians who followed the Samians' lead. While the Ionians copied those whom they should have regarded as different, the Ephesians took those who were different to be the same as thieves. Imagining in every sense proves to be the theme of Book VI, the most striking example of which is perhaps the difference in behavior of the Sybarites and Athenians after the capture of Miletus (21). Although the Sybarites and Milesians were "those cities of which we know that were especially bound in friendship with one another," the Sybarites did not grieve at Miletus' capture; but the Athenians "made clear their distress in many other ways as well as in this: when Phrynichus made a drama *The Capture of Miletus* and staged it, the audience burst into tears and fined him a thousand drachmas for reminding them of personal sorrows." A play, an imitation of what happened, reminds the Athenians of their grief, while the Sybarites, whom no daughter of Memory reminds, forget. A likeness has greater power than its original to produce an effect.

After the naval battle in which the Chians showed "brilliant deeds," the Lesbians mistook the survivors for thieves and killed them; and in this ruined state Histiaeus easily conquered Chios (26–27). "It is somehow customary," Herodotus says, "that there be a foreshowing, whenever great evils are about to happen to either a city or tribe, for even before these events there happened great signs to the Chians." The great signs were two in number. Of a hundred youths sent as a chorus to Delphi only two returned, while "a pestilence snatched up ninety-eight and carried them off": and in the city itself, a little before the naval battle, the roof of a schoolhouse caved in and killed all but one of 120 children, "while they were being taught letters."[3] "These events as signs the god showed forth to them, and afterwards the naval battle snatched them up and threw the city to its knees." Two disasters occur in succession, neither of which by itself can he interpreted, but after what befell the Chians Herodotus understands both as signs. They are not judgments on or punishments of some crime, as was the capture of Miletus, which the oracle addressed as "deviser of evil deeds" (19.2). These are simply signs that foretell great evils, though they might be thought great evils in themselves; but they differ from the disasters they foretell not only in magnitude but in kind. They are superfluities of the city, a chorus and schoolchildren, examples of leisure. They are the fine things, τὰ καλά, that Thrasybulus taught Periander were incompatible with a tyrant's safety.[4] Their destruction signifies, Herodotus implies, the destruction as well of the city's safety; but this implication is only warranted if the safe and secure cannot exist apart from the beautiful. Only if the necessary things—a strong army and navy in this case—depend on the "unbought grace of life," can Herodotus draw the conclusion he does. We ourselves would be inclined to believe the reverse, that the necessary things are the condition for the fine things, and without which the fine things are impossible (cf. 32). By describing these signs after the events they signified, Herodotus suggests this alternative. The order he employs in his narration is the order that makes sense, even though the pestilence and the roof's collapse temporally preceded the Chians' defeat and conquest. What signifies in Herodotus' own account the fragility of the καλά, signifies in time the destruction of a city, whose men were good and brave in the defense of Ionia.

That there is a problem in interpretation here Herodotus indicates in several ways. The Chians sent the chorus to dance and perhaps to sing at Delphi; it was designed to propitiate Apollo and gain his favor; and the schoolchildren were learning to read and write the language of their city. As the chorus was meant to signify something to a god, so the schoolchildren were

---

[3]Cf. Thucydides VII.29.

[4]Cf. pp. 148 ss. *supra*. According to Thucydides VIII.24.4–5, the Chians after the Spartans were especially successful after the Persian Wars in combining the beautiful and the safe (ηὐδαιμόνησάν τε ἅμα καὶ ἐσωφρόνησαν.

learning what the letters of the alphabet signified. What were already signs with a human sense became signs with another meaning: "the god" made the conversion. The god ignored their original significance—the dance addressed to Apollo and the alphabet to men—and made them foretell the future. He converted human things to a divine end. We know what a sacred dance means, and what is the purpose of letters; we do not know how to 'read' them differently. Herodotus claims that he knows, and yet he seems to give a double account of them. He first uses an impersonal προσημαίνειν and then a personal προδεικνύναι. The impersonal construction occurs in the general rule that Herodotus lays down, which he qualifies with the phrase, "it is somehow customary": but he says without qualification that "the god showed forth these signs." Similarly, in mentioning later the earthquake at Delos, he first says: "And this must have been a miraculous sign that the god revealed to men of the evils that were to come"; while in his second statement he only says: "Thus it was not strange or unfitting (οὐδὲν ἦν ἀεικές) for Delos to be shaken being previously unshaken" (98: cf. III.33).[5] To interpret this earthquake as "fitting" does not mean the same as to interpret it as an intentional sign. The gap between them is as great as that between an impersonal and a divine foreshowing at Chios. If no god intended these events as signs, they must be 'read' before they can yield their meaning; and they can only be 'read' after the events they signified occur. Herodotus is an interpreter with hindsight; he does not pretend to see the future, as an interpreter of dreams or an oracle must claim. To see a sign as a sign at the moment of its occurrence would mean that Herodotus knows the language of divine signs, that he knows the language the gods use in speaking to men; but he implies that all men are equally ignorant of that tongue (II.3.2).[6] But even if these were signs, a translation would be needed to make them intelligible to men. The sentence that immediately follows his remark on the appropriateness of Delos' earthquake glosses the names of three Persian kings, in whose time more evils befell Greece than in the twenty previous generations. "These names in the Greek tongue are equivalent to 'Doer' for Darius, 'Warrior' for Xerxes, and 'Great Warrior' for Artaxerxes, and the Greeks in their own tongue would correctly call thus these

---

[5]Cf. pp. 87–88 *supra*.

[6]Cf. pp. 31–34 *supra*: Cicero *de divinatione* II.131; Dio Chrysostom X.23-24 (ed. Emp.);Seneca *N.Q.*. II.32.2: *hoc inter nos et Tuscos, quibus summa est fulgurum persequendorum scientia, interest: nos putamus, quia nubes collisae sunt, fulmina emitti; ipsi existimant nubes collidi, ut fulmina emittantur (nam cum omnia ad deum referant, in ea opinione sunt, tamquam non, quia facta sunt, significent, sed quia significatura sunt, fiant): eadem tamen ratione fiunt sive illis significare propositum sive consequens est.*

kings." The three names have no meaning as long as no translation is given. A Greek would not know at first what they meant, whereas he would know at once that Delos means "Clear" (cf. IX.20).[7] Herodotus' translations, moreover, completely reverse the initial impression any Greek would have; for Δαρεῖος looks like ἀρήιος and Xerxes like ἐρξίης, but Herodotus says that ἀρήιος is the same as Xerxes and ἐρξίης as Darius. He thus denies that their looks can tell one anything at all. Translation from Persian to Greek cannot be done by likeness of letters to letters, but it depends on the sameness of meanings. To translate divine signs, however, depends entirely on likeness.[8] It is because a pestilence that happened before a city's capture looks like a portent that it is a portent. Divine signs are divine signs only if likeness is equivalent to sameness. They have a significance only if what seems cannot be distinguished from what is.

It might be objected at this point that Herodotus has plainly indicated his trust in the prophetic powers of the gods by his story of Croesus' experiment, which so conspicuously stands at the beginning of his *logos* (I.47-49). And yet Croesus failed to test what really needed testing. He arranged that his envoys to Delphi would ask the god on a specific day what Croesus was doing, and the oracle came through with flying colors. Croesus, however, should have asked what he was going to do on the following day, for only in that way could he test the god's knowledge of the future. The god shows that he knows the present. He shows that he sees and smells and is thus as universal as the sun, which Tiresias claims sees and hears all things (*Od.* XI.109). But the god's further contention that he understands the dumb and hears the silent i.e., he knows what human beings intend in their hearts, does not follow. Herodotus, then, raises the possibility that the gods are cosmic gods, whose omniscience embraces space but not time, the perceptible but not one's secret thoughts.

Herodotus showed that the god 'made good' his signs. Herodotus saved a pestilence and a roof's collapse from being thought the injustice of 'heaven' (cf. II.133.1-3). He did so by translating them into signs; but the jealousy of the divine, which Solon, Amasis, and Artabanus vouch for, makes Herodotus' interpretation more than doubtful.[9] Herodotus tried to understand why the innocent graces of life appeared so weak, and he suggested that the god intended their destruction as signs, by which he reconciled their appearance with their meaning. He saved the phenomena. He preferred the better to the

---

[7] Cf. pp. 121ss. *supra*.

[8] Cf. 19.2-3; 107; 118; I.34.1; 74.1-3; 78; VII.37.2-3; 57; VIII.65; Thucydides II.54.

[9] Cf. Chap. V, fn 32.

worse explanation. He showed his sobriety in fitting an ugly appearance to a higher principle. He did the opposite of the Ionians, who thought they had "sailed out of their minds" when they were in fact sane, and who attributed their madness to some divine transgression, which they believed was the only excuse for obeying Dionysius. Their metaphorical speech had justified their disobedience and concealed their baseness behind a seemly facade. The virtue that Herodotus constantly points to in this book is sanity, the ability to see things as they are and to act in accordance with that seeing. He illustrates what sanity is by showing us its opposite, the most extended account of which is Cleomenes' madness (74–84).

When it became known that Cleomenes had bribed the oracle at Delphi to expel Demaratus from the kingship, Cleomenes in fear retired to Thessaly and from thence went to Arcadia, where he had the Arcadians swear an oath that they would follow him wherever he led them (cf. V.29.7); and "gathering the chief Arcadians at Nonacris he was eager to have them swear by the water of the Styx"; and the Spartans on learning this "were afraid and brought him back on the same conditions by which he previously was king." In Homer and Hesiod only the gods swear by the Styx, and according to Hesiod if a god swears falsely "he lies breathless for a full year, nor does he ever approach ambrosia and nectar, but lies without breathing and speechless in bed, and an evil slumber covers him," and after this "disease" he stays away for nine years more from the other gods (*Theogony* 775–806). Now as soon as Cleomenes returned to Sparta "the disease of madness snatched him up," for he would thrust his scepter into the face of every Spartiate he met; so his relations locked him up and put a helot to guard him; and he, seeing the guard was alone, asked for his sword, and when the helot refused threatened him until in fear he gave it. Cleomenes then began to mutilate himself, cutting off his flesh in slabs, starting at his shins, and progressing to his belly, "which he minced up as for a sausage and thus died." Cleomenes' madness consisted is not seeing himself as himself but as another. He literally did not know himself. His madness began when he no longer recognized the Spartiates as Spartiates, but thrust his scepter into their faces as though they were helots, even as Odysseus had beaten Thersites with the scepter of Agamemnon.[10] His failure to recognize distinctions of rank finally led to his failure to recognize himself. He saw himself as other than what he was. Thus the Athenians said that the men they sent to fetch two statues from Aegina went mad—literally, "were of another mind"—when they began to "kill one another as enemies" (V.85.2). Cleomenes' suicide, then, showed that he had fallaciously doubled himself, the same kind of doubleness the Ionians were guilty of when they acted as if they were an army.

---

[10]*Iliad* II.265–269; cf. Xenophon *Memorabilia* I.ii.58.

Herodotus presents five different versions that try to account for Cleomenes' madness. Four of them in some way depend on the gods, while the fifth explains it in human terms. On the four divine accounts one is only implicit; for it would use the verses of Hesiod, which attribute to the waters of the Styx the power to make ill any god that swears falsely by it; so that Cleomenes in making himself like a god would have gone insane. A poet who has learnt from the Muses the truth and "falsehoods like the truth" would be the authority for this interpretation, and because of its doubtfulness Herodotus only suggests it. Many of the Greeks say that his suborning the Pythian oracle was the cause, but one could object that the Alcmeonids did not go mad even though they were said to have bribed the same oracle (123.2; V.63.1). The Athenians say that Cleomenes' clearing the temenos of the gods at Eleusis, while the Argives say his killing many Argives in the sanctuary of Argos and his burning "in disregard" the grove there, brought on his madness. These three explanations, which differ in the enormity of the crime they attribute to Cleomenes, agree that some violation of the sacred was involved; and since the Argive accusation is the gravest, Herodotus gives that in detail. What immediately strikes us is that Cleomenes' impiety is mixed up with his piety (cf. V.72.3–4), for his bribery of the Pythian oracle does not prevent him from consulting it, nor do the unpropitious sacrifices at the River Erasinus prevent him from sacrificing to the sea and in this way invading Argive territory. Cleomenes persists because the oracle said that he would capture Argos; but when he learns that the sacred grove he burnt belongs to the hero Argos, he believes that Apollo deceived him and at once returns to Sparta (cf. III.64.3–5). He believes that Apollo meant the grove of Argos and not the city; he believes that he confused the city with a grove of the same name; he believes, in short, that he took what was different for the same. It is a mistake that the Argives also make. Frightened by an enigmatic oracle, which they misinterpret, they decide to do whatever the Spartan herald proclaims to the Spartans; and Cleomenes, realizing that they imitate his army's actions, tells them to attack when the herald next announces breakfast, which completely deceives the Argives. They so much rely on the signals of the herald that they pay no attention to what the Spartans in fact do. They become so convinced that they have translated the signs correctly, just as they thought they understood the oracle's metaphors, that they forget that the signs are only signs. Their mistake is the same as the Scythians', who took camp-fires and the braying of asses as proof that the Persians were still there (IV.134.3–135.3).[11] Thus the Argives are as wrong as Cleomenes; indeed, they are as mad as he. The scepter that merely signified his authority became in his hand a weapon, with which he

---

[11]Cf. pp. 115–117 *supra.*

literally exacted punishment; just as the call to breakfast seemed a proof to the Argives that the Spartans were breakfasting. The literal and the figurative again appear together.

On Cleomenes' return to Sparta his enemies accused him of not capturing Argos because he was bribed; but Cleomenes protested his innocence on two counts, and "whether he lied or told the truth," Herodotus says, "I cannot clearly say." Cleomenes asserted that the oracle meant the sanctuary of Argos and not the city, and since he did not believe it just to capture Argos unless the god still showed his favor, he sacrificed in the Heraeum, and when flames flashed from the chest of Hera's statue, he knew the truth that he should not capture Argos; for if the flames had come from the head, he would have captured it "from top to bottom" (κατ' ἄκρης), but since it flashed from the chest, he knew "he had done as much as the god wished"; and the ephors, before whom he pleaded, "thought that he had spoken what was convincing and likely (πιστά τε καὶ οἰκότα)." Cleomenes avoids conviction by the sameness of two names and by a metaphor. The metaphor depends on a likeness of an acropolis to a head, which in turn depends on poetic usage having established the phrase κατ' ἄκρης in this sense.[12] The god must not only speak in images but in poetic images: the flame flashes out of an image of Hera.

Now the Spartans deny that Cleomenes went mad "from any daimonion," but rather say he associated with Scythians and having learnt from them to drink undiluted wine went mad; and they assert that since then, whenever they wish to drink wine neat, they say, "Let it be in Scythian fashion." It might seem at first glance that the Spartan account has nothing to do with the gods, and in the strict sense that is true; but if we consider that the Spartans accuse Cleomenes of having learnt an alien custom, we realize that they merely replace the violation of sacred things with the violation of a law. He drank "more than was due" (μᾶλλον τοῦ ἱκνεομένου), more than what the Spartans had established as due; just as Leutychides declared that Demaratus was king "unduly" (οὐκ ἱκνεομένως), since Spartan law barred a bastard son from the throne (65.3,4: cf. 82.3). The Spartan explanation, then, is not entirely of the same kind as Herodotus' of the tippler Cambyses' madness, whose epilepsy made it "not unlikely" or "not strange" that his mind was also unsound (III.33).[13] The Spartans rather link a somatic cause with Cleomenes' violation of law. They seem to take the same position as the Scythians do, who say that it is not fitting that a god drive men mad; but the Scythians said this of Bacchic

---

[12]Cf. Leumann, M., *Homerische Wörter* (Basel, 1950), p. 56. κατ' ἄκρης occurs only here and at 18; and neither φλόξ nor ἐκλάμπει occurs elsewhere.

frenzy, when their king Scyles was initiated into the rites of Dionysus, the god of wine (IV.79.3).[14] The Scythians killed Scyles because he violated Scythian customs; the Spartans say Cleomenes went mad because he violated Spartan customs and learnt Scythian ones. The Spartan account looks completely different when viewed from the Scythian side. The corruption they see in Anacharsis' and Scyles' adoption of Greek orgiastic rites, the Spartans see in Cleomenes' adoption of theirs. Faced with this impasse, Herodotus is silent about what caused Cleomenes' madness; he looks, instead, at another aspect of it, which he partly borrows from the Spartans and partly from the other Greeks. Many Greeks attributed Cleomenes' madness to his bribing the Delphic oracle to declare Demaratus illegitimate, and the Spartans to his drinking more than was fitting and just; but Herodotus makes no one responsible: "I think that Cleomenes paid this as retribution to Demaratus" (84.3).[15] Herodotus does not give a cause, any more than he made "the god" causally responsible for the pestilence at Chios. It was as a sign that the pestilence is justified, and it is as retribution that Cleomenes' madness and suicide make sense. Again Herodotus saves the phenomena, not in terms of cause and effect, but in terms of the surface alone. He makes us look at the appropriateness of Cleomenes' madness in light of his injustice to Demaratus. He makes us see an 'ought' in Cleomenes' death, what may be called its 'poetic justice.' He makes us see as belonging together what is and what ought to be. He lets appear in this special case the theme of Book VI: σωφροσύνη or sanity.

Herodotus does not say that Cleomenes' madness compensated for Dorieus' but for Demaratus' failure to become king (V.42.1–2). Dorieus deserved the kingship by his merits, and if he had stayed in Sparta and put up with being ruled by his inferior, he would have obtained the kingship; but his disbelief in the coincidence of merit and success, a disbelief that shows itself in his disregard of oracles and customary rites, prompted him to leave Sparta and bring about his own death (V.48). Cleomenes acted unjustly against Demaratus in terms of the law, Dorieus was wronged and deprived of his natural right by the law; Cleomenes was in no way responsible. The violation of the law and not of nature was punished in Cleomenes' madness. Sanity, then, would seem to be based on the conviction that what the law says is. It would seem to be based on the support of human affairs by the divine.

There is, however, another meaning of sanity which parallels its meaning in this story. Herodotus indicates in Book VI why the deeds of his last books

---

[14]Cf. pp. 119–120 *supra*; Plato *Leges* 637a2–e7.

[15]Cf. 72.1; 91; IV.205. Of 14 instances of τίσις seven are Herodotus' own; they have a different character from these two (72.1; 84.3): III.109.2; 126.1; 128.5; VIII.105.1; 106.4.

need the λόγος of his earlier books. When Mardonius came to Ionia, Herodotus says, "I shall here tell the greatest marvel for those of the Greeks who do not accept that Otanes gave as his opinion to the seven (conspirators) that the Persians must have a democracy; for Mardonius put down the Ionian tyrants and set up democracies in the cities" (43.3; III.80).[16] Unless the reader has been converted to believing that a free discussion took place among the Persians, he will be unable to understand an event that he cannot doubt occurred. Only if he had lost the view that democracy is a Greek discovery can he comprehend this fact in light of that speech. We saw, however, that Herodotus' conviction that the speeches of Otanes, Megabyzus, and Darius were in fact spoken turned on the necessity that the truth, if certain conditions are met, will be spoken. It was the necessity of λόγος itself that guaranteed the event, and not only the customary truth-telling of the Persians. The possibility that the truth be told coincided with its necessity, just as the willingness of Praxaspes did not differ from the necessity that came over him to tell the truth. Mardonius' establishment of democracies ceases to be unexpected if one admits that it was not impossible for Otanes to think of it. The fact finds its explanation in thought, and it would be distrust in thought that made Mardonius' action miraculous. "By distrust," Heraclitus says, "many things escape being known" (Fr.86). Sanity, then, means not only the coincidence of law and fact but the coincidence of speech and deed. It means not only seeing things in their facticity but in their λόγος. To see deeds soberly means to see them in the light of λόγος, just as to see λόγος soberly requires the light of deeds. Herodotus wrote the first four books under the necessity of a λόγος, which inevitably led him to ignore and distort certain deeds in Egypt, Persia, Scythia and Libya; but the deeds of the last four books are not allowed to dictate their own account without the benefit of that λόγος. Books I–IV would seem insane were they not corrected and illuminated by Books VI–IX, which, in turn, would be senseless were they not informed by Books I–IV. Neither the θεωρίη of I–IV nor the πρῆξις of VI–IX is intelligible by itself. If the tension between them was the underlying theme of Book V, it is their mutual adjustment that constitutes that of Book VI.

Herodotus shows what the reconciliation between speech and deed means by the double use he makes of the phrase τὸ ἐόν ("what is" or "the truth") (37; 50). In the first story, Croesus told the men of Lampsacus to release Miltiades, "for otherwise he would wipe them out as a pine tree; and when they wandered in their speeches perplexed as to what this saying meant" an old man finally said the truth, that a pine tree once cut does not grow again but utterly dies; and in the second story Cleomenes asked Crius what was his name, and when

---

[16]Cf. pp. 83–84 *supra*.

he told the truth, Cleomenes said, "Now cover your horns, Ram (Crius), with brass, for you will meet with great evil" (cf. IX.91). The truth in the first story lies concealed in a simile, the truth in the second is a name; but the truth about the simile is a fact, while the truth about the name seems to appear only after Cleomenes converts it into a metaphor. Both stories concern threats. The simile of the pine-tree becomes a real threat when the deed which it suggests is grasped; whereas the name of Crius becomes a deed only metaphorically. τὸ ἐόν of the simile is what is true, τὸ ἐόν of the name signifies nothing but the name. Croesus showed his intention in a natural simile; Cleomenes gave an intention to a conventional name. Cleomenes attributed to Crius' name something that ordinarily would not belong to his name; or rather he apparently drew out from the name something that was already there. He discovered and made use of its meaning; and the old man at Lampsacus did almost the same with Croesus' simile.[17] The gap between τὸ ἐόν as meaning and as name is that between discovery and invention. Where the old man deciphered a likeness, Cleomenes made one. If the old man stands closer to the Herodotus of Book IV, who discovered there that the Scythians had likened snow to feathers, Cleomenes resembles the Herodotus of Book VI, who interpreted Cleomenes' own madness as retribution and the disasters of Chios as signs. He uncovered the intention of these events, which apparently bore as little significance as Crius' name. He gave them a sense. But to give them a sense is not the same as to discover a sense that is already there. One knows that Croesus intended something by his simile, while Cleomenes transforms into sense what Crius unintentionally told him. Both Cleomenes and Herodotus made sense of what was given them, but that does not make it true. The old man's discovery was true, only Crius' name was true. Thus the gap between them proves to be that between what is and what ought to be, between what is true and what makes sense. It is the gap that Herodotus in Book VI tries to close.

To put a "good face" on some unjust action, to assimilate the worse to the better reason, would be one way of closing that gap, and Herodotus gives us many examples of it. The "pretext" of the Samians by which they saved their sanctuaries and private goods; the "screen" of Mardonius, who put the punishment of Eretria and Athens before his real intention of conquering as many Greeks as possible; the "pretext" the Athenians "gladly caught hold of" when the Aeginetans gave earth and water to Darius; the "pretexts they dragged out" for not giving back the Aeginetan hostages; and the "pretext"

---

[17]That Lampsacus was once called Pityus ("Piney") adds point to the discovery by an old man—he remembered the name; but at the same time it shows how different his discovery was from Cleomenes'.

and "screen of speech" Miltiades presented against the Parians in order to satisfy a private resentment[18]—all these excuses might seem merely the tribute vice pays to virtue; and yet the Samian and Athenian pretexts cannot so easily be dismissed. If Herodotus himself accuses the Ionians of foolishness in not accepting the Persian proposals, the Samians seem more than hypocrites when they allege the disorder of the Ionians and the power of Darius as their reasons for withdrawal; and the Athenians seem more than justified when they allege Aegina's betrayal of Greece as the reason for their accusation. Herodotus himself says Cleomenes "worked for the common good of Greece" in wishing to arrest those Aeginetans who were "most responsible" for their submission to Persia (61.1). It is extremely doubtful, then, whether "pretext" has a good or bad sense, whether the impure motives of the Samians and Athenians completely condemn what they did. If we look at the action alone, it seems to be honest and fair; if we look at the intention alone, it seems to be unjust. "Looks" and intention seem incompatible and as far apart as false and true. Leutychides, when he tries to persuade the Athenians to give back the Aeginetan hostages, tells a story that points up this difficulty (86). Glaucus had the best reputation for justice of all the Spartans of his time, and a Milesian, on the strength of this, deposited half his money with him and gave him tokens by which he could know to whom he should give it back; but when the Milesian's sons showed their right to the money, Glaucus claimed that he did not remember any such Milesian; but wishing to act justly, he inquired at Delphi whether he should swear an oath and thus rob them; and the oracle warned him that a man who swears falsely leaves no posterity;[19] then Glaucus begged for forgiveness, "but the Pythian said that to make trial of the god and to act are equivalent." From a divine point of view intention and act are the same; the god is indifferent as to whether Glaucus returns the money, which he did, or even thinks about not returning it: no trace of Glaucus' family is left in Sparta. The god does not care whether Glaucus in fact was just; and such high standards would automatically condemn both the Samians and Athenians. They would be guilty of bad intentions even though what they did saved themselves or worked for the common good of Greece. The show of justice that they and Glaucus put forward does not jibe with their hidden designs; but Herodotus seems less willing than the oracle to dismiss that show. He lets a screen negotiate between the just and unjust. He lowers his standards. His acquiescence is another indication of his prudence and sobriety.

---

[18]13.2; 44.1; 49.2; 86.1; 133.1 bis; cf. 94.1; 137.2; IV.165.3; p. 122 *supra*. πρόφασις and πρόσχημα occur 8 times out of a total 26 here; in IV, with the next highest, 5 times.

[19]Cf. Hesiod *Theogony* 226–232; *OD* 219–224; 320–334.

It is not surprising that Leutychides on this occasion did not convince the Athenians. He used a story that suits the Spartans more than the Athenians. Its sacred character would make it more persuasive at Sparta. Sparta is a city that always looks to the sacred. Its laws are sacred laws, and its actions are guided by Delphi. Oracles show the Spartans how to adjust every departure from the law to the law; they show them how to fit nature to law (52–55).[20] The wife of Aristodemus gave birth to twins; and when the Spartans wished the older to rule "according to law," they did not know how to distinguish them, "so like and equal were they," and their mother claimed that she herself did not know, "wishing that both in some way might be kings." Perplexed by a natural likeness, the Spartans consulted the oracle at Delphi, which told them to have two kings, but to honor more the older (or worthier); and again perplexed they were advised to spy on the mother and see whether she always washed and fed one of them first; and when they observed that she did, they reared him at public expense as a sign of his greater dignity. The Spartans not only follow their ancient law, they believe that a mother would also; they take it for granted that she would cherish the older more and identify the older with the dearer. They solve the doubleness that nature produced on the grounds that a mother would naturally follow the law; and they solve the doubleness itself by consulting an oracle. They change their law of a single king by oracular guidance, and they preserve their law of primogeniture by identifying nature with law. This mutual adjustment of nature to law and law to nature indicates the grain of truth in the playful Greek story about Anacharsis; who is supposed to have said that he found all the other Greeks busy at every kind of wisdom, but only the Spartans spoke and answered soberly (IV.77.1.). Spartan σωφροσύνη rests on their ability to fit what ought to be to what is, and what is to what ought to be. They combine, as it were, the truth of Croesus' simile with the truth of Crius' name.

The Spartans' account of their twin kingship is told by no other Greek; it is an exclusively Spartan story, so much so that "they agree with no poet" (52.1). They do not depend as the other Greeks seem to do on poetry, but stand as much apart from it as did the Scythians, whose account of their own origins did not agree with the Pontine Greeks, who based their version on Hesiod, nor even with Aristeas "possessed by Apollo" though he was, let alone with the common story held by both Greeks and barbarians (IV.5–13).[21]

---

[20]In the Spartan section of this book, 50–86, Herodotus uses or has the Spartans use the word φημί 23 times out of a total 38 in the whole book. Note the frequency of poetic words: ἄγη 61.1; λάσθη 67.2; εἴδομαι 69.1 (cf. VII.56.2); λιταί 69.2; ἀιδρείη 69.4; μέμονα 84.2.

[21]Cf. pp. 102–105 supra. For the Spartan contempt for poetry, cf. Plato Leges 680b1–d3; and consider VII.159; 161.3, where the Spartans, without

Spartan sobriety is directly related to their provincialism. By keeping to themselves they preserve a constancy that neither Athens nor Persia shares; indeed,
the Persians "especially adopt foreign customs," and are quite willing to
sacrifice to gods in whom they do not believe.[22] The Persians' tolerance
merely shows the reverse side of Cambyses' madness, which appeared in his
contempt for images of alien gods, and of Xerxes' setting fire to Greek
temples. The Spartans' sobriety, then, might be called the reflexive virtue, the
virtue of remaining true to oneself. It is what connects them with the Egyptians
and Scythians, who both especially avoid foreign customs.[23] It connects them
even more closely than the account, agreed upon by the other Greeks and the
Persians, would suggest, which affirms that their kings, on the female side,
were originally Egyptians (53–54). This ὁμολογία between Greeks and Per
sians guarantees the "correctness" of their joint account, just as the agreement
of "barbarians" with Egyptians guaranteed the accuracy of Egyptian history
after Psammetichus, and the common account of Greeks and barbarians about
the Scythians' origins was most convincing to Herodotus (II.147.1; 154.4).[24]
Moreover, Herodotus only admits the correctness of the Greek account up to
Perseus, for the Greeks make Zeus his father, and are unable to assign him a
mortal father, as they can to Heracles. Their failure to provide a double
account does not affect the Persians, who say that Perseus was originally an
Assyrian.[25] The agreement between Greeks and Persians breaks down at the
vital point, the presence or absence of gods; and Herodotus remains silent
about how native Egyptians showed their right to Dorian kingdoms, but wisely
refers the reader to others, who must have written of Io (the ancestor of the
Heraclidae) whom the Greeks portrayed in the likeness of the Egyptian Isis.
The alien origin of the Spartan kings necessarily leads back to stories about
divine origins, which Herodotus as carefully avoids relating here as he did in
Book II; instead, he resorts to the same device that served him there. He discusses Spartan laws (56–60: cf. I.65.3–5).

Sparta's double kingship contains another kind of doubleness. Not only
are the two kings served double portions at every public sacrifice and at every
meal whether private or public (cf. IV.66: VII.103.1); and not only does each
choose two messengers to consult the oracle at Delphi and have two votes in

---

saying that it is, quote part of an Homeric line (*Iliad* VIII.125), while the
Athenians explicitly use Homer as an authority; also V.94.2, where the
Athenians' argument comes from Homer (note the poetic plural (ἁρπαγαί).

[22]I.135; cf. VI.97.2; 118.1; VII.191.2; 197.4; IX.41.4.

[23]II.79.1; 91.1; IV.76.1; cf. II.158.5; IX.41.4.

[24]Cf. pp. 63–4, 104–5, *supra*.

[25]Cf. II.44.4–5; 50.3; 91.2–6; 146; and I.181.2–182 with VII.61.3.

council: but they have two priesthoods and a double function in peace and war. One priesthood belongs to Zeus Lacedaemon, the other to Zeus Uranius. Zeus Lacedaemon is a local god, Zeus Uranius is universal. One takes care of Sparta as a separate land, the other takes care of the Spartans whenever they invade any other territory. In order to reconcile a local habitation with more than local operations they need two gods, who together bind their earth to heaven, the part to the whole. These two kinds of gods inevitably remind us of the Egyptian and Persian Zeus, one a ram-faced Zeus of Thebes, the other the whole disc of heaven which the Persians call Zeus (I.131.2: II.42). Thus the Spartans recapitulate the two major barbarian peoples, who contributed as well to two major parts of Herodotus' own *logos*. And Herodotus now remarks that the Spartans agree, on the one hand, with most barbarians in Asia and the Persians in their royal funerals, and, on the other, with the Egyptians in the practice of the arts, each herald, flutist, and cook handing down his art to his son (cf. II.37.5; 65.3; 166.2–167). The Assyrian origin of Perseus, whose son is supposed to have given the Persians their name, and the Egyptian origin of Danae, the mother of Perseus, would seem to be confirmed in the double agreement that Spartan laws have with Asian and Egyptian laws. Herodotus has replaced the Greek and Persian accounts with his own, which finds not origins but agreements. They do not show Sparta's derivative character but its lack of uniqueness. Just as Otanes had shown Athenian democracy as a possibility that must occur in a free discussion, so now Spartan laws are shown not to differ from those of the barbarians. Both Athens and Sparta belong to the *logos* of Books II–IV.

The Spartans do not pick a herald for his "loudness of voice" but for his being the son of a herald, nor can he be dismissed for lack of this natural ability. An "ancestral art" is a contradiction in terms.[26] An art cannot be learned unless the learner can be taught, who must come to the art already equipped with certain prerequisites. The weak voice of a herald may make little difference, but it matters a good deal whether the Spartans have a good or bad king. When their king dies the citizens loudly lament, saying that the last king, whoever he was, was the best king; and yet Cleomenes died mad and only obtained the throne on the basis of seniority, while Dorieus knew that by excellence he deserved it (V.42.1). The Spartans thus gloss the difference

---

[26]The "art" of prophecy is the critical case of an art that seems unlearnable but still transmittable: Euenius obtained ἔμφυτον μαντικήν (IX.94.3, but consider 95); but Herodotus uses μαντηίη at II.83 (consider 84) after he says that among the Egyptians the τέχνη of μαντική is assigned to no human being (cf. II.49.2; 57.3; IV.67.2; 172.3); see further Plato *Symposium* 202e7–203a1.

between nature and custom by praising each king once dead as the best; just as the Egyptians called each of their kings καλὸς κἀγαθός (II.143.4). What would show up the one defect of monarchy—the accidental coincidence of merit with rank—the Spartans conceal in their lamentations, and not only in them, as the story of Demaratus makes clear (61–70).

A Spartan baby-girl was ugly, and her nurse, noting that her parents were grieved at her lack of beauty, used to take her to the temple of Helen, where she stood in front of her statue and prayed that Helen remove the ugliness of the child. The nurse did so on the grounds that the daughter of prosperous parents should be beautiful; she believed that what ought to be must be, just as the Spartans praise each dead king as the best king. A woman who appeared before her as she was leaving the sanctuary answered her prayers, and the girl became the most beautiful of Spartan women. This metamorphosis occurs by divine intervention. It somehow inverts the claim of the Greeks and Scythians that the Neuri every year change themselves into wolves, which did not persuade Herodotus though they swore to its truth (IV.105.2). Whereas the Neuri alternate between the human and the bestial—the higher and the lower—and they do so by their own magic, the Spartans claim that a goddess effected a change from the ugly to the beautiful, so that the proprieties would be observed. And for similar reasons Ariston ("Best") refused to acknowledge his responsibility for the failure of his two wives to bear children—the legitimacy of kingship would fail with his sterility; and he concealed the desire that "chafed" him behind an oath (62.1). He made his illegitimate desire to have another man's wife conform with the need to maintain justice, and he effected this conformation by an oath. He so much elevated his desire that it no longer was illegitimate; and yet the illegitimate still plagues him and his son Demaratus ("Prayed-for-by-the-people"). Ariston's son was born before he had been married to his new wife ten months, and when he was informed of his birth he counted on his fingers the months and swore that it could not be his; but he later regretted this remark—perhaps he recognized his sterility—and believed that the child was his. Later, Cleomenes bribed the Pythian oracle to deny Demaratus' legitimacy, and Demaratus, deprived of his throne, beseeched his mother under oath to tell him the truth of his parentage. His mother then offered a double account of his legitimacy. To Ariston's denial she replied that women sometimes bear in the seventh as well as in the tenth month. It was Ariston's ignorance, she said, that made him utter his denial. He made the mistake of confusing the customary with the natural; he did not see that nature does not follow the strict counting of custom, which turns what usually happens into a law without exceptions. Demaratus' mother, in short, adjusts what ought to be to what is, while her reply to the accusation that she committed adultery with an ass-keeper, adjusts what is to what ought to be. She said that on the third night after her wedding "an apparition resembling Ariston" slept with her and crowned her, and when Ariston saw that she swore to its truth, he understood that the matter was divine; and since the crown evidently came from the heroon of Astrabacus, the god of muleteers, she asked Demaratus to believe himself either a hero's son or Ariston's. She offers both a natural and a more than natural explanation. She does in the first what the Spartans had done when confronted with twins—adjusted the law to the fact; and she does in the second what Cleomenes had done when accused of bribery before Argos— attributed his retreat to a divine sign.

The Spartans' ability to find in what seems what is, and in what is a seeming, recurs in their justification of their failure to aid the Athenians at Marathon (106.2-3). To the Athenians' plea that they should not let the "most ancient" Greek city fall to barbarians, the Spartans oppose their unwillingness to break a law that forbids them to leave unless the moon is full on the ninth day of a new month (cf. VII.206.1; VIII.72; IX.7.1). A celestial sign protects the Spartans from any accusation of betrayal or indifference. They gloss the fact of their absence with so fair an excuse that we cannot distinguish the show of legality from its intention. The divine gives to the human a fairer appearance (cf. VIII.94).

When the Persians at Marathon saw the Athenian hoplites begin to attack, "they charged them with an utterly fatal madness, seeing they were few, and, worse, charging at a run, unsupported by either cavalry or archers—thus the barbarians guessed (κατείκαζον)" (112.2-3; cf. VIII.10.1). The Persians make a mistake. They look at the Athenians in what they believe is a perfectly rational way: they are few, they do run, they are unsupported; and yet they really do not see what is before them. They conclude that they are madmen when they are perfectly sane. The Persians make the same mistake as Xerxes did later, when he learned that the Spartans at Thermopylae were combing their hair; from which "he was unable to conjecture the truth, that they were preparing to kill and be killed" (VII.209.1). The Persians are so 'rational' in their reasoning that it has the same effect as the excessive imagination of the Ionians, who likened themselves to madmen when they were sane. The Persian error seems to arise from their trust in λόγος at the expense of what appears before them. They so closely identify what ought to be with what is that they deny that any son ever killed his father or mother. They are unconsciously forced to lie, although they believe lying to be most shameful. If they were confronted with the mad Cleomenes asking for his sword, they would be compelled to give it back; for otherwise they would have to lie and be unjust, for they believe that the failure to give something back the second greatest disgrace. They do not understand the connection between lying and justice. It is the Persians' failure to see that lying might be necessary for justice that constitutes part of their madness. They do not understand the importance of seeming. Their λόγος stands so far apart from what they see around them that they cannot fit them together. They cannot make a proper likeness; they are unpoetic. They have no gods that can publicly appear in an image. Either they conjecture from the dreams of kings or from eclipses. There is nothing divine that can appear as Astrabacus did to Demaratus' mother, or Pan to Philippides. There are no oracles that openly explain the will of the gods. Herodotus seems to attribute the greater sanity of the Greeks to their anthropomorphic gods and heroes, who are what they seem to be and hence permit the 'saving of the phenomena.'[27] They sanction the adjustment of what is to what ought to be. It is appropriate that the Athenians should be stationed in the Heracleon at Marathon, and again on their swift return should camp in the Heracleon at Cynosargus (108.1; 116: cf. IX.101.1). For the Spartans to worship Lycurgus after he established good laws among them might violate the strictest truth; but if the Pythian oracle cannot decide whether he is man or god (I.65-66), perhaps it is not unfitting that they should not too sharply distinguish between 'how like a god' and the god himself. That it can lead to great abuses the tricks of Pisistratus show, but the stability of Sparta, based as it is on the constancy of their laws, owes much to the more than human reverence that they accord Lycurgus. The Persians' utter reasonableness, on the other hand, in adopting from others what they think better than their own customs, leads to their underestimating the political importance of tradition. They do not see how the sound in theory can be in practice unsound, and vice versa. They could be Herodotus' guide in Books I-IV, where he wished to discover the true λόγος, but incompetent to guide him later through the seemings that are necessary for sound practice.[28]

The Athenians were the "first of all the Greeks we know of who ran against enemies, and the first who endured seeing Median dress and the men who wore it; for up till then even the name of Medes was for the Greeks a terror to hear" (112.3). Everyone has remarked that Herodotus forgets the former battles he has himself recorded in which Greeks fought bravely against the Persians; but one thing makes this battle different from all those. It is the first battle the Greeks won (Pl. *Menex.* 240d). Herodotus attributes the Athenians' victory to their seeing Median dress as simply Median dress, the men who wear it as simply men, and to their hearing the name 'Medes' as simply a name. The Athenians see what is before them; they do not imagine anything.[29] It is their avoidance of all imaginings that justifies their title of being first. Herodotus interprets the Greeks' previous defeats as indicative of their failure to see what is as what is. Although the Spartans arrived after the battle

---

[27]Cf. p. 46 *supra.*

[28]Cf. p. 22 *supra.*

[29]Cf. Thucydides IV.34.1; but consider VIII.132.3 with IX.90-91.

of Marathon, "they nevertheless desired to look at the Medes" (120). The
Medes they saw were dead Medes, but the sight must have rid the Spartans of
the terror their dress, appearance, and name must have once invoked. At any
rate, they were not terrified at Thermopylae (cf. VII.207; 226; IX.46). In
θεωρίη, then, lies the highest kind of σωφροσύνη. It is what the Persians call
madness. Herodotus thought that the Greeks had jokingly invented the saying
of Anacharsis, which attributed the practice of every kind of wisdom to the
other Greeks but sobriety to the Spartans. He thought it was unserious because
it separated wisdom from sobriety, a separation that the Athenians' 'insane'
sobriety, based on θεωρίη, shows to be impossible.

In the last twenty paragraphs of Book VI Herodotus gives a kind of sum-
mary of its theme. It easily falls into two sections, one concerned with the
Alcmeonids, the other with Miltiades (121–131; 132–140).[30] They both
illustrate the phrase "to save the phenomena."[31] Herodotus expresses surprise
at and his own rejection of the story that the Alcmeonids would have signalled
to the Persians, and thus brought Athens under the Persians and Hippias. He
marvels that the story was even invented, when they "evidently were haters of
tyranny," and had the reputation for having bribed the oracle at Delphi, which
"openly" liberated Athens, whereas Harmodius' and Aristogeiton's murder of
Hipparchus only exacerbated the surviving Pisistratids. If an obscure factor in
the sequence of events that led to the Pisistratids' expulsion obtained so much
glory (cf. 109.3), it seems incredible that the Alcmeonids' actions, which
immediately preceded Athens' liberation, could have failed to prevent such a
story. Thus the evident itself refutes it. Moreover, the evident agrees with
what λόγος would decide (οὕτω οὐδὲ λόγος αἱρέει);[32] for if one thinks of a
motive for their betrayal—some resentment they might have had against the
populace—, the evident again refutes it: the Alcmeonids were the most
honored and notable family among the Athenians. Herodotus finds, then, in
the perfect coincidence of the phenomena with reason the grounds for vindicat-
ing the Alcmeonids. But we have only to consider the stories Herodotus
chooses to tell right afterwards, as he intended us to do, to doubt his argument. He explains how the Alcmeonids became very wealthy and famous
throughout Greece. Their wealth comes from Croesus, their fame from
Clisthenes the tyrant of Sicyon. Their evident hatred of tyrants does not seem
to have touched their ancestors; for we now recall that the second attempt of

---

[30]The story of Agariste's suitors is written in an Homeric style: the word
μνηστήρ occurs seven times; cf. Fränkel, E., *Geschichte der Griechischen
Nomina agentis* (Strassburg, 1910), Pt. I, p. 213.

[31]Cf. Aristotle *de gen. et corr.* 325a17–23; *EE* 1236b21–23.

[32]Cf. II.33.2; 43.3; III.45.3.

Pisistratus to establish his tyranny was based on an alliance with Megacles, whose marriage to Clisthenes' daughter is now described (I.60–61.2). How can this evidence be reconciled with the previous evidence? One could suggest the following solution. The origins of something splendid or beautiful might not be splendid or beautiful but quite as sordid as the Alcmeonids'. It would, however, be a mistake to ignore the result in favor of the origins. In an attempt to reduce the result to its origins, the result might no longer be seen for what it is. This is the argument by which Amasis won over the Egyptians to his rule (II.172).[33] He made a golden foot-basin into a statue of some god, and when the Egyptians began to worship it, he told them its origin and compared himself to it, who once base had now become their king and deserved to be honored as such. Not what he was but what he is should guide them. Now Herodotus seems to defend the Alcmeonids on the same grounds. It would be mad to reject the surface impression of the Alcmeonids and rely only on their past, if the new result can neither explain the surface nor discover any motive which does not contradict λόγος itself. Thus Herodotus, as far as the Alcmeonids' guilt is concerned, finds it safer and more just to ignore their past.

Alcmeon once helped the messengers of Croesus at Delphi; and Croesus later invited him to Sardis and offered him as much gold-dust as he could carry on his person all at once. Alcmeon put on a large chiton with deep folds and the largest boots he could find: and pouring gold-dust in his boots and dress, sprinkling some in his hair, and putting more in his mouth he emerged "looking more like anything than a human being: his mouth was stuffed and everything else swelled up." Alcmeon's greed is so great that he ceases to look human. He becomes in fact what the suitors of Agariste are metaphorically, "swelled up on their own merits or their native land." Thirteen suitors had come to Clisthenes' court, and Clisthenes inquired of all of them about their native land and family. He then tested their "manly excellence, temper, education, and character, both individually and all together"; and he tested the younger suitors at gymnastics and, "most important, at symposia." He tested them in σωφροσύνη. Clisthenes at first preferred Hippoclides because of his own excellence and family connections with the tyrannical Cypselids; but at the final feast the suitors held a contest in music and social wit; and Hippoclides was so carried away by his dancing—"he danced somehow pleasingly to himself"—that he began to dance on a table, first Laconic figures, then Attic, and third "supported his head on the table and gesticulated with his legs." Clisthenes was so outraged at his shamelessness that he told him that he had danced away his marriage, to which Hippoclides replied what later became

---

[33]Cf. pp. 64–66 *supra*.

a proverb: "It is no concern of Hippoclides." Hippoclides assumed a shape as grotesque as that of Alcmeon; he too looked like anything more than a human being; but the cause was exactly the opposite. Alcmeon became non-human by his greed, Hippoclides by his indifference. His excessive lack of concern led to the same effect as Alcmeon's over-anxiousness. Both neglected appearance. Both went beyond what is seemly. They did not take care to maintain their likeness to human beings. Each makes up half the simile of Amasis, who, reproached for his idleness, compared the human condition to a bow, which cannot always be kept strung but must be unstrung when not in use; so, too, if a man remained only in one state he would go mad (II.173.3–4). The playfulness of Hippoclides and the earnestness of Alcmeon must be combined. Croesus laughed at Alcmeon who did not laugh at himself; and Hippoclides found himself amusing, but no one else seconded him. It is difficult to fit these two conditions together. Herodotus himself fits them by the very juxtaposition of these two stories, neither of which yields its meaning without the other; but he never shows their union except in his own *logos*. His defense of the Alcmeonids steers exactly a middle course between the seriousness of the explicit defense, which excludes any doubt, and the absurd story he himself produced which undermines it; but the absurdity of Alcmeon only corrects but does not destroy the original defense. The two halves together form the true defense, whose final proof rests on another Agariste, who dreamed that she gave birth to a lion—a sign of tyranny—and in a few days gave birth to Pericles, who seemed but was not a tyrant.[34]

If these stories point to the adjustment of the playful to the serious on the human level, the following two stories show the adjustment of the human to the divine (135; 139–140). They show the "ought" of oracles being made to coincide with fact and gloss an evident wrong.[35] The Parians wished to kill Timo, the priestess of the chthonic gods, who treated with Miltiades about Paros' capture and revealed to him "the sacred things that are unspeakable to the male sex"; but the oracle prevented them, "asserting that Timo was not responsible, but Miltiades had to end not well, and she appeared as his guide into troubles." All the Greeks say that the Parians guarded their wall and doubled its height at vulnerable points; only the Parians give this account of Miltiades' failure. The Parian account links the injustice of Miltiades with the

---

[34]Cf. V.56.1; 92β3; Thucydides II.65.9; Plutarch *Pericles* 7.1 (155C); Strassburger, H., *Historia*, 4, 1955, pp. 1–25.

[35]For the "ought" of the oracle (135.3), cf. I.8.2; II.161.3; IV.79.1; VI.64; IX.109.2; and for the "ought" of Herodotus' *logos* (either in the sense of what he must say or what must be thought), cf. I.57.2; 179.1; II.16.2; 20.3; 24.1; III.9.2; 45.3; V.54.1; 62; 67.3; VII.185.1; 214.2; IX.65.2.

violation of the sacred, the humanly unjust with the divine. It links what did happen with what ought to have happened, and thus absolves Timo of any guilt. Miltiades himself had employed a similar kind of screen in the capture of Lemnos. The Lemnians had promised hundreds of years ago that they would recompense the Athenians for their injustice, whenever a ship travelled in a single day from Attic land to Lemnian; and Miltiades, having made the Chersonesus subject to the Athenians, had sailed from there to Lemnos and reminded the Lemnians of the oracle. One city agreed that the Chersonesus was Attic, another did not (140.2). It did not agree to this ambiguity of a name, which could equally stand for the original land and its colony. Miltiades screened the apparent wrong of his attack behind an oracle. He interpreted it in such a way that what he did coincided with what the oracle said must be. Under its auspices he was more successful than when he could only allege the medism of Paros (133.1).

What the last paragraphs of Book VI reveal is the double theme of Book VI. On the one hand, the stories of Alcmeon and Hippoclides point to the human simply, as the mean between the excessive unconcern of Hippoclides and the excessive concern of Alcmeon; and on the other, the stories of Timo and Miltiades point to the connection between the human and the divine. The human cannot be treated by itself but requires for its understanding an interpretation of the divine. But the divine has a double interpretation. The divine is jealous and destroys the beautiful, and the divine is gracious and allows the beautiful to appear. One is forced to wonder, then, whether there is some relation between the human as the mean between the serious and the playful—the tensed and relaxed bow of Amasis—and the divine as both jealous and gracious. Is the humanly serious to the humanly playful as divine grace is to divine jealousy? Does divine grace support one and divine jealousy destroy the other? Does human excellence have a support in the whole outside these extremes? Or must the human simply tend toward being as grotesque as Alcmeon or as topsy-turvy as Hippoclides? Are the Greeks, who preserve a mean between the excessive piety of the Egyptians and the impiety of the Persians, a genuine and permanent third? These are the final questions of Herodotus, whose answers lie in the last three books of his *Inquiries*.

VII. PERSIA AND GREECE

Herodotus has presented in Books V and VI the main characteristics of Athens and Sparta. Neither Athens nor Sparta altered the triple argument of Books II–IV, but they did clarify that argument by indicating how we could discern in it the deeds of those two cities. Greece appeared as derivative in a double sense: first in the Egyptian and barbarian origin of its gods, second in the sameness of Spartan laws with the laws of Egypt and Persia, and in the agreement of Athenian democracy with Otanes' speech. The battle of Marathon, however, showed that the superiority of Athens to Persia—the superiority of the derivative to the original—rested on the Athenians' ability to see the Persians as they are. For the first time things were seen for what they were. The derivative proved stronger than any one strand of Herodotus' *logos* precisely because it suffered from none of the faults each strand, uncomplemented by the other two, was subject to. The Persians relied too heavily on a specious λόγος, which led them to underestimate the Athenians, whose perfect understanding of what confronted them seemed to stand in need of no accounting. It so exactly conformed with the situation that, if the previous books had not prepared us, we should have failed to realize its significance. The Athenians showed in practice the superiority of θεωρίη. To make us aware of how difficult it is to see things as they are, and then to act on that seeing, Herodotus devoted Books II–IV to the separate analysis of what he thought were the three fundamental ways of seeing; and he then described how they were present in Athens and Sparta. He now turns again to Persia, whose way of seeing he had uncovered in Book III. There the importance of λόγος itself for the Persians had been examined; but how that was connected with their invasion of Greece was hardly considered. To be sure, the practical consequences of their trust in speech and reason had been shown (Cambyses' madness, for example); but it was not clear how it led to the Persian Wars themselves. It is the question which Herodotus now tries to answer.

The opening paragraphs of Book VII at once remind us of Book III.[1]

---

[1]Cf. pp. 68–76 *supra*.

Herodotus here tells of Darius' preparations against Greece, which the revolt of the Egyptians "enslaved by Cambyses" interrupted, while there he told why Cambyses invaded Egypt. The resentment of an Egyptian doctor, the deception of Amasis, and the chance speech of Aprias' daughter that revealed the truth were the causes of that invasion; but as far as Cambyses was concerned, it was only the last cause that prompted him to act. Such was the Persian story; but the Egyptians made Cambyses half-Egyptian, although they should have known, Herodotus says, that Persian law forbids a bastard to take precedence before a legitimate son. Here in the 7th book Darius is asked to decide whether Artabazanes, his eldest son, or Xerxes, the eldest of his sons born while he was king, should become the next king. Artabazanes appealed to the universal custom of men, which always assigns the throne to the eldest, and Xerxes appealed to Cyrus, his mother's father, who gave the Persians their freedom. Xerxes' appeal to his lineage was supported, "as rumor has it," by Demaratus' contention that the Spartans by custom crowned the first son born to the father while king; and Darius is supposed to have acknowledged the justice of this and, on the strength of it, made Xerxes king. Herodotus, however, thinks that Xerxes would have been king even without this legal support. "for Atossa held all the power." Whereas Herodotus refuted the Egyptians' claim about Cambyses' parentage by showing up their unaccountable ignorance of Persian law, he now casts doubt on the force of Demaratus' argument by pointing to what far outweighed it, the power of Xerxes' mother. This difference indicates how drastic was the shift that Book V effected. No matter how decisive customs might be in general, other forces easily suspend them in some particular situation. Neither the universal custom for Artabazanes, nor the Spartan custom for Xerxes, alone persuades Darius; they are both superfluous in light of Atossa's power; but we may note, in accordance with the contraction of Herodotus' scope in the last four books, that the Spartan exception to a universal custom gives Xerxes' accession a show of legality that it otherwise would not have had. Instead of the conflict between a Persian and an Egyptian story, Herodotus now presents an agreement between Persian practice and Spartan law; and instead of the Persians' invasion of Egypt, which illustrated two parts of his *logos,* Xerxes now suppresses the Egyptian revolt in an offhand fashion as he prepares for a full-scale attack on Greece (7; cf. III.12.4). Cambyses invaded Egypt for the sake of avenging the lie that Amasis had perpetrated; but Herodotus was far less interested in it as a cause than as illustrative of the Persians' trust in speech. Now, however, Xerxes' reasons for invading Greece are important in themselves; for unlike Cambyses' quick anger at a single lie, Xerxes had to be persuaded in many ways before he was willing to undertake the invasion. True and false speech in theory, which was the major concern of Book III, is replaced by diverse opinions about the advisability of invading

Greece. λόγος, one might say, is replaced γνώμη (5-18).[2]

Mardonius gave a threefold reason for invasion. One, Herodotus says, was to persuade Xerxes to avenge the wrongs the Athenians had done, another he urged as "an addition" or "a digression," that Europe was very beautiful, with all kinds of cultivated trees and an excellent soil, "and worthy for only a king among mortals to possess"; and between these two he pointed to the "good report" Xerxes would acquire, and the fear Xerxes would instill in everyone who might later wish to attack Persia. Xerxes himself, when Mardonius finally persuaded him, offered slightly different reasons (cf. I.46.1; 73.1). He first told the assembly of the best Persians that, ever since Cyrus established the empire, the Persians have never rested but always expanded, and that he, wishing to have no less honor and fame than his forebears and to add no less power, saw that the invasion of Greece could satisfy his ambition at the same time that it would punish the Greeks for their attack on Sardis and the Persian defeat at Marathon. Xerxes rearranged the order in which Mardonius had put these reasons. For Mardonius the acquisition of more land was a mere aside and vengeance most important. Mardonius' secret ambition to become ruler of Greece led him to distort the order, whereas Xerxes had no reason to conceal the truth behind a pretended concern for justice. Once Greece is disposed of, he knows that no one will further resist him, and "both guilty and innocent will bear the yoke of slavery." Greece is the only obstacle to his making the Persian empire "coterminous with the sky of Zeus," so that the whole earth will be under one earthly master (8γ1). Herodotus had admitted that the whole earth was one, and only conventional names separated it into Europe, Asia, and Libya; but he did not conclude that it should have one master because it was one. Xerxes believes that the singleness of the sky can be duplicated on earth because the sky is the Zeus that the Persians worship (I.131.1).[3] The universality of Zeus persuades him that a universal empire is its necessary counterpart. He wishes to extend the local horizon to the natural horizon. Neither the sky nor the other six things the Persians worship are local: earth is everywhere, the sun and moon shine everywhere, fire burns everywhere, water is found and winds blow almost everywhere. As their gods are not particularly associated with some particular place, they are not thought of as being effective only within certain boundaries.[4] The seven walls that

---

[2]Out of 170 instances of γνώμη 40 are in VII (more than any other book), and 26 of these are said of or by Persians.

[3]Cf. pp. 34-4, 150, 170 *supra.*

[4]Cf. I.172.2; IV.94.4; Tacitus *H.* 4,64: *quomodo lucem diemque omnibus hominibus, ita omnes terras fortibus viris natura aperuit.* The Persians' ready acceptance of alien practices also aided their expansion; I.135; VII.62.1; cf. Xenophon *Cyropaedeia* III.iii.21-22; and (on the Romans)

Deioces built around Agbatana, each of whose battlements was a different
color, probably symbolized the seven planets (I.98.4–6); but they equally well
represent the seven Persian gods, which Xerxes believes can be brought down
to earth.[5] When Xerxes crossed the Hellespont, a Greek is supposed to have
said: "Oh Zeus! Why do you in the likeness of a Persian and with the name
Xerxes instead of Zeus wish to depopulate Greece, leading all men? For even
without them you could have done it" (56.2; cf. 203.2). The speaker believes
that Zeus has a human shape even when he is not Xerxes. He believes that
Zeus has a particular shape though endowed with universal power. Xerxes
does not make this mistake; he does not see himself as Zeus, but the earth as
another sky. Just as the sky contains and comprehends all the planets and stars,
so the earth contains all the cities and nations; and since there is one sky and
one earth, nothing prevents the worshipers of universal gods from becoming
the rulers of all men. Xerxes refuses to admit a distinction between heaven and
earth; he does not see any disproportion between them. And his refusal to
acknowledge their disproportion exemplifies the natural *hubris* or impiety of
the Persians (I.89.2; cf. 189.1–2; II.32.3). In contrast to this, we must remember that Spartan kings held the priesthood of Zeus Lacedaemon as well as Zeus
Uranius (VI.56.1).

After Mardonius "smoothed over" any objection that the Persian
counselors might make to Xerxes' proposal, Artabanus brings forward two
major reasons for not mounting the expedition. He protests against Mardonius'
deliberate underestimation of the Greeks' military skill, and he points to the
power of chance, which once put Darius' army in jeopardy when Histiaeus
alone opposed the Scythians' demand to destroy the bridge across the Danube.
He believes that prudent judgment, even if it fails, is better than an imprudent
success. "I find the greatest profit in good deliberation; for even if anything
comes out contrary to it, nonetheless it has been well deliberated, and it has
been overcome by chance; but he who deliberates badly, if fortune attends
him, has a windfall, but nonetheless it has been badly deliberated." Artabanus
testifies to the superiority of reason even in practice. The Persian trust in
λόγος, in what ought to be, is unaffected by fact. Fact must measure up to
what should happen in order to be praiseworthy; but there is no plan that can
guarantee their coincidence. Chance keeps them apart. It is a disproportion that
can be traced directly to what "the god" wishes. "You see how the god blasts
with lightning living things that excel, nor does he permit them to make a
great show, while he does not even graze those that are small. You see how he
always hurls thunderbolts against the largest houses and trees; for the god is

---

Arrian *Tactica* 33.
[5]Cf. p. 25 *supra*.

wont to dock all that excels." Divine jealousy allows nothing but himself to be outstanding, and he maintains his own superiority by destroying everything that seems to rival him. Artabanus seems to echo the opinion of both Solon and Amasis, but each gives to the same opinion a different cast (I.32.1-2; III.40.2-4).[6] Even the wise men of Greece, Egypt, and Persia remain Greek, Egyptian, or Persian. Solon talks about human things only; he does not mention, as Artabanus does, trees and animals; nor does he give any proof of god's direct intervention, while Artabanus points to thunder and lightning. Artabanus speaks of "the god," Solon and Amasis of "the divine." If the Persian Zeus is the whole disc of heaven, Artabanus can see thunder and lightning as his weapons. Solon says that every day in a man's life is different, no matter whether he is prosperous or not; Artabanus takes into account only the destruction of great things, for the small things he believes escape unscathed. Solon thought that the disproportion between the divine and the human was so great that he miscounted the number of days in a man's life, as if the Greek calendar's failure to coincide with the solar year led him to exaggerate the difference.[7] The Egyptians had more wisely adjusted their year to the solar year, an adjustment so exact that they could predict, they believed, from the moment of birth what would befall everyone (II.4.1; 82.1). Amasis partly seems to believe this. He advised Polycrates to throw away what he most valued, as though that would magically put a stop to the alternations of success and failure; and when Polycrates got his ring back, Amasis dissolved the alliance, "because he realized that no man can save another from his future, and that Polycrates would end badly." He believed that he could predict Polycrates' miserable death, as he once believed that the future could be controlled. Solon, Amasis, and Artabanus, then, agree that earthly things are unstable, but they do not understand that instability in the same way. Amasis and Artabanus look at great prosperity or great things. Solon at all human things; but Solon and Artabanus think that there is no remedy, while Amasis does. And yet Amasis sees something that neither Solon nor Artabanus sees: he sees the soul (cf. I.32.8). He advised Polycrates to pain his soul so that his material prosperity would continue. Even though he thought divine jealousy could be appeased by the sacrifice of something that affected the soul, he did consider the soul as more important than the body. To be unmaimed, healthy, handsome, untouched by troubles, and the father of fine children, which Solon set down as the only conditions for prosperity, Amasis somehow saw were insufficient. The state of the soul had also to be taken into account, and Artabanus' failure to understand the soul prevents his sound advice from being followed.

---

[6]Cf. pp. 80-82, 132-3 *supra.*
[7]Cf. pp. 17-8 *supra.*

In spite of his initial anger at Artabanus' lack of daring, Xerxes decides on second thoughts to abandon the project; but during the night a tall and handsome man appears in his sleep and forbids him to change his mind. Xerxes pays no attention to the dream, and apologizes to the reassembled Persians for his youthfulness that made him "boil over, so that I threw out words more unseemly than they should have been against an elder." On the following night the same dream appears again. The first dream addressed him as "Oh Persian," the second as "Oh son of Darius," and while the first merely told him to revert to his original plan, the second threatens him: "As you have become great and mighty in a short time, so you will be humbled just as quickly." Xerxes becomes very afraid at this and sends for Artabanus, to whom he expresses his fear that he might displease the god if he does not invade Greece; and in order to make sure that the god sent the dream, he urges Artabanus to dress in his robes, sit on his throne, and then sleep in his bed, for he would then know that the dream came from outside and was not his own. Artabanus at first refuses to obey the command, "because he did not think himself worthy to sit on the royal throne"; but once compelled he tries to persuade Xerxes that dreams are not divine. He says that the association of bad men has corrupted Xerxes' judgment. "just as they say about the sea, though it is most useful to men, when the blasts of winds rush upon it, they do not allow the sea to enjoy its own nature; so I was not so much pained because you disgraced me as because, when two opinions were proposed to the Persians—one set on increasing pride, the other on stopping it and saying that it is bad to teach the soul to search always for more than it has—you preferred the more perilous of these opinions for yourself and the Persians" (16.2). Artabanus compares the soul to the sea, which left to itself enjoys its own nature, but stirred up by wrong counsels seeks more than it has. He applies this to his proof that dreams are not divine; for Xerxes merely dreamt at night of what he had considered during the day, and his dream was thus an after-image of his original decision. But though Artabanus objects to Xerxes' command to assume the external appearance of Xerxes, he does admit that if the dream appears continually, he too would acknowledge it as divine. He then does what Xerxes compelled him to do, and the same dream appears to him; again it threatens, but he dreams in addition that hot irons are about to put out his eyes, so that "shouting out loud he starts up in his sleep" and admits his error (cf. I.8.3; III.38.4). It is appropriate that the decision to conquer the world rests on Xerxes' and Artabanus' confidence in a dream, where all distinctions between "mine" and "thine" disappear, and everything seems possible. Xerxes had envisioned only two possibilities—the conquest of Greece by Persia or the conquest of Persia by Greece: "There is no middle to our mutual hatred." East and West must become one. They must acquire the same unity in fact as they would have in dreams, which Xerxes believes cannot distinguish between

Artabanus dressed in his robes and himself. What Artabanus could so easily have dreamt (himself as king), Xerxes compelled him to act out. Xerxes transferred the absence of "mine" and "thine" in a dream to the world of waking. He denied that the dream was his dream, and if a dream can become the property of anyone, so too can the earth. An empire without limits obtains its real support not from the universality of the Persian Zeus but from the world of dreams. The earth can only be seen as one in a map or dream (cf. I.209.1).

Artabanus did not regard the soul as having its own inherent desires. By comparing it to the sea he denied it any internal source of motion.[8] As whatever we dream about would reflect the business of the day, the soul in itself would be imperturbable. The nature of the soul is simple, so that if a dream continuously urges the dreamer to seek for more, it cannot be characteristic of the soul when asleep, but it must be more than human. Since Xerxes has already changed his mind, his next dream should have praised his decision; and if it did not, the dream could only come from a source more external than his daily life, the gods. Artabanus distinguished so sharply between the soul and its motion that only the gods could account for a recurrent dream. His failure to put the soul and its motion together was aided by his ranking as equal one's own good judgment and one's acceptance of another's. "I have judged it equal to be wise oneself or to be willing to obey him who speaks well." He does not believe, as Hesiod does, that the first is better than the second: "He is altogether best who thinks all things by himself, reflecting on what in the future will finally turn out better; and he too is good who is persuaded by a good speaker; while he who neither thinks for himself nor listens to another and takes it to heart, he is quite useless" (OD 293-297; cf. 286).[9] By not differentiating between the man who thinks for himself and the man who obeys another who thinks for himself, Artabanus was bound to think that all Xerxes' opinions were derived from others. Out of deference perhaps to his master, Artabanus could not imagine that Xerxes might have conceived some inordinate desire by himself. He is thus compelled to deny any difference between knowledge and trust, $\epsilon\pi\iota\sigma\tau\eta\mu\eta$ and $\pi\iota\sigma\tau\iota\varsigma$.[10] Even if in all practical affairs it might seem that the man who has thought how he must act cannot be told apart from the man who willingly obeys him—their actions would be the same—, the difference proves to be important when one sets out to conquer the world.[11] Artabanus' failure to distinguish them allows Xerxes to put his trust in a dream, which has nothing to do with thinking. A dream ignores the dif-

---

[8]Contrast Sophocles *Antigone* 929ss.; Semonides fr. 7, 27-42.

[9]Cf. Livy XXII.29.8-9.

[10]Cf. Chap. III, fn 30.

[11]Cf. Plato *Meno* 97a9-98c4.

ference between true and false, and thus elevates trust to the level of knowledge. Touch, the most fundamental of the senses, could tell the true from the false Smerdis, but in his dream Artabanus could not tell whether hot irons were about to blind him or not. He took a threat in a dream as equivalent to a true threat. A nightmare had the same effect as the actual punishment would have had because he did not believe that his own soul could have originated it. The fear of punishment made him abandon his better judgment. The problem of trust, which dominated Book III, becomes in Book VII the problem of courage.

Xerxes' failure to distinguish between dreaming and waking, and Artabanus' failure to distinguish between an imagined and a real threat, as well as his mistake in identifying knowledge and trust, suggest that the failure of the Persian expedition turns on a general failure to draw distinctions. This failure is shown most clearly in the way that the Persian army was ordered. It was divided into two parts, and between them a space was left for Persian infantry and cavalry—Herodotus gives their particular numbers and calls them four times "chosen"—which preceded or followed the chariot of Xerxes. Herodotus contrasts these ordered groups with the rest of the army, which in front was "jumbled up with tribes of every kind without distinction" (40.1.), and which behind went "higgledy-piggledy" (41.2); and, apart from the Persians, "the army as a promiscuous mixture of every kind" crossed the Hellespont (55.2; cf. I.103.1; IX.32.1). This crowd of soldiers resembles the way in which all the people of the earth would have appeared to us had Herodotus not sorted them out, explained what differentiated the tribes of Libya from those in Scythia, and how they agreed with one another when compared with the Egyptians or Persians. We would not have expected Xerxes to have ordered his army with the precision of Herodotus' own *logos*, but it seems strange that he did not arrange it by tribes as soon as he began his march. Its disorder has the appearance any mixture of different kinds of things would have. It has no *logos*. The heterogeneity of Xerxes' army does not jibe with the homogeneity of the sky in which he confided. He pays attention to celestial but not to terrestrial phenomena (cf. 37.2–3; 57). He does not see the inarticulate form of his army because he accepts what is immediate without reflection. His confidence rests on two premises that are incompatible: he thinks on the unity of the earth and of the sky while he trusts the immediate phenomena. In his second conversation with Artabanus he shows his inability to put them together (45–52).[12]

---

[12]One could say that as the Egyptians' error is to confound νόμος with φύσις, and the Scythian-Libyan error to confound τέχνη (ποίησις) with φύσις, so the Persians' error is to confound τύχη with φύσις—the result of not separating what is from what is not susceptible to λόγος; consider III.34–35; 64.3;

When Xerxes saw the Hellespont covered over with his ships and the beaches and plains full of men, he blessed himself and then wept: and called upon to explain why he did what were "far separated from one another," he told Artabanus that the shortness of every human life came to him on reflection, if out of so large a number none would be alive in a hundred years. Artabanus then went further in sadness, saying that no man, no matter how short his life, does not often wish to die rather than live; but Xerxes cut him off: "About human life let us cease, Artabanus, being as you define it (διαιρέαι), nor let us remember bad things having good things at hand." Artabanus then suggested other grounds for his disquiet about the expedition, and ended thus: "That man would be best, if in deliberation he trembles, reflecting on everything that might happen. but in action is bold." Xerxes again cut him off: "Reasonably, Artabanus, you distinguish (δαιρέαι) each several thing, but do not fear everything nor reflect on everything alike; for if you want to reflect on everything alike in the case of every suggestion, you would never do anything at all; and it is better to be completely bold and suffer half from evils than to fear everything and suffer nothing at all." Xerxes finds the instability of human affairs so great that he prefers the risk of a great loss to the ignominy of inaction. He does not deny what Artabanus has articulated, but he prefers to forget it. He does not wish to have second thoughts. He felt at the sight of his army a mixture of joy and sorrow. He sees but does not wish to act on that mixture. He is willing to accept it as simply the way things are. He accepts it as he accepts the mixture of tribes in the army, which he does not at first order and marshal into kinds. He completely separates action from reflection. λόγος, in its simplest sense of articulation, stands for him completely apart from ἔργον. It is only a hindrance to action, and even Artabanus seems to believe that it must be abandoned in action itself. Courage for both of them would be thoughtlessness. As a result of this separation the army is known in only two ways: its total number and the number of tribes (60). No one knows what is between these extremes: how many men each tribe contributed. Only after the troops are numbered into 170 ten-thousands are they arranged into tribes. A circle was drawn around ten thousand men, and using this as a measure another group would be herded into the same circle, and so on until all had been counted. Men are treated in batches that fail to take into account the differences among the tribes. They are either treated as "so many men" or as "this" and "that" tribe, while the obvious combination

---

78.5; 86.2; 128.1; 151.2; note the frequency of τύχη, its compounds, συμφέρω, and συμβαίνω in III: 4.1; 10.2; 14.7; 39.3; 40.1bis; 40.2ter; 40.3bis; 40.4; 42.1; 43.1,2; 44.1; 50.1; 71.2; 77.2; 78.1; 121.2; 125.4; 129.1; 139.3.

of "so many men of this tribe" is ignored. The Persians see either the troops as human ciphers or as kind—the same kind of disjunction as that which Xerxes made between thinking and doing: either the universal or the local. Xerxes' trust in λόγος was a trust in the universal gods of the Persians, and his trust in ἔργον was a trust in the mixed body of his troops.

Herodotus presents a catalogue of Xerxes' infantry, cavalry, and navy (61–99). The catalogue of infantry reminds us of Homer's Catalogue of Ships: the 29 Persian commanders of 46 tribes recall the 29 groups into which Homer divided the Achaeans. But there are certain differences. Herodotus, unlike Homer, refuses to give the names of the native commanders: "I am not compelled by necessity for the purpose of my inquiry." They are "unworthy" and come more as slaves than as generals, since the Persian generals hold all the power. Homer, on the other hand, not only gave the names of the native rulers but often their genealogy as well. Herodotus tells us instead the names that the nations once had, or the different names that they have among different people; but, most important, he tells us the various kinds of arms that they carried, which Homer does not mention at all. It points up the fundamental weakness in the whole: the lack of uniformity in its equipment. The Persians would have been perfectly justified in numbering it as a whole had they armed it all alike (cf. IX.62.3; 63.2). Now some are armed like the Greeks, while others have only stakes and wicker shields. Again Xerxes accepts the mixed as given. He does not see its weakness because he thinks the Persian commanders suffice to make it uniform. He does not see that a unity in command cannot wipe out these differences in kind; nor that the symmetrical hierarchy of commanders—divided into those who command ten thousand, a thousand, a hundred, or ten—does not make up for these differences. The perfection of the order only emphasizes how little it applies to the matter it is supposed to shape. The gap between λόγος and ἔργον remains as far apart as before.

Xerxes' reliance on an abstract chain of command, which ignores the differences among the tribes' equipment, is coupled with his reliance on the overwhelming superiority of their numbers. In his talk with Demaratus he indicates what he believes binds these two elements together (101–105). He asks him whether the Greeks will resist, expressing his own view that not even the collection of all men in the west would hold their ground against him. Demaratus replies as follows: "Poverty has always been endemic to Greece, but virtue is an alien importation, produced by wisdom and strict law, and by its use Greece wards off both poverty and despotism." Xerxes can scarcely believe his assertion that numbers will make no difference to the Spartans, and he presents a case for regarding their freedom as a disadvantage: "If they were ruled by one man in our fashion, they would prove by their fear of him to be better than their nature, and would advance, though less, against more, being compelled

by the whips; but left by themselves to be free, they would do neither."[13] The
link, then, that Xerxes sees between the schematic and the inarticulate character of his army is compulsion or necessity. Necessity as bodily whippings
gives it shape and makes it manageable. Demaratus objects to his disjoining
freedom from necessity; he says that there is a middle term: "Being free they
are not altogether free (the Spartans); for their master is law, which they are
more inwardly afraid of (ὑποδειμαίνουσι) than your troops are of you—at least
they do whatever it commands, and it always commands the same, forbidding
them to flee from battle before any multitude, but to remain in position and
conquer or die." The law is an invisible whip, more compelling than any evident force. Its force cannot be measured numerically, as Xerxes tries to do
when he figures out that one Spartan would have to be equivalent to a thousand
men in order to balance the strength of his army. His mistake is based on the
Persian belief that the many is the strong (I.136.1; cf. III.80.6; VIII.69.2).
The numerical disproportion between Spartans and Persians is specious. The
law, by always commanding the same, far outweighs this disproportion. It
affects the soul rather than the body; its own consistency instills a persistence
and constancy into its subjects that cannot be called simply compulsion. To
fight under the law is to fight under a necessity that is felt as a persuasion.
Therein lies the difference between the Greeks and the barbarians. Necessity
and persuasion are the theme of Book VII.[14] It is the wider horizon within
which Herodotus examines the virtue of courage.

Before Demaratus was willing to answer Xerxes' question, he asked him
whether he should tell the truth or say what Xerxes would be pleased to hear;
and urged to tell the truth he did, only to hear Xerxes' laughter and his
explanation of why he thought Demaratus spoke nonsense. Demaratus then
replied that Xerxes himself compelled him "to tell the truest of speeches," and
that in the future he would keep silent, "but now being compelled I spoke."
Xerxes again laughs at what he said and gently dismisses him. Demaratus tells
the truth under compulsion; he believes the truth will displease Xerxes, for he
assumes that he will persuade Xerxes, but Xerxes laughs at what he says and
does not take it seriously. He takes pleasure in what Demaratus took no
pleasure in saying. He, and not Xerxes, found the truth unpleasant. The alternative he established—between a compelled speech that would persuade Xerxes
because it was true and a lie that would persuade because it was pleasant—was
not exhaustive, as Xerxes laughter showed. Xerxes, however, accepted this

---

[13]Cf. 22.1; 56.1; V.118.2; VIII.15.1; p. 150 *supra*.

[14]ἀναγκαίη and related words occur more often in VII than in any other
book (27 out of 68); but πειθώ and derivatives occur most often in I; but
ἐθέλειν occurs 40 times out of 187 in VII, more than any other book.

disjunction, not in speech but in action. He believed that the pleasure of freedom precluded martial discipline, which only the pain of compulsion could
bring about. Demaratus showed him that they could be merged: "I claim the
ability to fight neither ten men nor two, and I would not even willingly fight
one; but were there a necessity or some great conflict that urged me, I would
with the greatest pleasure fight anyone of those men who say each is worth
three Greeks." Demaratus says that under necessity he would take pleasure in
fighting. In action he would combine what he could not do in speech. Spartan
law brings about that mixture of freedom and compulsion in which the virtue
of military courage consists. No Spartan law taught Demaratus to tell the truth,
and he was not pleased to tell it. In order to find an example of someone willing to be truthful, we have to go back to the Persian Praxaspes, who willingly
forgot his promise to conceal the truth when a necessity overcame him to tell it
(III.75.1-2).[15] We could also cite Herodotus himself, whose own *logos* everywhere exhibits his willingness to submit to the necessity of the *logos*, and this
nowhere more explicitly than in Book VII. He does not record the names of
the native commanders in Xerxes' army because he is "not compelled by
necessity" to do so; but he does record the names of eleven native captains of
the fleet, ten because they were "most renowned," and the eleventh because he
is "most surprised that a woman waged war against Greece" (98–99).
Artemisia took part in the war, "though under no necessity," because of her
"audacity and courage." She belongs by necessity to Herodotus' argument
because she willingly participated in the war. Since most of the others came as
slaves, i.e., unwillingly, their names are excluded; while her willingness gives
her a place in an argument that only obeys the dictates of necessity. Her
courage differs from that which Demaratus defines as the Spartan kind; for the
Spartans, or at least Demaratus, would not willingly fight unless compelled.
Artemisia's audacity is beyond law: in order to escape from an Athenian ship
she rams and sinks one of Xerxes' (VIII. 87.2-88).[16] Spartan courage is

---

[15] Cf. pp. 83–4 *supra*.

[16] The problem raised by Artemisia is the same as that raised by
Themistocles—great wisdom without the kind of justice Aristides shows,
whom Herodotus regards (νενόμικα) as the best and justest in Athens
(VIII.79.1); whereas Themistocles "even before being thought to be wise
appeared as truly wise and of good counsel," when he used the advice he gave
to the Athenians, borrowed from Eurybiades, for his gain (VIII.109.5–110):
"he was acclaimed and thought much the wisest of the Greeks throughout all
Greece" (VIII.124.1). Wisdom has a wider range than justice. The difference
between Aristides and Themistocles has something to do with Artemisia's
eliminating in her own person the difference between men and women; consider VIII.68α1; 104–106; 125; cf. pp. 24–26 *supra*.

imported and not as natural as hers. As a product of wisdom and strict law it does not have the same spontaneity: but it does not suffer from the superficiality of Persian whips; nor again is it as deep as Herodotus' own necessity to obey the argument. What law commands stands, rather, between the necessity of λόγος and the necessity of whips.

Demaratus remarked that law instilled more fear into the Spartans than Xerxes personally could into his own troops. He attributed the effect of the law to the sameness of its commands on every occasion. He seemed to define courage as persistence, as staying one's ground until one conquered or died. Immediately after this talk, Herodotus gives two examples of Persian courage (106–108). Mascames resisted every Greek attempt to expel him from Doriscus in Thrace, the only one of the Persian governors to do so; while among those defeated, Xerxes believed Boges alone to have been brave. Boges, "though he could have departed from Eion under a truce and returned to Asia, was not willing, lest the king might think that he had survived out of cowardice, but he persisted up to the end." Boges' fear of Xerxes would seem to contradict Demaratus' assertion that only a law could inspire such courage; and yet Demaratus could still point to a fundamental difference. The Spartans, he said, would be no worse than others in single combat; but collectively they would be the best.[17] Xerxes can here and there affect someone with the same sense of honor as does the law; but he cannot make it general. His presence at the battle of Salamis made his navy fight better than they had at Artemisium in his absence; but it is not a concerted effort (VIII.69.2; 86; cf. IX.62.3).[18] Each man separately then thought Xerxes was watching him, but this still visible and external despotism cannot match the invisible pervasiveness of the law, which makes the Greeks not only fear it but each other as well. Xerxes' own persistence in honoring Mascames (carried on by Artaxerxes for his descendants), and his continuous praising of Boges, who was still praised in Herodotus' own day, prevented him from realizing that nothing can replace public praise or blame.[19] He could not understand that common opinion, which is custom and law, is more effective than private recognition.

Two things most frightened Artabanus: earth and sea (47.2–49; cf. 118–121.1.). He meant the particular earth of Greece and its sea-coast—the earth unable to support the vast army Xerxes brought, nor any of its harbors large

---

[17]Cf. 225.2; V.3.1; 8; IX.102.3; pp. 133-4 *supra*.

[18]Note the difference at Plataeae between the Greeks themselves ordering and stationing themselves into position (ἐτάσσοντο) and Mardonius' doing the ordering for his troops (ἔταξε); IX. 28.2-32; cf. 22.3-23.

[19]Cf. 111.1; 115.3; 117.2; and note Herodotus' own persistence: 108.1,3; 110; 112; 113.1; 115.2.

enough to protect his ships from sudden storms. He thought Greece was too weak in its resources; but though he proves to be right on both counts, Greece proves also too strong in its men. What especially harms Xerxes benefits the Greeks, for Demaratus had partly attributed to the necessity of her poverty the excellence of her strength (cf. IX.122). This necessity, however, is incomplete, for if it were complete, wisdom and law could never have imparted virtue; and the very possibility of virtue, which depends on choice, would disappear. The Greeks recognize that the absence of choice eliminates responsibility: only those Greeks who surrendered to the barbarians, when they were not compelled and their affairs were in good order, had to pay a tithe to the god at Delphi (132.2). There must be choice before one can praise or blame, and some of the Greek cities seem to have obtained the conditions necessary for the exercise of choice. Herodotus suggests that these conditions are rooted in the nature of Greece itself. When Xerxes' army came to the River Echidorus on the edge of Macedonia, lions only attacked the provision-carrying camels, and did not touch any other beast or man (125; cf. I.804–5; IV.129). "I wonder at the cause," Herodotus says, "whatever it was that compelled the lions to abstain from the others and attack the camels, an animal they had never seen before nor had any experience of." The absence of compulsion makes Herodotus wonder, just as he did at Artemisia's joining Xerxes' expedition, uncompelled though she was. In both cases he cannot find a direct cause of their actions. It is the lack of a visible cause, rather than the lack of cause simply, that surprises Herodotus. It can only be due to an innate audacity, specifically attributed to Artemisia, and commonly believed of lions (cf. 180; 220.4; 225.2). That this leonine free choice, moreover, should occur in Greek territory does not appear to be accidental. It fits in with what we have learned about the digressive nature of Greece. Herodotus had wondered at the impossibility of breeding mules in all of Elis, "since the land is neither cold, nor is there any other evident cause" (IV.30).[20] He does not doubt that a cause exists, though he only records without accepting the Elians' own story, that it came about through a curse. He imitated its obscurity by making his account a digression in his main narrative about Scythia: there seemed no necessity for either his digression or Elis' anomaly. One was an interruption in his argument, the other ran counter to the simple causes of extreme heat and cold that accounted for so much in Libya and Scythia; but Herodotus said that his *logos* sought digressions from the very beginning. The digressions are a part of his *logos* in a way that the cause in Elis does not seem to belong to the collection of climatic causes. If, however, we consider Greece itself a digres-

---

[20]Cf. pp. 106, 121 *supra*. For the digressiveness of wonder see I.23; III.12.1; IV.85.2; VIII.8.2; IX.25.1.

sion in the midst of Egypt, Persia, and Scythia-Libya, then the grounds for
Herodotus' departure from a strict sequence would he based on Greece's own
anomalous position. Greece cannot be understood in terms of any one of the
three principles Herodotus discovered in Books II–IV; but that does not mean
that these principles are inadequate to account for her. It means that all three
principles must be considered together and not separately. Their union in
Greece makes Greece better in fact but not other in principle than any of its
three parts separately. Their union excels its own parts as the climate of Greece
is the fairest mixture of weathers (I.142.1; 149.2; III.106.1). Its climate is
temperate, just as its λόγος is a temperate mixture of the three parts of
Herodotus' own λόγος. As a mixture Greece must not be confused with
Xerxes' army, which is a mixture of a different kind. His army contains all the
nations in which Herodotus had originally discovered his triple λόγος—
Egyptians, Persians, Scythians and Libyans—but they are merely added or
jumbled together without being combined. They are there by necessity, which
neither attends to their differences nor orders them into a whole; and it cannot
do the second because it fails to see the first. The Persians' use of external
necessity grows directly out of their trust in a λόγος, which they believe to be
always simple. They believe other people are better in proportion (κατὰ λόγον)
to their proximity to themselves, which combines so naively a trust in the
senses with a trust in λόγος (I.134.2–3).[21] They believe that the universality
of their gods leads at once to the universality of empire, for they do not
understand that in so far as the gods are theirs they are not universal, and in so
far as they are universal they are not theirs. Hence they must force the two to
fit. The Greeks, on the other hand, believe that only the uncompelled who surrender are guilty: so those who choose to fight the Persians have also come
together uncompelled. They are persuaded to join into a whole, for they are
already a whole. Their free choice is based on the lack of necessity in the very
composition of Greece, whose principles, one might say, have been persuaded
to come together. Unlike the separate necessities that dominate Egypt, Persia,
Scythia and Libya, their combination in Greece has tempered the immediate
force of each. Whereas the λόγος of Egypt appeared in its earth and water, the
λόγος of Scythia-Libya in its rivers and cold, sand and heat, and the λόγος of
Persia in its seven gods (especially the sky), the λόγος of Greece does not
appear at first sight in anything bodily. It has borrowed, directly or indirectly,
from all three λόγοι, but in the course of time they have become domesticated.[22] They have hid their roots so deep that they appear to be specifically

---

[21]Cf. p. 92 *supra*.

[22]The elements do show up in Athens and Sparta, but indirectly as sea-
or land-power—more a Thucydidean than an Herodotean theme; but Herodotus
does indicate it in the two lists of naval power he presents, one before the

Greek. They appear to be truly one. That they are not one or only precariously so, Herodotus indicates later; but he now wishes to show how his λόγος has taken on the guise of being Greek. He wishes to show how the necessity of the universal λόγος has become a persuasion in Greece.

Xerxes desired to see the outlet of the Peneius, "and as he desired so he did," and when he saw it, he greatly wondered and asked his Thessalian guides whether the river could be diverted into another channel (128-130).[23] Herodotus then relates how Thessaly was transformed from a lake into a plain, when Poseidon, as the Thessalians say, or an earthquake, as he himself says, opened up a chasm between Olympus and Ossa, through which the lake's waters are emptied into the sea, just as now the Peneius collects all the waters from the interlocking mountains and carries them off. After this digression Herodotus gives the guides' answer to Xerxes, who, on learning that there was only one outlet, supposedly said that the Thessalians were wise to have surrendered at once, for he could have so easily blocked the Peneius' outlet and submerged all Thessaly. Xerxes turns out to have attributed more wisdom to the Thessalians than they at first showed; for only their kings surrendered, while the rest were willing to resist if the Greeks helped them (6.2; 172-174). They did not recognize the necessity Xerxes saw so clearly because they did not see the earthquake that formed Thessaly as a necessity. Believing as they did that Poseidon opened up the channel, they interpreted the earthquake as the act of a god who willed to make Thessaly, and thus his action was not reversible by any man. Their belief gave them a freedom of choice which Xerxes did not think that they had. Because their land was divinely granted, they were willing to defend it. Poseidon as a local god supports them in a way Poseidon as the equivalent of 'earthquake' would not. Herodotus finds the same kind of local restriction in the wrath of Talthybius, which affected Sparta but seems to

---

battle of Artemisium, the other before Salamis (VIII.1-3; 42-48; consider also VIII.55). The first list presents the cities in an exact order of power—the Athenians first, the Spartans in the middle, the Locrians last—, while the second list presents an inexact order in terms of geography—the Spartans are first and the Aeginetans in the middle (cf. 93.1); and here the origins of the cities are given: over both fleets the Spartan Eurybiades had the greatest authority. The ground for Athens being listed first lies open to view, in its being first in power, but the ground for Sparta's being first lies hidden in the past (cf. VII.159; IX.26-28.1). One might say that the coincidence of ground with appearance characterizes Athens, while a lack of this coincidence characterizes Sparta (cf. Thucydides I.10.1-3; VI.31.4; also 46.3); see further Benardete, S., *Hermes* 91, 1963, p. 15 fn.

[23]Cf. pp. 87-89 *supra*.

have by-passed Athens (133–137). Although the Athenians and Spartans both killed a herald of Xerxes, Herodotus cannot say what "unwished-for" thing happened to the Athenians—he does not consider the devastation of their land to have occurred "through this cause"; but the wrath of Talthybius, the herald of Agamemnon, struck the Spartans. Unable to obtain favorable auspices they were grieved, and they asked whether anyone wished to die for Sparta. Two Spartans "willingly" assumed the task of paying the penalty for the murder, and Herodotus says that their daring was "worthy of wonder." It surprises him because they were "naturally well-born and among the wealthiest Spartiates." Nothing in their domestic or private affairs, from which they might have wished to escape, compelled them (cf. 163–164). Herodotus also finds the words that they spoke worthy of wonder. They told Hydarnes that he would not have urged them to enlist on the Persian side had he known how sweet freedom was; and they refused to reverence Xerxes in the Persian fashion, though his bodyguards tried to compel them, saying that it was not their custom to reverence a human being, nor had they come for this purpose. These two sayings show that they were completely free in their choice, since they resisted both temptation and force. Xerxes refused to kill them—out of magnanimity he said—but nevertheless the wrath ceased. The gods would seem to have recognized and been satisfied with their intention, but the Spartans say that it was reawakened during the Peloponnesian war, when the sons of these two men were killed by the Athenians (cf. VI.60). Herodotus thinks this story a digression, for he says at the end of it: "I shall return to my former *logos*." It seems to him one of the most divine events, "for that the wrath of Talthybius struck heralds nor ceased before it was fulfilled, so much pertained to justice"; but that it should strike heralds who were the sons of those heralds, marks it clearly for him as a "divine thing." That the punishment was over and above what justice would have demanded shows that it was divine. The divine shows itself in what is more necessary. It is clearly divine because it is obscurely necessary. It has the same character as Elis' failure to breed mules—attributed to a curse—and its own failure to strike Athens. Moreover, its lack of necessity—from a human point of view—is exactly like the two Spartans' willingness to die. They were willing to die for the sake of auspicious sacrifices: a divine law persuaded them.

Nothing more suggests the absence of necessity among the Greeks than their disagreement about what they should do when faced with Xerxes' invasion (138; cf. 9β2). Many eagerly medized, and those who did not trembled; and most conspicuously the Athenians, whom not even "fearful oracles from Delphi, casting them into fear, persuaded to leave Greece" (139–144). The Athenians' "choosing Greece to remain free" prompts Herodotus to praise her: "Here I am compelled by necessity to declare my opinion, invidious though it is to the majority of men, but nevertheless, in what way it appears to me to be true, I shall not hold back." Herodotus is compelled to declare his opinion because it appears to him to he true. "Willy-nilly" he must speak.[24] The conclusion that his thinking necessarily arrived at seems to entail its own avowal. Although Herodotus sometimes suppresses what he knows, if it is unjust, unpleasant, or not part of his *logos,* here his knowledge coincides with the necessity to publish it. He is compelled in spite of the displeasure he will arouse, just as Demaratus thought he was compelled to speak the truth in spite of its unpleasantness; but Xerxes compelled Demaratus, while necessity itself compels Herodotus. Its pressure has nothing to do with physical torture. It is not an unpleasant truth for Herodotus. Not in persuading him of its truth but only in forcing him to declare it does it appear as a necessity. He shows his courage in not yielding to opinion, for he cannot yield without distorting his *logos.* His faithfulness in abiding by the truth parallels the Athenians' own faithfulness, and their refusal to yield to the Delphic oracle's threats. They do not depart from their decision, even though the first oracle said that neither head nor body, feet nor hands would be left of Athens. They are not as frightened of this as Artabanus was of a dream in which hot irons put out his eyes. Artabanus at once changed his mind—he did not understand the soul—while the Athenians are persuaded to consult the oracle again as suppliants. They attempt to persuade Apollo, but the prophetess declares that Athena herself was unable to persuade Zeus with all her "many words and great cunning," and Zeus only concedes that a wooden wall would remain unsacked. Some of the older men though that the acropolis was meant, since they remembered that a fence once surrounded it; others thought that it meant the city-wall, and some, ships; but these could not interpret the last two lines of the oracle, which the oracle-mongers took to mean that they must be defeated in a naval battle around Salamis. Themistocles, however, in his first appearance in Herodotus, persuaded the populace that the words "Oh divine Salamis" pointed to the enemy's defeat and not their own. He argued that otherwise the oracle would not have employed the word "divine" but something like "wicked." The Athenians decided that this was preferable to the other opinion that did not allow them to fight, "nor even, in general, raise arms in defense." They preferred an interpretation that left them some freedom of choice; they learned that the word "divine" did not spell their necessary defeat.

Even after the Athenians heard of Xerxes' offer to leave them autonomous, help them acquire whatever other land they wished, and restore the sanctuaries that he had burnt, they did not relax their determination to fight (VIII.140–144; IX.7α1–β). They tell the Spartans why they would never surrender: "That the Spartans fear lest we might come to an agreement with the

---

[24]Cf. pp. 52-3 *supra.*

barbarians is admittedly very human; but ill knowing the temper of the
Athenians you seem to be afraid, because no sum of gold anywhere on earth
nor any land however surpassing in beauty and excellence would we willingly
accept for our medizing and enslavement of Greece. There are many great
things that prevent us from doing so; first and greatest are the statues and
homes of the gods that have been burnt and demolished, for which we must
necessarily seek revenge rather than agree (ὁμολογέειν) with him who has done
this; and again Greece itself, being of the same blood and same language
(ὁμόγλωσσον) and the common temples of the gods, sacrifices, and our same
ways, which it would not be good for the Athenians to betray." The gods
prevent them from agreeing, or rather the homes of the gods. ὁμολογία would
be possible if their gods were the same as the Persians'. The gods are Greek
gods, peculiar to the land of Greece; they are not universal gods like the Persians'; they are as local as the Greek language. γλῶσσα prevents λόγος from
being the only consideration: difference of tongue excludes sameness of
λόγος.[25] So much has the local prevailed over the universal that the Athenians
assure Alexander who brought Xerxes' offer: "As long as the sun goes in the
same path as it now goes, we shall never agree with Xerxes." Although
Herodotus had contemplated a change in the sun's path, so that it would go as
high up in Scythia as it now does in Libya, the Athenians do not consider that
possibility (II.26.2; cf. 142.4; V.92α1).[26] Their resistance depends on the
part being stronger than the whole; it depends on the gods having made their
home in Greece; it depends on the divine rather than the human (cf. VIII.41.2–
3).[27]

---

[25]Cf. 9β; VIII.135; p. 37 supra. βάρβαρος occurs most frequently in
VIII (63 times), while there are 45 in VII, 38 in IX, out of a total 196. οἶκοι
(VIII.143.2) here alone has the meaning temple, οἰκήματα here (144.2) and at
II.175.3 in the same sense (cf. IX.116.3). Thus it is clear why Herodotus post-
poned his telling of the Macedonian kings' origins till just before the
Athenians' reply to Alexander and Sparta (VIII.137–139; cf. V.22.1). Note its
similarity with the Scythian story (IV.5–6); and with Iliad II.100–108, where
the sequence, Pelops "horse-smiter," Atreus "herdsman of his people," and
Thyestes "rich in sheep," has its counterpart in the three brother, ὁ μὲν ἵππους
νέμων, ὁ δὲ βοῦς, ὁ δὲ νεώτατος...τὰ λεπτὰ τῶν προβάτων (137.2); also the
doubling of names at 139 (unique in Herodotus) as in the passage of the
Iliad—there are seven in each list; note the poetic γενέτωρ, 137.1.

[26]Cf. p. 150 supra.

[27]See George Saville, The Character of a Trimmer (Works, ed. Raleigh),
p. 97: "Our Trimmer is far from Idolatry in other things, in one thing only he
cometh near it, his Country is in some degree his Idol: he doth not Worship
the Sun, because 'tis not peculiar to us, it rambles about the World, and is no

And yet there is another sense of the divine. Herodotus often refers to the Peloponnesian War in the course of his later books; references that would not surprise us if we believe that Herodotus puts down everything he knows; but if, as we hope to have shown, he is always selective in his writing, we must consider why he should do so. The earthquake at Delos prompts him to remark: "In the time of Darius the son of Hystaspes, Xerxes the son of Darius, and Artaxerxes the son of Xerxes (three successive generations) more evils befell Greece than in the twenty generations prior to Darius, evils that partly befell it from the Persians, and partly from the chief (cities) themselves warring over empire" (VI.98.2).[28] Herodotus does not make a distinction between the earthquake as a sign of the Persian Wars and the earthquake as a sign of the Peloponnesian War. God showed his utter indifference to both Greeks and Persians in making a single earthquake serve as a double sign. If the Persian War shows the triumph of justice and freedom, the Peloponnesian War seems to have had nothing to do with either freedom or justice. The earthquake does not point to the providential care of Greece, but rather to the unimportance of Greek freedom and justice from a divine viewpoint. Solon concluded that the divine was jealous and troubling after he had given two examples of human happiness, one of which he described in terms of the human καλόν, the other in terms of the divine ἀγαθόν.[29] Divine jealousy, then, may only express the disproportion between the beautiful and the good. The beautiful may be at odds with the whole; it may find no support in the divine; and that may be the lesson that Herodotus drew from the war between Athens and Sparta. It would be the truth in the story of the man who likened Xerxes to Zeus (56.2). If Greece united represents an informed mixture of principles and elements, by which it defeated the elemental chaos of the barbarians, the Peloponnesian War would show how weak that mixture really was. Egypt, Persia, Libya and Scythia not only reveal themselves more clearly than Greece but as more enduring. The highest in man would be the accidental in the whole, and Greece would be only a digression.

The Athenians' decision to fight was supported by a previous decision of theirs, when Themistocles persuaded them to use in common the money from the silver-mines and build two hundred ships. He intended these ships to be used in the war against Aegina, a war that saved Greece, Herodotus says, "having compelled the Athenians to become a maritime people." Not only, then, Themistocles' persuasiveness but also an external necessity brought about

---

less to us than others; but for the Earth of England, tho perhaps inferior to that of many places abroad, to him there is Divinity in it..."

[28]Cf. pp. 159–161 *supra*; also Thucydides I.23.2-3.

[29]Cf. pp. 133–4; 150–1 *supra*; also pp. 80–1; 91–2 *supra*.

the Athenians' choice. Themistocles later refers to the two great gods of Athens: Persuasion and Necessity (VIII.111.2). The Aeginetan war gave them the occasion to acquire the means for their defense against Persia; it was a necessary but not sufficient condition for their decision to do so. It allowed them to make the right choice. Such an allowance is not always present, and Herodotus cites a number of examples to show how necessity sometimes prevents the possibility of choice. If Xerxes' army did not become one, in spite of the uniformity of the compulsion, Greece could not become one because of the local differences in the degree of compulsion. Various mixtures of compulsion and persuasion affected the Argives, Gelon, the Corcyraeans, the Cretans, and the Thessalian—the Thessalians said that "no compulsion is stronger than powerlessness"—, but Herodotus most explicitly defends the Argives.[30] It proves to be a defense as well of his own *logos*.

The Argives said that an oracle advised them to keep quiet and not participate in the war, but nevertheless they asked the Spartans for half the leadership of the army, and their fear of the oracle did not prevent them from requesting a thirty-year truce with the Spartans. When the Spartans refused the first condition and said that others must consider the second, the Argives broke off negotiations, preferring submission to the barbarians to the greed of the Spartans. Another version of the Argives' refusal, which asserted that their request for half the leadership was merely an excuse, offered two proofs of the Argives' treachery, but Herodotus cannot "accurately tell" whether they occurred, "nor do I declare any other opinion about them than that which the Argives themselves say, for I know so much, that if all human beings brought their own private troubles into the middle, wishing to exchange with their neighbors, once they had peeped at the troubles of their neighbors, each of them would gladly carry away what they themselves had brought: so not even the Argives acted most shamefully." The Argives had just lost six thousand men at the hands of the Spartans; and they would be wiped out completely unless the Spartans agreed to let another generation grow up in peace, who in

---

[30] 148–152 (Argives); 153–167 (Gelon); 168 (Corcyraeans); 169–171 (Cretans); 172–174 (Thessalians). Gelon refuses to help Greece merely out of χάρις (i.e., without any necessity; consider 156.2–3; 164; 166); he demands some share in the leadership, for he does not see the necessity (cf. VIII.2.2–3); the Corcyraeans persuade the Greeks of their innocence even though they are guilty—the necessity they appeal to is indistinguishable from a true necessity; the Cretans are compelled by an oracle to desert, even though they are not (except in name) the same Cretans whom the wrath of Minos affected (170.2; 171); and the Thessalians' submission to necessity does not prevent them from being eager, nor do they have any regrets (cf. IX.1).

thirty years could assure the next generation. These private sorrows do not
have a common measure. They have a compulsion that someone who has not
suffered from them cannot calculate. Everyone would prefer the sorrows he
knows to those of another that are unknown. He would thus be unable to compare the decision he took with the decisions of others, who in turn could not
blame what he did because they would regard his sorrows as incomparably
greater than their own. Private misfortunes do not have a common λόγος.
They are, as Psammenitus once said to Cambyses, greater than lamentation:
silence alone can express them (III.14.10). Herodotus sees the force of the
Argives' argument in the incomparability of their sufferings, just as he
believes that only the example of Eurytus compelled the Spartans to dishonor
Aristodemus (229–231). Both were suffering extremely from sore eyes, and if
both had returned to Sparta, the Spartans would not have blamed their unwillingness to fight at Thermopylae; but since Eurytus did not use his blindness as
an excuse, the Spartans were able to compare his conduct with Aristodemus'
and find it wanting. No comparison, however, exists for Argos, and the
uniqueness of its situation persuades Herodotus that, if they did not rise above
necessity, they did not act as basely as the other Greeks believed. He does not
feel free to blame them (cf. VIII.73.3). His argument is reminiscent of the one
he used in Book III to show the madness of Cambyses (III.38.1). If Cambyses
had not been mad, "he would not have tried to laugh at sacred things and
customs; for if one bid all human beings to select the most beautiful customs
from all customs, each one would, after considering them, choose his own: so
each believes his own customs are by far the most beautiful." To blame the
actions of others is like laughing at the customs of others, which seem to the
outsider to be base. Herodotus' proof of this rule was Darius' question to
Greeks and Indians whether either would be willing to follow the custom of
the other in the matter of eating or burning the dead. We saw then that the
question turned entirely on the body, whose privacy made it impossible to
decide among conflicting customs; but that if the question were put in terms of
the soul, it proved possible to discover reasons for preferring one custom to
another. Now Herodotus, after he has explained here why he accepts the
Argives' account, remarks: "I am obliged to tell the things that are said, but I
am under no obligation to be persuaded by them, and let this saying hold for
my whole *logos*." Herodotus has an obligation to his *logos* that prevents him
from suppressing the stories unfavorable to Argos; but he cannot extend his
obligation so far as to believe them all: they contradict one another. His *logos*
as a whole must be consistent; he cannot allow it the privilege that he willingly
allows Argos. Its private sufferings prevented it from choosing what would
have been nobler; but this local necessity, this necessity of the body—the
oracle advised Argos to guard its head, "and the head will save the body"—
does not and cannot apply to λόγος. The law of non-contradiction means that

λόγοι are comparable, and as such Herodotus must either reject all of them or accept one. He must follow a necessity in λόγος itself that does not attend to any other necessity. It seems at least to be unaffected by the body.[31]

An oracle prevented the Cretans from helping Greece, and Herodotus mentions in the course of his account the "greatest Greek slaughter of all we know," which occurred between the cities of Rhegium and Tarentum (170.3–171.1; cf. 5.3; I.214.1). He says, "The affairs relating to the people of Rhegium and the Tarentines have been a digression in my *logos*." A digression describes the greatest Greek slaughter; its being Greek does not justify his including it in his *logos* as anything more than a digression. In magnitude there is nothing Greek that surpasses the barbarians' deeds. Herodotus extended his Samian account because the island contained the three greatest Greek works, though Egyptian and Babylonian works easily surpassed them (II.148.1–3; III.60).[32] The Egyptian works were "greater than any reckoning" (λόγου μέζω), a claim that Xerxes now echoes about his own power. He wishes the Greek spies to report that his power is "greater than any reckoning" (147.1; cf. VIII.140β2). It is so great that Herodotus must guess at its numbers, or even refuse to compute the number of followers (184–187). Numerically there is a disproportion between the Greeks and barbarians which the epitaph at Thermopylae only exaggerates but does not alter: "Here four thousand from the Peloponnesus once fought three million." This disproportion equally applies both to the rivers of Greece when compared with those of Asia—not even the largest Achaean river sufficed for the army—and to the best horses Greece produces: in a race against his own horses Xerxes found that the Thessalian mares were left far behind (196). The superlatives of Greece cannot compete with the superlatives of the whole. They cannot compete if bodily strength or size is considered, for Xerxes can draw upon the resources of the whole known world. And yet the Persians' belief that number is strength fails to be borne out when tested. Even when Demaratus tried to explain where they erred, he could not persuade Xerxes to take him seriously; nor can he now persuade him that the Spartans have come to Thermopylae to conquer or die (208–212). A Persian horseman was amazed when he saw the Spartans stationed outside the camp, some exercising, and others combing their hair; and "no one pursued him, but he found great indifference (ἀλογίη)." Xerxes could not understand what the horseman had seen, but asked Demaratus to interpret what to him appeared laughable; and Demaratus, having protested Xerxes' laughing at what he had previously said, explains: "These men have come to fight with us over this pass, and they are preparing for this; for their custom

---

[31]Cf. pp. 73–80 *supra*.
[32]Cf. pp. 61–2, 81 *supra*.

is, when they are about to risk their soul, to adorn their heads." Xerxes had graciously allowed Greek spies to see his preparations because they were greater than any reckoning; but he cannot understand how the Spartans can be indifferent when their numbers are so easily calculable. Their carelessness seems incompatible with any concern about fighting. He does not see how the beautifying of the body can coexist with the courage necessary in the soul. Zopyrus willingly mutilated his face for the sake of capturing Babylon: he had to sacrifice his external beauty in order to show the excellence of his soul (III.153–160).[33] The Persians' inability to unify the generosity of appearance with the necessity of discipline recurs in their treatment of two prisoners (180–181; cf. VIII.92.1; 11.3). They sacrificed the most beautiful and the first of the Greeks that they captured, whose name Leon ("Lion"), Herodotus thinks, also persuaded them to regard him as a good omen; but they admired Pytheas so much for his virtue—he fought until he was completely minced up—that they cured his wounds and exhibited him to the whole fleet. They look at the beautiful and the best differently. They cannot put together the indifference of beauty and the caring of virtue, whose union was the truth that Xerxes could not understand when he heard what the Spartans were doing at Thermopylae. He found everything Demaratus said unconvincing, who ended his speech thus: "Now you are attacking the most beautiful of Greek kingdoms and the best."

When Xerxes finally decides to attack the Greeks at Thermopylae, he first sends in the Medes, who though they kept up the attack all day were unable to dislodge them: "They made it clear to everyone and not least to the king himself that there were many human beings but few men" (210.2; cf. 9γ).[34] The difference between the Greeks and barbarians shows up in the difference between human beings and men. It makes impossible the numerical calculation of their relative strengths. It cancels out the disproportion between them on a new reckoning: it replaces the body as the measure with the soul (cf. 153.2–4). The new balance that is struck makes Greece the equal if not the superior of Persia; and not only of Persia but of the known world taken together. A small part of the earth proves a match for the whole. Its superiority does not rest on different principles, any more than as men the Greeks cease to be human beings. It rests rather on the co-presence of the same principles, which have taken hold there and penetrated to the soul of its inhabitants (cf. IV.95.2). These principles appear in the local setting of Greece more persuasive than compulsive, as they are when found separately in other countries. In becoming local they have assumed the guise of customs: they have become something to

---

[33]Cf. p. 85 *supra*.
[34]Cf. Chap. V, fn 22; VIII.68α1; 93.2; IX.20; 107.1.

be trusted rather than something to be obeyed. But this trust is mixed with the knowledge that the Greeks have of fighting, for their courage, like all courage, is an uneasy mixture of knowledge and trust: "The Spartans fought in a manner worthy of estimation, displaying in other ways among those who did not know that they knew how to fight and in this—whenever they turned their backs, they apparently fled all together, and the barbarians seeing them in flight advanced, noisily shouting, while they, once overtaken, turned back to face the barbarians, and by wheeling round they slew an innumerable multitude of Persians" (211.3).[35] The Spartans could only have performed such a maneuver if they listened to the commands of their officers. They would have had to be silent. Their order reflects the order of Greece itself: a κόσμος both beautiful and secure (cf. VII.86: IX.59.2). Whereas the Persians "by regiments and in every sort of way attempted" to break through, the Greeks "were marshalled by regiments and by nations, and each fought in turn." A schematic order fits with a local order. They are not incompatible as they are among the barbarians, whose lack of order appeared in Herodotus' not knowing how many men each nation supplied. It appears again in the battle itself: on the last day the regimental captains used whips to drive their men forward (223.3).

Having made us admire the apparent unconditionality of Spartan courage at Thermopylae, Herodotus presents Demaratus' last conversation with Xerxes (234–237). Xerxes asks him to suggest the least troublesome way of subduing Sparta; and he recommends frightening them with the threat of invasion from an island off their coast, since a war at home would make them abandon any attempt to help the rest of Greece. A private misfortune can even compel the Spartans to leave their post. Some necessity can always be devised to break even the highest kind of courage, and the breaking-point for the Spartans is the threat of invasion and conquest. The local in the last analysis seems always to prevail. Demaratus asserts that if Xerxes does not adopt his proposal, all the Peloponnesians will fight him at the Corinthian Isthmus: "Expect that you will have more violent battles than these that have been." Demaratus believes that the Peloponnesians would fight at the Isthmus; but Herodotus pointed out that if Athens had been unwilling to remain, the Isthmus would have been useless (139.2; cf. IX.9.2). Demaratus never mentions Athens. He has no understanding of sea-power. He does not know that if Xerxes controlled the sea, "the Spartans, betrayed by their allies, not willingly but by necessity, as the barbarians would have captured their cities one by one, would have been isolated, and once isolated they would have displayed great deeds and nobly died. Either they would have suffered this, or seeing the rest of the Greeks medizing they would have come to an agreement with Xerxes." Herodotus, then, was

---

[35]Cf. IX.59.2; 62.3; Chap. III, fn 23; Thucydides VI.72.4.

compelled by necessity to declare his opinion about Athens because the Spartans' predominance in Book VII tended to exaggerate their power and their will to resist. He had to correct these two impressions before the battle of Thermopylae would convince the reader of them. He did not wish to be accused of envy at the moment of their triumph.

Xerxes did not accept Demaratus' advice, for Achaemenes pointed out that a detachment of three hundred ships would dangerously weaken Xerxes fleet; and he also accused Demaratus of advising this in bad faith. Xerxes refuses to believe Demaratus spoke with ill will, judging by what he has said before and by the truth "that a citizen envies a successful citizen, and is hostile in silence, nor would a citizen advise what he thought best if another consulted him, unless he had attained a high degree of virtue; but such men are rare; while a stranger is most well-disposed to a successful stranger, and he would advise what is best if consulted." Xerxes judges Demaratus free from reproach on a particular and universal ground. He is fond, like all the Persians in this book, of general rules.[36] The rule which he now formulates admits of few exceptions, and these, he thinks, are not common enough to make the rule useless; but only the virtuous man upsets the rule about fellow citizens, while Xerxes does not consider any exception to the rule about mutual strangers. He seems to think that nothing could compel a stranger to offer deliberately bad advice. Herodotus says immediately after this that Xerxes commanded Leonidas' head to be cut off and impaled, and he remarks: "It is clear to me by many other proofs, and in this fact there is not the least, that king Xerxes was most angry against Leonidas while alive of all men, for otherwise he would never have thus departed from custom about the corpse, since the Persians especially are accustomed of all people that I know to honor men brave in war" (238.2).[37] Herodotus gives a general rule among the Persians that the compulsion of anger overrode. The example shows that a necessity may be so great that all rules are suspended, on which very same principle Herodotus himself had justified the Argives' conduct. He had also denied there the same indulgence to his own argument. He implied that no pressure could be brought to bear which could force him to accept as true what he believed to be false. He seemed to exclude his own *logos* from any kind of external necessity. Now, however, Demaratus' suggestion that a war at home would compel the Spartans to abandon the rest of Greece, contrary to the example of Thermopylae (233.1), was followed by Xerxes' statement that nothing could induce a stranger to give bad advice; which was followed in turn by Xerxes' abandonment of a Persian custom; and which immediately precedes Herodotus'

---

[36]Cf. 2.3; 8α1; 9γ; 10δ2–η2; 39.1; 46.3-4; 49.4; 50.2; 51.3.
[37]Cf. 136.3; III.2.2; 15.2; IX.78.3-79.

own avowal of an error: "I shall go back to that point of my former λόγος where there was an omission" (239: cf. 220.3).[38] His omission consists in not telling the "wonderful manner" in which the Spartans learned about Xerxes' intention to invade Greece. It not only involves Leonidas' wife, which would have made it suitable when he told about the oracle that gave the alternative— Leonidas or Sparta—but Demaratus as well, who ran the risk of detection to let the Spartans know (cf. I.123.3; V.35.3). Herodotus believes, "and the likely sides with me," that Demaratus as an exile was not well-disposed toward the Spartans, "but one may conjecture whether he did this out of good will or gloatingly" (cf. 104.2; VIII.65). The general tenor of Demaratus' life would indicate his ill will, but this single action can be interpreted in two ways. Herodotus does not decide. If we decide that he acted out of good will, then he must be one of those rare men who offer their best advice to fellow-citizens; but in that case he may violate the other part of Xerxes' rule, that stranger is most well-disposed to stranger. Demaratus might have then deliberately given bad advice, just as he now seems to have helped the Spartans. We see, then, that Herodotus was forced into a dilemma. Had he put this story where it would have explained why the Spartans consulted the oracle, the question of Demaratus' good will would have been out of place; but since Xerxes' asser- tion of a rule compelled Herodotus to use Demaratus' own behavior to cast doubt upon it, he found that the other part of the story was out of place. He preferred this dislocation to the other because it allows us to formulate a rule: not even Herodotus' own *logos* is so strict that necessity cannot compel it to abandon its 'proper' order. The 'proper' position for this story differs from that which it now occupies; but that propriety depends only on the need to preserve a temporally correct sequence. Its present position is not temporally but 'logically' correct. It necessarily belongs here if Herodotus is concerned with understanding how universal principles, like the one Xerxes proposed, are modified under particular conditions. The last eleven paragraphs of Book VII—from Aristodemus' "failure of soul" to Demaratus' good will or gloating—would confirm this. They would confirm not only that Herodotus was concerned with necessity and persuasion in light of the body and soul throughout VII, but that the apparently improper position of this last story points to Herodotus' overall intention in Books V–IX: how Greece in its digressiveness shows the modifications the triple λόγος of Books II–IV there underwent.

A treatise entitled *On Sevens* and preserved in the Hippocratic corpus contains a chapter (XI) on the seven parts of the earth, which are said to

---

[38]The asyndeton of the sentence, ἐπύθοντο Λακεδαιμόνιοι..., indicates the departure from strict sequence of this story.

resemble the seven parts of the human body.[39] The writer compares the Peloponnesus, *magnarurn animarum habitationem,* to the head, the Corinthian Isthmus to the neck, Ionia to what lies *inter viscera et praecordia,* the Hellespont to the legs, the Bosporus to the feet, Egypt to the belly, and the Black Sea to the lower intestine. Whether this is to be taken seriously or not, it does point up the subtler view of Herodotus. He seems to think that continental Greece reveals man as man, not in the sense of a correspondence between its shape and that of the human body, but rather that Greece, because of its fortunate mixture of grace and compulsion, allows man to appear in his excellence, the excellence of his soul. Inasmuch as Herodotus shows Greece as the non-bodily embodiment of his triple λόγος, it is not open to the same objection as the Hippocratic likeness, which seems arbitrary and provincial. And yet Herodotus does not avoid the difficulty we had noted before.[40] Herodotus still regards the soul metaphorically. It is not explicitly the theme; it is only observable through the screen of historical events; it is not the subject, except incidentally (Artabanus and Xerxes), of the actors in his *Inquiries.* The soul as it were guides the argument without being the argument; and it cannot be the argument without the *Inquiries* becoming a work of philosophy. The *Inquiries* is philosophical; an inquiry into the truth about man and his horizon dictates its stories; but the stories are not themselves about λόγοι but about ἔργα; and in attempting to discover a λόγος in ἔργα a disproportion arises that cannot be explained.[41] Herodotus goes too quickly from his triple λόγος to its application, for he does not consider whether Egypt, Persia, Scythia and Libya necessarily had to be there in order for him to discover the λόγος, or that they accidentally proved to be examples of it. He cannot decide whether or not the mimetic parallel between the Nile and the Danube, with its far-reaching effect on his understanding of Egypt and Scythia, had to be a consequence of his account of εἰκασία; any more than he can decide whether or not Persia, with it customs about truth-telling and cosmic gods, had to be situated in Asia. What Herodotus fails to explain is the heterogeneity of his own triple λόγος: what necessity of itself binds the three λόγοι together. His failure to consider their togetherness as a problem compels him to rely completely on Egypt, Persia, Scythia and Libya, as though their being there was sufficient proof for the ground of their being there. It compels him to take geography more seriously than reason might warrant; for his reasoning cannot

---

[39]Cf. Roscher, W. H., *Die hippokratische Schrift von der Siebenzahl* (Paderborn, 1913), pp. 117–130; Mazzarino, S., *Fra Oriente e Occidente* (Firenze, 1947), pp. 65ff.

[40]Cf. pp. 30–1; 62–3; 119–120 *supra.*

[41]Cf. Plato *Phaedo* 97b7–100b9.

account for this reasonable articulation of the earth.

Although Herodotus does not solve this problem of his λόγος, he does show in fact that the heterogeneity of the earth forbids any part, even the best part (Persia), from conquering the whole earth. The superiority of Greece, however, lies in its lack of partiality, and therefore Herodotus' work ends with a thinly veiled warning to Greece that not even Greece can preserve a universal empire (IX.122). The very conditions that make for the superiority of Greece prevent its expansion except with the loss of its superiority. It cannot remain free unless it maintains its virtues, and it cannot expand without sacrificing its virtues. This fundamental defect cannot be overcome on the political level, but it remains to be seen whether on the non-political level superiority cannot coexist with universality. It remains for us to look at Herodotus himself.

Before we can turn, however, to Herodotus, we must first turn back to Persia, with which he both begins and ends his *Inquiries*. The first story in his *Inquiries* was a Persian story. It presented Greek stories in a Persian guise, which transformed them in two ways. It removed the role that the gods had played in the Greek versions, and it denied there was any necessity in the actions of Io, Helen, Europe, or Medea. The Persians said that sober men pay no attention to the rape of women; for if the women had not been willing, they would not have been raped. Although they use a word (ἁρπαγή) that implies compulsion and force, they seem to mean by it what the Phoenicians do when they say, in contradistinction to the Persians, that Io willingly sailed off with the Phoenicians after she realized she was pregnant (I.5.2). The willing and the compulsory act are one and the same. This Persian denial of necessity does not seem to jibe with what a Persian says in the ninth book (IX.16; cf. 41.4–43). He predicted that few would be left of Mardonius' army at Plataea; and having shed tears at this prediction, his surprised table-companion asked him why he did not warn Mardonius, to which he replied: "Stranger, whatever must come from the god, no human being can turn aside; for no one is willing to obey him who speaks trustfully. Though many Persians are certain of this, we follow nevertheless bound by necessity; and that is the greatest sorrow in human things, to reflect on everything and rule over nothing." A Persian is so convinced of his doom that he does nothing to avert it. His conviction deprives him of the will to resist, just as the Persians' belief that no woman is unwillingly raped would rob them of the will to exact vengeance. Thus complete necessity and complete freedom lead to the same indifference. Herodotus shows how false that disjunction can be in the story that immediately follows the Persians' assertion (IX.17–18). The Phoceans had medized "not willingly but by necessity" (cf. VIII.38), and those who had come to join Mardonius' army at Plataea were ordered to stay by themselves in the plain; whereupon the entire cavalry of the Persians surrounded them. A rumor soon arose that they were about to be slaughtered, and their general Harmocydes tried to encourage them: "Phoceans, clearly these men are about to hand us over to a foreseen death, maligned as I suspect we have been by the Thessalians; but now every one of you must prove himself a brave man; for it is better doing something in defense to die than to let ourselves be destroyed by a most disgraceful fate; so let every one of them know that being but barbarians they have stitched a death for Greeks." Herodotus cannot "accurately say" whether the cavalry encircled them in order to kill them or to try their mettle. At any rate, seeing the Phoceans prepared to resist, the cavalry rode off, and Mardonius commended the Phoceans for their bravery. In a doom far more certain than that which the Persian predicts, there appears away out. Necessity has to be resisted in order to be overthrown.

The Persians think that either they are helpless before or masters of necessity. In a story about the remote past they recognize no necessity—the learned (οἱ λόγιοι) among them tell it—, but in the present they recognize only necessity. They so reworked Greek stories in the light of λόγος that they only admitted the necessity of λόγος itself; but confronted with a factual event they interpreted it to exclude all choice. Nothing for them stands between choice without bounds and necessity without loopholes. As one of his last stories Herodotus tells of Xerxes' love affair (IX.108–113).[42] He fell in love with his brother's wife, but she refused him; and he could not compel her out of respect for his brother: "and the same consideration held also for the woman, for she knew very well that she would not meet with force." Xerxes then arranged a marriage between her daughter Artaynte and his son Darius, by which he hoped he could get a hold over her. Having made the contract and done what was customary (τὰ νομιζόμενα) he brought Artaynte to Sousa, but he soon transferred his love from her mother to Artaynte and met with no resistance. Amestris, the wife of Xerxes, had woven for him a robe "worthy of sight," large and multi-colored. Xerxes took such pleasure in the robe that he wore it when he went to visit Artaynte; and being pleased as well with her he promised to give her whatever she asked for. Artaynte made him swear an oath on his promise, and when he had done so, she "fearlessly" asked for the robe he was wearing. Xerxes tried in every way to persuade her to ask for something else, but he felt at last compelled by his oath to relent. She wore the robe and "gloried in it": and Amestris, suspecting that Artaynte's mother was responsible and not Artaynte, waited for the king's birthday, on which day the king grants whatever request is made, and asked for the wife of Masistes, Xerxes' brother. Xerxes was "very unwilling" to agree, for he knew that she was innocent and what Amestris intended, but "compelled by the law" he granted it. He then tried to undo the damage by begging his brother to divorce

---

[42]Cf. Schulz, E., *Die Reden im Herodot* (Greifswald, 1933), p. 11.

his wife and marry one of his daughters; but Masistes refused to comply because his wife was the mother of his children, and he himself found her pleasing (cf. V.39–40). He told Xerxes not to force the matter, but suspecting more mischief from Xerxes' anger at his refusal, he ran home only to find his wife already mutilated. The story concerns two kinds of compulsion, the compulsion of love and the compulsion of law. Xerxes does not sense the compulsion of love as a compulsion—he is pleased with Artaynte—but he does sense the compulsion of an oath and a law as compulsion. He cannot violate either because the oath has partially transformed his love into the compulsion of law. He had willingly submitted to the oath, as he had freely offered Artaynte anything she asked for; but he came to realize that an unrestricted offer was impossible. His love made him believe that there were no restrictions; it made him forget not only the law but property as well. The robe was his robe, made for him and no one else. As a gift of Amestris he could not do with it as he wished; but as a sight-worthy object it did not belong to anyone. In itself it was meant to be seen, and it made no difference whose it was. It is like the wife of Candaules, who as a beautiful woman ought to be seen, but as the wife of Candaules cannot be seen by Gyges.[43] Candaules took pleasure in his wife not only because he loved her, but because he thought she was the most beautiful woman; so Artaynte took pleasure in the robe not only because it was beautiful but because it was hers. The transition from the story of Gyges to that of Xerxes shows the argument of Herodotus' *Inquiries*. It began with Herodotus' becoming free of all the restrictions of custom and law: he went to see everything. He could afford to look because he had no other desire than to look. He did not want anything he saw for his own. It now ends with Artaynte's pleasure not in seeing a robe but in having it as her own. The absence of necessity that characterizes Herodotus' λόγος cannot but be fatal if it becomes acquisitive: a dream persuaded Xerxes to undertake the conquest of the whole earth. Gyges would have been right if he had said that one must do what is one's own; he is wrong when he says that one must look to one's own (cf. II.32.3; IX.122).

"Who I know first began unjust deeds against the Greeks, with just an indication of who he was I shall go on in my *logos*, going alike through small and large cities of human beings; for cities that were in ancient times great have become small, and those great in my time were formerly small. Knowing, then, that human happiness never remains in the same place, I shall make mention of both alike" (I.5.3–4). Herodotus' most comprehensive justification for the way in which he will proceed is equally the most deceptive assertion he

---

[43]Note phrases χρῆν γὰρ Κανδαύλῃ γενέσθαι κακῶς (I.8.2) and τῇ δὲ κακῶς γὰρ ἔδεε πανοικίῃ γενέσθαι (IX.109.2).

ever makes. He implicitly identifies human happiness with political greatness (freedom and empire). In the light, however, of the stories that Solon tells about Tellus the Athenian and the Argives Cleobis and Biton, where the question of individual happiness is shown to be not necessarily connected with political greatness, one can say that the political perspective which Herodotus here suggests as his own, and which would entitle him to be called primarily an historian, runs counter to the actual procedure of Herodotus, which consists in the questioning of that perspective. That perspective is questioned in a double way, from the perspective of the divine, which stands outside of while it supports the political, and from the perspective of the subpolitical, which the importance of women in Herodotus most plainly exemplifies. Herodotus' suspension of judgment as to the truth of the Persian versions of the stories of Io, Europe, Medea, and Helen, which replace the divine in the Greek versions of these stories with the subpolitical, is in fact an agreement with the Persians as to what constitutes the political perspective, for the Persians are the first to identify it as freedom and empire (I.126.6). Where Herodotus differs from the Persians is in their failure to estimate correctly the subpolitical, which most shows itself in the privacy of the body and its affections, as the indispensable ground for the political. That the Greeks do not see the political solely as the political, and that the Persians do not see the subpolitical in its bearing on the political, explain in large measure why the unity of Herodotus' *Inquiries* is so difficult to grasp. Herodotus himself acts on behalf of the Greeks as the discoverer of the political perspective at the same time that he corrects that perspective with his own understanding of its upper and lower limits. His own understanding of those limits emerges from his understanding the mistakes which the Persians, Greeks, Egyptians, Scythians and Libyans make about them. It is only in Herodotus' redrawing the limits of the political that the political in its independence from and dependence on the non-political comes to sight. It is only through Herodotus' *theoria* that *praxis* gets its proper stamp.

SECOND THOUGHTS

Herodotus never uses δίκη in relation to Athens. It is peculiarly Persian: of its fifty instances, 25 are said either by or about Persians. The Persians distinguish between justice and moderation: the rape of Helen was an act of injustice but all who are sensible are indifferent since women are never raped against their will (1.4.2). Herodotus distinguishes between the injustice of Croesus and his own indifference when it comes to his survey of large and small cities alike (1.5.3–4). The latter is Herodotus's form of moderation. I should have made it clearer than I did that if injustice for Herodotus does not consist, as the Persians believe it does, in the sacking of cities in retaliation for a private wrong, but in the permanent subjugation of a people,[1] then Herodotus's enigmatic linking of Croesus with his general plan is resolved immediately in the implication that as the instability of human happiness follows exactly on the rise and fall of empires, so human happiness depends necessarily on injustice. This is something Solon does not know and cannot inform Croesus of, but Croesus himself expresses it when he has lost his kingdom and calls out Solon's name. Croesus did not believe that his deaf and dumb son, whom he did not reckon to be his, marred his imperial happiness at the time when he questioned Solon, though Solon himself would certainly have counted it as such (1.32.6), any more than the loss of his other son, for whom he was in mourning for two years, stirred in him any memory of Solon's counsel. That Croesus exemplifies the thesis of Solon in a non-Solonian way is enough to indicate that we are not at Herodotus's final position. The death of Cyrus does not fit very easily into Solon's view, for his defeat at the hands of the Massagetai neither deprives the Persians of happiness nor casts a shadow over his own life. Only if a particular custom about burial, with its attendant belief, holds, does the Queen's plunging Cyrus's head into a sack of blood affect the estimation of whether his life were happy or not. Croesus, after all, survived the loss of Sardis, and we do not know whether Croesus kept to his sudden realization of Solon's truthfulness, or he became satisfied over time

---

[1] Cf. Caesar *de bello Gallico* 7.77.14–16.

with the life of a slave. A king who could advise Cyrus to unman his people, perhaps out of resentment that otherwise they might one day regain their freedom, though he could not, cannot be trusted to carry Herodotus's message. His advice to Cyrus to invade the territory of the Massagetai has all the signs of an act of revenge (1.207).

Freedom and empire, or freedom and injustice, is Herodotus's broadest theme. Just as he began with it, he ends with it: the very last word of the book is "to be a slave." Cyrus advises the Persians to preserve their freedom along with their injustice rather than lose their freedom and empire together (9.122). Herodotus, then, is just as much a political historian as Thucydides. His singling out in his first sentence the cause of the war between Greeks and barbarians, against the backdrop of human events and magnificent deeds, already points in the same direction, as does his labeling his discussion of Persian laws a digression (1.140.3). One could therefore infer that the first four books are the ultimate and remotest causes of that war. Herodotus, in other words, replaces the Trojan War, which for the Persians is the originary cause, with the principles and structures of laws and customs that are to be found in Persia, Egypt, and Scythia. The just takes on the guise of law. Herodotus goes one step further than the Persians in demythologizing events. The Persians already have Egypt (with Io) and Scythia (with Medea) in their rationalistic account of Greek myths; but they are blinded by their own injustice not to discern in these countries the truth about Greece (cf. 4.1.1, 118, 167.3). Herodotus sets out to liberate cause ($\alpha\iota\tau\iota\eta$) from blame. The first step in such a liberation is to cut out the heroic age.[2] In dismissing the Persian debunking of the heroes and the gods that stand behind them, Herodotus does not restore the heroic age but implicitly accepts the Persian view that it never existed.[3] The iron age is at the center of Herodotus's inquiry. He therefore takes for granted the unavoidable presence of injustice, for without it human happiness has no ground. The beautiful and the good thus take precedence over justice simply and give a new meaning to justice. Justice simply, the justice of the heroic age, takes refuge

---

[2]The founding of Cyrene, which begins at 4.145, may be said to be Herodotus's account of the heroic age, which is nothing but the confluence of Egypt, Persia, and Scythia in Greece. The language of the account is highly poetic.

[3]The separation of narrative from causality, with their subsequent conjunction, goes back to Homer, where the causality is traced to the gods. The Persians, in rejecting divine causality, replace it with the notion of $\tau\iota\sigma\iota\varsigma$, or the automatic fulfillment of a pattern of right that has no other ground than the narrative itself. The rationality of the Persians is inseparable from their belief in poetic justice.

at the edges of the known world, where people are still tribal and have not yet acquired wisdom and deepened their ways (4.46.1, 95.2). The tension within the polis between art and freedom is the internal counterpart to the tension between empire and freedom, for just as the city in becoming great risks the loss of the freedom for which it may have originally been compelled to expand, so the city in its division of the arts and knowledge, or the state of non-barbarism, has no intrinsic connection with freedom.

The first book is almost evenly divided between the fall of the Lydian empire and the rise of the Persian. In both cases, a period of some five hundred years that precedes the era Herodotus describes is mentioned (1.7.4; 95.2). Herodotus concentrates on the two centuries that follow. This allows for a synchronicity between Lydian and Persian events; and it seems at first that the second book breaks radically with this scheme. The Egyptian logos is almost equal in length to the Lydian and Persian accounts combined. Herodotus, however, differentiates sharply between what the Egyptian priests say about their past and what of Egyptian history finds confirmation among others (2.147.1). Psammetichus was the first to let in the light: he set out to discover the first language. The period of joint knowledge lasts for 146 years till the time of Cambyses' invasion of Egypt. These 146 years are divided among five kings whose reigns vary in length. Herodotus writes up Lydian history over a period of five kings or 170 years, and Median-Persian history lasts for 179 years and again covers the reigns of five kings. The problematic length of the second book has to do primarily with its first 146 chapters, for without them the last quarter of the book covers the same period as the two parts of the first book. Now Egypt is important for Herodotus inasmuch as the Egyptians are the religious people.[4] Through them Herodotus introduces the problem of the sacred, or the second and non-rational root of political life: iron stands for the first root. The most obvious indication of this theme is the introduction of the word "priest" for the first time at 1.140.2 and its virtual disappearance after 3.38: "priest" occurs twice more at 6.81. Now 3.38 ends with Herodotus's citation of Pindar: "Law is the king of all."[5] Since the citation follows a discussion of Cambyses' violation of the sacred and Darius's discovery of the difference between Greeks and some Indian tribe about burial, one can say that the theme of sacred law, which began with Gyges' saying, "Each must look to his own," ends at 3.38 and overlays the tripartite syn-

---

[4]Εὐσεβής occurs only in Book 2 (133.2; 144.6), as does ὁσίη and θρησκείη (18.2; 37.3; 45.2; 171.2), and of the sixteen occurrences of ὅσιος half are in the second book.

[5]"Law" (νόμαιον, νόμιμα, νόμος) occurs 76 times up to 3.38 and 66 times thereafter; νομίζειν 65 times up to 3.38, 60 thereafter.

chronicity of Lydia, Persia, and Egypt.[6] The story of the tyrant Periander immediately follows the Pindar citation. The political in its independence from the sacred emerges with the discussion of tyranny and reaches its climax with the killing of the magi by the conspirators around Darius and the free discussion they have about the best possible regime independent of any sacred considerations. Cambyses' lawless actions, in tearing off the veil from the sacred, make it possible for Herodotus to turn to the political. Knowledge (ἐπιστήμη) becomes possible with the destruction of trust (πίστις).[7] This destruction carries a price: truth is not possible if there is truthtelling. The difference between Cambyses and Herodotus is that Cambyses wants to punish lying.

If the section of Egyptian history that begins with Psammetichus matches more or less the chronology of the two parts of Book I, the first three sections of Book II can be labelled a digression. They give the cause behind the cause for the Persian invasion of Egypt, which occupies the beginning of Book III and starts off the beginning of Book II (2.1; 3.1).[8] The relation between the first three sections of Book II to the last section is the relation, writ small, of the first four books to the last five. The need to give the causes of the cause is due to the compulsion Herodotus's logos is under to speak about the divine (2.3.2). The gods of Egypt force Herodotus to diverge from his scheme. We have, then, two structures—straight history from Croesus to Cambyses and sacred law—that overlap for much of their course. The second book, however, in its entirety matches the fourth book, three-quarters of which concerns the Scythians, and the last quarter Libya and the history of Cyrene. Egypt stands to Scythia-Libya as religion stands to poetry. Egypt reveals the original status of the Greek gods before the poets transformed them, and Scythia-Libya reveals the character of poetic transformation in general. Scythia, however, cannot just be matched with Egypt; it must also be considered in light of the

---

[6]The fourth section of Book II (147.2) begins with the Egyptians' liberation after the priest of Hephaestus had been king.

[7]One has to understand "the logos that is" (τὸν ἐόντα λόγον) about Cyrus (1.95.1), which Herodotus prefers to tell instead of the three other tales he knows, in light of Deioces' self-concealment, so that he would seem to be of a different sort if his equals were not to see him (1.99.2): Cyrus as a boy plays at being king and proves to be the legitimate king because it could not be the case that he really was the son of a shepherd.

[8]Book I begins with the lifting of the veil over sight (Candaules' experiment), Book II begins with a failed attempt to lift the veil on hearing (Psammetichus's experiment), Book III begins with the discovery, by speaking, of the truth Amasis tried to conceal through sight, and Book IV begins with the concealment of what is by a symbolic sight (Scythian experiment).

discovery of the political after sacred law has been dropped. Scythia as the home of the essence of freedom, without the encumbrance of political life, coincides with Scythia as the source of Herodotus's understanding of poetry. There is apparently a deep connection between Greek poetry and Greek freedom. Such a connection is to be found in the gods of the poets.[9] The gods of the poets are between the rational and natural religion of the Persians, for whom nothing but man is holy (1.140.3), and the excessive piety of the Egyptians, in which man is wholly unsanctified and utterly contemptible in his own eyes. It is between Herodotus's discussion of the Egyptian gods in light of their poetic transformation into Greek gods and his discussion of sacred beasts that he sets aside the Egyptians and Greeks from all other peoples (2.64). Everyone else, he says, except the Egyptians and Greeks, has intercourse in temple precincts, for they observe that all animals ($\kappa\tau\dot{\eta}\nu\varepsilon\alpha$) and birds do so. The Egyptians, in other words, abstain because they are less than the other animals, the Greeks because they are more. The gods of the poets allowed man to look up at and down at himself, but no one was to bow down before another human being (7.136.1). There was something of man as a whole in the highest of the beings, but he was not the equal to what he at most merely resembled: neither the Persians nor the Egyptians have heroes.[10] Pride and moderation became for the first time coincident notions. This paradoxical achievement went along with the recognition of the other, the clearest expression of which is Aeschylus's *Persians*, where in the absence of any mention of justice the Persians are shown to be as noble in their suffering as the Greeks. The possibility of the *Persians* depends on the *Iliad*, where Achilles gives back to Priam the body of Hector for burial. So distinctive is this that Virgil ended the *Aeneid* with the killing of Turnus and thus denied to the Romans anything comparable to Achilles' action. The Greeks thus became the first civilized people of the West; and since no other poet has ever celebrated the defeat of tyranny from the perspective of tyranny, it may not go too far to say that the Greeks were also the last civilized people.

---

[9]In his discussion of the various causes the Greeks assign to the flooding of the Nile, Herodotus splits the refutation of Ocean between 2.21 and 2.23. Greek poetry is thus put right next to what Herodotus believes is the true cause (the sun). "Ocean" is a name without a referent; it names that which is not; it surrounds a possible cause, the melting of snow. Herodotus calls the sun a god.

[10]The Persians have a rational account of Io, the Egyptians worship Isis with the horns of a cow (in just the way the Greeks paint Io [2.41.1]), the Greeks regard her as a heroine. It is for this reason that Herodotus begins with the story of Io.

The verb for mourning (πενθέω) occurs twice in Herodotus (6.68.3; 7.220.4). In both cases it refers to the Spartan manner of mourning for their dead king, which, Herodotus says, is the same as the practice of the barbarians (6.58.2). The noun for mourning (πένθος) occurs nine times. With one exception it is always of barbarian mourning. The one exception concerns the Milesians, who mourned for the capture of Sybaris, a city with which they had the strongest ties of friendship (6.21.1). Herodotus immediately adds that the Athenians burst into tears when Phrynichus presented his tragedy, *The Fall of Miletus*, and fined him for reminding them of their own evils (οἰκήια κακά).[11] Greek poetry, Herodotus seems to imply, transposed the ritual of mourning into its imitation, and in this form the barbarian origin of everything Greek lives on (cf. 2.82.1). Greek poetry is the distancing of the near and the drawing in of the foreign in the form of the beautiful. Sophocles' Ajax becomes un-Greek at the very moment he regrets the gift he received from Hector in recognition of his valor. In casting himself as the supreme patriot, he fails to realize that not the best of the Achaeans but the best of the enemy had already bestowed upon him the honor he believes should have come from the Greeks. Ajax kills himself with Hector's sword as if he had betrayed the Greeks by accepting it and thus deserved to be punished. Ajax took the beautiful for a crime. He is the barbarian that always lurks within the civilized. The word "barbarian" occurs for the first time in the play when Agamemnon and Teucer debate Ajax's right to burial (1263, 1289, 1292).

After Solon had given two incompatible answers to Croesus's single question—Who was the happiest of those Solon had seen?—and listed first and second what amounted to a difference between the beautiful and the good, Solon accounted for his answers in an oblique manner. Without his account, we would have said that Solon was reflecting the tension between the political and the tragic view of life, and the subordination of the latter to the former was Solon's version of what Greek poetry had achieved, the unity of human pride with self-knowledge. Solon's own account, however, seems to deny the possibility of self-knowledge, for if one always has to look to the end of a life, he who lives the life is left out of the picture.[12] By a false understanding of the connection between the lunar and solar calendars, Solon exaggerates the

---

[11]The verb to shed tears (δακρύειν) is only used of barbarians: 1.87.2; 112.1; 3.14 bis, 32 ter; 7.45, 46.1 bis.

[12]The problem inherent in the Solonian formulation is hinted at in Plato, where the syntax of the sentence in which it is stated is contrary to its presumed meaning: "To honor *the living* with praises and hymns is not safe, until someone runs through *his entire life* and puts on it a beautiful end" (*Laws* 802a1–3).

haphazardness of life, so that a life is nothing but a string of beads of various qualities, each one of which, if it happens to be the last, carries the whole meaning of a life. That man in his entirety is nothing but circumstance and luck seems to have nothing to do with either of Solon's stories. His emphasis on chance discounts the soul and makes man nothing but body. He likens the human body to a piece of land that is not fertile in all respects, but supplies some things and lacks others. Solon suggests to Croesus that he must not attempt to put together the import of his first story with that of the second, for the gods, in signifying that it is best not to be born, do not support the strictly human and political life of Tellus.[13] Croesus fails to understand Solon, for under pressure from Persian expansion he consults the oracle at Delphi. One can then say that for Solon chance keeps apart the meaning of his two stories, and it is always fatal if one believes that human life has a plot, or that there is a strict coincidence between who one is and what befalls one. The story of Atys and Adrastus, whose names signify this kind of coincidence, illustrates what happens when the beautiful in the form of shame comes together with chance and forces chance to be experienced as fate. The suicide of Adrastus is the human acknowledgment of the divine judgment on Cleobis and Biton. The tragic form of his story points to how the Greek poets helped to keep the tragedy of life apart from life itself. Herodotus emphasizes their apartness by beginning the story with the remark that "a nemesis from god seized Croesus, to the extent that one can make an image of it (ὡς εἰκάσαι), because he held himself to be the happiest of all human beings" (1.34.1). Croesus himself did not get the message, but Adrastus took it tragically.

The emergence of the political as such, which is the burden of Solon's first story, and becomes thematic after 3.38, seems to be the necessary but not sufficient condition for Greekness. The story of Gyges separates Herodotus from the barbarians, who never with impunity see anything for what it is, and poses the question of the relation between barbarian and Greek shame. Shame is the law's expression of man's ignorance by way of prohibition. The law completes man by saying no to man. The law clothes man and thus turns philosophy—man's awareness of his own ignorance—into shame.[14] If Greek

---

[13]This attempted fusion makes Cyrus laugh when Croesus asks permission to reproach Apollo (1.90.3). Cyrus himself tries to push the human into the divine (1.204.2; cf. 1.189-190.1). The Egyptians make the divine intrude into the human as far as possible.

[14]The three accounts of divine jealousy that Herodotus puts in the mouth of a Greek, an Egyptian, and a Persian express the universal awareness of a limitation on man if he is to remain human and a universal ignorance of what that limitation is apart from the law.

shame shows up in Adrastus's suicide, and Greek *theōria* in nakedness and Herodotus's own sightseeing, what holds together these three aspects of Greekness—poetry, nakedness, and "history"—with the political?[15] This is perhaps Herodotus's deepest theme. It is a working out of what Homer shows if one thinks together the *Iliad* and the *Odyssey*. In the *Iliad* he shows in the experiences of men the need of the gods if man is to be human; in the *Odyssey* he shows the rebestialization of man as well as the possibility of human understanding without the gods. As Achilles represents the first, so Odysseus represents the duality of the second. The more difficult structure of the *Odyssey*, which Herodotus repeats in the split within his single book, is a necessary consequence of this duality.

---

[15]Thucydides suggests one of these elements as constituitive of Greekness when he juxtaposes the Athenians first giving up the carrying of weapons with the Spartans first stripping completely at games (1.6.3–5). Both are a sign of self-confident power: no one poses a threat to us even when we are most exposed. He further expands on Herodotus's theme by beginning as if he agreed with Pericles—"We" do not need a Homer—and then going out of his way to remark on the music contests on Delos in which Homer competed long ago (3.104). Thucydides, though he presents himself as Homer's truthful rival, cannot but imitate him in his own fictions.

I. Index of Proper Names

This and the following three indices are meant to serve as a subject index

II. Passages Discussed Not in Their Herodotean Place

III. Index of Ancient Authors

IV. Index of Greek Words